Romanticism and Linguistic Theory

Also by Marcus Tomalin:

LINGUISTICS AND THE FORMAL SCIENCES

Romanticism and Linguistic Theory
William Hazlitt, Language and Literature

Marcus Tomalin

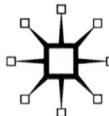

© Marcus Tomalin 2009

All rights reserved. No reproduction, copy or transmission of this publication may be made without written permission.

No portion of this publication may be reproduced, copied or transmitted save with written permission or in accordance with the provisions of the Copyright, Designs and Patents Act 1988, or under the terms of any licence permitting limited copying issued by the Copyright Licensing Agency, Saffron House, 6–10 Kirby Street, London, EC1N 8TS.

Any person who does any unauthorized act in relation to this publication may be liable to criminal prosecution and civil claims for damages.

The author has asserted his right to be identified as the author of this work in accordance with the Copyright, Designs and Patents Act 1988.

First published 2009 by
PALGRAVE MACMILLAN

Palgrave Macmillan in the UK is an imprint of Macmillan Publishers Limited, registered in England, company number 785998, of Houndmills, Basingstoke, Hampshire RG21 6XS.

Palgrave Macmillan in the US is a division of St Martin's Press LLC, 175 Fifth Avenue, New York, NY 10010.

Palgrave Macmillan is the global academic imprint of the above companies and has companies and representatives throughout the world.

Palgrave® and Macmillan® are registered trademarks in the United States, the United Kingdom, Europe and other countries.

ISBN-13: 978–0–230–21833–8 hardback
ISBN-10: 0–230–21833–4 hardback

This book is printed on paper suitable for recycling and made from fully managed and sustained forest sources. Logging, pulping and manufacturing processes are expected to conform to the environmental regulations of the country of origin.

A catalogue record for this book is available from the British Library.

Library of Congress Cataloging-in-Publication Data

Tomalin, Marcus.
  Romanticism and linguistic theory: William Hazlitt, language and literature
    p.cm.
  Includes bibliographical references and index.
  ISBN-13: 978–0–230–21833–8 (alk. paper)
  ISBN-10: 0–230–21833–4 (alk. paper)
    1. Hazlitt, William, 1788-1830—Knowledge—Philology.
    2. Grammar, Comparative and general—History—18th century. 3. Grammar, Comparative and general—History 19th century. 4. Language and languages—Philosophy—History—18th century. 5. Language and languages—Philosophy—History—19th century. 6. Romanticism—Great Britain. I. Title.

PR4773.T66 2008

824.7—dc22   2008016327

10 9 8 7 6 5 4 3 2 1
18 17 16 15 14 13 12 11 10 09

Printed and bound in Great Britain by
CPI Antony Rowe, Chippenham and Eastbourne

'This is one of those subjects on which the human understanding has played the fool'.

William Hazlitt, 'English Grammar', 1829.

Many of the topics presented here were first considered in the context of lectures and classes that I gave for the Faculty of English at the University of Cambridge during the period 2003-2008. Therefore, I am indebted to several generations of undergraduates as well as to various members of the 'Language' SGC who provided me with the opportunity to refine my ideas. In particular, Eric Griffiths, Raphael Lyne, Dan Wakelin, and Laura Wright have been unfailingly supportive. I am also grateful for the chance to speak at the 2008 'Hazlitt Day-School' which took place at Hertford College, Oxford. In particular, the discussions that I had there with Uttara Natarajan, Duncan Wu, Tom Paulin, and Simon Bainbridge (amongst others) were extremely helpful. In different ways, Nick Roe, Julia Simon, Will Poole, Rhodri Lewis, and Cathy Philips also provided valuable guidance when it was most required. Although I made use of various libraries while preparing this book, the Cambridge University Library deserves an especial mention, particularly the staff of the Munby Rare Books Room. Their careful assistance was always exemplary. Further thanks are due to Palgrave Macmillan, first for agreeing to support this venture, and then for overseeing the preparation of this manuscript so carefully. Paula Kennedy and Steven Hall, especially, have been invariably helpful and encouraging, while Mary Payne has proved to be a meticulous proof reader.

Over the years, numerous Tomalins, Trencsényis, and MacDonalds have endured conversations about some of the topics discussed in this book, and the chance to explain my ideas was always beneficial (for me at least). I am grateful to them for their patience and I thank them – especially my mother, who probably learnt more about Indian Jugglers than she ever expected. Finally, as usual, Sarah is implicated throughout.

All quotations from Duncan Wu's *The Selected Writings of William Hazlitt* 9 vols. (1998) are reproduced with the kind permission of Pickering & Chatto Publishers.

Despite my vigilance, I assume that there are lingering errors in this text. If so, then they are due entirely to my own ignorance, carelessness, and stupidity. I wish the mistakes well, though, and I trust that they will bring joy to all attentive readers.

This book is dedicated to my father:

Malcolm (Raymond) Roy Tomalin
1935-2007

Contents

1	**Introduction**		*page* 1
	1.1	Romanticism and Language	1
	1.2	Hazlitt on Language and Linguistic Theory	7
	1.3	Reception and Analysis	14
	1.4	The Way Ahead	22
2	**Linguistic Theory in the Eighteenth Century**		25
	2.1	Theories and Theorists	25
	2.2	Philosophy of Language	25
	2.3	Philosophical Grammars	30
	2.4	Grammar Textbooks	38
	2.5	Lexicography	44
	2.6	Language and Style	51
	2.7	Tories and Radicals	57
3	**Philology and Philosophical Grammar**		60
	3.1	Hazlitt and Philosophical Grammar	60
	3.2	Nonsense and Redemption	63
	3.3	Horne Tooke's Theory of Language	65
	3.4	Indeclinable Words	72
	3.5	Winged Words	79
	3.6	Rejecting Metaphysics	84
	3.7	A Light in the Darkness	91
4	**The Implications of Style**		93
	4.1	The Influence of Pedagogy	93
	4.2	Vulgarisms and Broken English	94
	4.3	The Grammars of English	98
	4.4	Perspicuity: Purity, Propriety, and Precision	102
	4.5	Familiarising the Perspicuous	108

5	**The Languages of Literature**		122
	5.1	Grammar and Literature	122
	5.2	Verbal Criticism	129
	5.3	Common Language	141
6	**Victorian Perspectives**		148
	6.1	Hazlitt's Influence?	148
	6.2	Journalism and Urbanism	150
	6.3	The Progress of Philology	154
Notes			165
Bibliography			181
Index			188

1
Introduction

1.1 Romanticism and Language

The epigraph to this book is taken from an essay that Hazlitt wrote towards the end of his life. It was published in *The Atlas* in 1829, and it contains his final thoughts concerning the nature of the difficulties that perhaps inevitably bedevil the study of English grammar. It is a topic that had fascinated him for many years and which had prompted him to publish his own grammar textbook, *A New and Improved Grammar of the English Tongue* (henceforth *Grammar*) in 1809. Although twenty years had intervened between the publication of the *Grammar* and the appearance of the *Atlas* essay, Hazlitt adopts the same basic position in both texts: he repeatedly implores his audience not to allow themselves to be 'hoodwinked and led blindfold by mere precedent and authority', and he speaks disparagingly of those who unquestioningly accept the linguistic precepts with which they had been indoctrinated as children.[1] As these remarks suggest, the system of grammatical analysis that was standardly taught in British schools was, for Hazlitt, a detestable absurdity:

If a system were made in burlesque and purposely to call into question and expose its own nakedness, it could not go beyond this, which is gravely taught in all seminaries, and patiently learnt by all school-boys as an exercise and discipline of the intellectual faculties.[2]

The conventional pedagogical practices seem farcical: diligent children are required to master an analytical system which is so profoundly flawed as to be inherently self-parodic. Ever attentive to the fallibility of apparent authorities (be they political, intellectual, linguistic, or otherwise), Hazlitt maintains that dire consequences inevitably follow from an overly servile adherence to tradition, especially when the particular customs involved are fundamentally misguided. Despite his dissatisfaction with the grammar-based pedagogy of the day, he is pessimistic about the possibility of reform, offering an amusing sketch of the sufferings that would have to be endured by a zealous pedagogue who took a novel approach:

> A schoolmaster who should go so far out of his way as to take the Diversions of Purley for a textbook, would be regarded by his brethren of the rod as 'a man of Ind,' and would soon have the dogs of the village bark at him.[3]

This passage is characterised by a distinctly Hazlittian density. The 'Diversions of Purley' is a text that will be discussed at length in this book. It is, essentially, a treatise concerning the analysis of natural language, the first volume of which was published in 1786 by the noted radical John Horne Tooke. Appropriately enough given his subversive political views, Horne Tooke rejected conventional grammatical systems, and argued that etymological analyses were essential if the structure of natural language were ever to be correctly understood. Consequently, the 'Diversions of Purley' provides a provocative alternative to conventional wisdom, and therefore, if a schoolmaster were to compel his pupils to use this inflammatory publication, he would be perceived by his conservative colleagues (the ominously designated 'brethren of the rod') as being guilty of a secular heresy. Hazlitt's phrase 'a man of Ind' is, of course, adapted from *The Tempest*, and it is usually revealing to contextualise such allusions:

Caliban
Doe not torment me: oh.

Stephano
What's the matter?
Haue we diuels here?
Doe you put trickes vpon's with Saluages, and Men of
Inde? ha? I haue not scap'd drowning, to be afeard
now of your foure legges: for it hath bin said; as proper
a man as euer went on foure legs, cannot make him
giue ground: and it shall be said so againe, while Stephano
breathes at' nostrils.[4]

When Stephano and Caliban encounter each other, two different races and cultures collide, and, when the former accuses the latter of trying to torment him with 'Saluages, and Men of Inde', these crude ethnographical classifications provide Hazlitt with a convenient analogical perspective. Like Caliban, the radical village teacher would be viewed as a strange, exotic, possibly infernal, threat. However, for Hazlitt, the fearful response of the schoolmasters would be (like Stephano's) ultimately misjudged and self-deluding, revealing prejudice and ignorance rather than valour and authority. The implications of this small allusion to *The Tempest* are considerable, and it is typical of Hazlitt to allow a discussion of something as seemingly mundane and enervating as the teaching of English grammar to accumulate connotations which problematise broader, more fundamental, social conflicts. Ultimately, it seems, when viewed from an Hazlittian perspective, even the abuses of misanalysis suffered by the words and phrases of the English language become a pretext for the advocacy of radicalism and reform.

It should be clear by now that the argument Hazlitt presents in his 1829 essay highlights the close connections that exist between language and dominant social structures. Given this basic sociolinguistic fact, it is no surprise that, during the past thirty years or so, the sociopolitical implications of Romantic attitudes towards linguistic theory have been explored from a range of different perspectives. In recent work, for instance, Richard Turley has convincingly stressed the centrality of philology during this period:

So thoroughly was the Romantic imagination transformed by its encounter with philology, which routinely addressed 'ultimate' questions about the origins and construction of language, that our conception of Romanticism is necessarily flawed without taking proper account of the relationship.[5]

For Turley, an exploration of Romanticism as a complex socio-political, intellectual, and artistic movement necessitates a clear understanding of contemporaneous philological debates, and it is apparent that there was a widespread perception in the late eighteenth and early nineteenth centuries that natural language and linguistic theory merited serious consideration. Many writers, including Horne Tooke, Lord Monboddo, Wordsworth, Coleridge, Leigh Hunt, Charles Lamb, Percy Shelley, and Thomas De Quincey (to name just a few), mused upon a range of philological topics with varying degrees of exhaustiveness. Sometimes their concerns were literary, sometimes philosophical, sometimes philological, sometimes pedagogical (assuming that these sub-types can be cleanly separated) and their writings will be referred to from time to time in later chapters. However, in order to provide some kind of context at this initial stage, it may be helpful briefly to consider certain contemporaneous language-focused pedagogical anxieties, for Hazlitt was certainly not the only person to express an interest specifically in the educational practices adopted by schoolteachers. In his endearingly arch 1821 essay, 'The Old and the New Schoolmaster', for instance, Charles Lamb describes a coach journey between Bishopsgate and Shacklewell during which his eponymous narratorial persona, Elia, encounters a man whom he later realises is a schoolmaster. The particular questions asked by the latter during their conversation cause Elia to reflect (in a gleefully unapologetic manner) upon the parlous state of his own general knowledge, and this remarkably unremarkable encounter culminates in a series of meditations upon certain changes in pedagogical practice that had occurred in British schools since the Renaissance. Elia broods particularly upon the content and style of education in sixteenth-century grammarschools, and he invokes the great Latinists of the past, figures such as William Lily, John Colet, and Thomas Linacre:

> Rest to the souls of those fine old Pedagogues; the breed, long since extinct, of the Lilys, and the Linacres: who believing that all learning was contained in the languages which they taught, and despising every other acquirement as superficial and useless, came to their task as to a sport! Passing from infancy to age, they dreamed away all their days as in a grammar-school. Revolving in a perpetual cycle of declensions, conjugations, syntaxes, and prosodies; renewing constantly the occupations which had charmed their studious childhood; rehearsing continually the part of the past; life must have slipped from them at last like one day. They were always in their first garden, reaping harvests of their golden time, among their *Flori* and their *Spicilegia*; in Arcadia still, but kings; the ferule of their sway not much harsher, but of like dignity with that mild sceptre attributed to king Basileus; the Greek and Latin, their stately Pamela and their Philoclea; with the occasional duncery of some untoward Tyro, serving for a refreshing interlude of a Mopsa, or a clown Damaetas![6]

Halcyon days then, it seems – days in which benign grammatical monarchs would reap the crops of their erudition in the fields of their childhood. The 'perpetual cycle of declensions, conjugations, syntaxes, and prosodies' provided a reassuringly predictable rhythm for the life of the intellect, and a deeply hierarchical estimation of the value of different subjects ensured that linguistic concerns were prioritised, allowing 'every other acquirement' to be spurned for being comparatively facile and purposeless. In order to demonstrate the depth of this sentiment, Elia quotes at length from the Preface to Colet's *Accidence*, and notes the conformist tendencies of such works:

> How well doth this stately preamble [...] correspond with and illustrate that pious zeal for conformity, expressed in a succeeding clause, which would fence about grammar-rules with the severity of faith-articles! – "as for the diversity of grammars, it is well profitably taken away by the king majesties wis-

dom, who foreseeing the inconvenience, and favourably providing the remedie, caused one kind of grammar by sundry learned men to be diligently drawn and so to be set out, only everywhere to be taught for the use of learners, and for the hurt in changing of schoolmaisters." What a *gusto* in that which follows: "wherein it is Profitable that he Can orderly decline his noun, and his verb." His noun!⁷

The sixteenth century was an age, then, in which 'grammar-rules' were guarded and preserved with the same zealous care as the articles of religion, and in which monarchs could intervene to ensure that the Classical languages were taught in an appropriate manner. No doubt Elia's celebration of the '*gusto*' which he identified as being such a distinctive characteristic of this particular kind of language teaching, caused Hazlitt to smile when he first read the essay. However, having evoked this golden age of theologically-driven philological study, Elia effects an immediate transition by describing the early nineteenth-century approach to the task of educating the young. As he puts it, '[t]he fine dream is fading away fast; and the least concern of a teacher in the present day is to inculcate grammar-rules'.⁸ Rather than being obliged systematically to decline nouns and to conjugate verbs,

[t]he modern schoolmaster is expected to know a little of every thing, because his pupil is required not to be entirely ignorant of any thing. He must be superficially, if I may so say, omniscient. He is to know something of pneumatics; of chemistry; of whatever is curious, or proper to excite the attention of the youthful mind; an insight into mechanics is desirable, with a touch of statistics; the quality of soils, &c. botany, the constitution of his country, *cum multis aliis.*⁹

This passage may be brief, but it highlights some of the consequences that had ensued as a result of the many intricate and protracted reconfigurations of educational practice that had been propagated during the seventeenth and eighteenth centuries. An understanding of the grammatical structure of the Classical languages was, by the 1820s, no longer considered to be a fundamental acquirement; a knowledge, even a shallow one, of modern scientific theories (pneumatics, chemistry, mechanics, statistics, botany, and the like) was deemed essential in all contexts; a bowing acquaintance with the study of socio-political and constitutional matters could be helpful, and, as Elia's mournfully nostalgic Latin tag phrase indicates, there were many other equally important and fascinating modern topics besides these which could be profitably introduced to the eager student.

Elia's remarks are just one example selected from numerous early nineteenth-century writings which suggest that, by this period, the general belief in the self-evident advantages of a grammar-based education had started to wane, that the Classical languages had been inevitably devalued, and that general perceptions concerning the importance of grammatical analysis had shifted. In this context, Leigh Hunt's account of his experiences while studying Latin and Greek at Christ's Hospital, is pertinent. Hunt entered the school in 1792 (soon after Lamb had left it) and, writing in his *Autobiography* fifty-eight years later, he recalled that he had not valued highly the kind of language-focused learning that he had been required to endure:

Being able to read, and knowing a little Latin, I was put at once into the Under Grammar School. How much time I wasted there in learning the accidence and syntax, I can not say ; but it seems to me a long while. My grammar seemed always to open at the same place. Things are managed differently now, I believe, in this as well as in many other respects. The boys feed better, learn better, and have longer holidays in the country. [...] They now have these holidays with a reasonable frequency ; and they all go to the different schools, instead of being confined, as they were then, some to nothing but writing and ciphering, and some to the languages.[10]

Gradually, then, between the 1790s and the 1850s, the pedagogical practice at Christ's Hospital (at least) had altered. Along with reforms concerning meals and vacations, the emphasis of the syllabus had changed too, much to Hunt's retrospective delight, and the type of contrast that he highlights here seems generally to be in accordance with Elia's musing in 'The Old and the New Schoolmaster'. Equally revealing, though, are Hunt's remarks concerning his early literary encounters with the most admired Classical authors:

How little did I care for any verses at that time, except English ones ; I had no regard even for Ovid. I read and knew nothing of Horace ; though I had got somehow a liking for his character. Cicero I disliked, as I can not help doing still. Demosthenes I was inclined to admire, but did not know why, and would very willingly have given up him and his difficulties together. Homer I regarded with horror, as a series of lessons, which I had to learn by heart before I understood him. When I had to conquer, in this way, lines which I had not construed, I had recourse to a sort of artificial memory, by which I associated the Greek words with sounds that had a meaning in English. Thus, a passage about Thetis I made to bear on some circumstance that had taken place in the school. An account of a battle was converted into a series of jokes ; and the master, while I was saying my lesson to him in trepidation, little suspected what a figure he was often cutting in the text. The only classic I remember having any love for was Virgil ; and that was the episode of Nisus and Euryalus.[11]

This joyously unashamed description of a reluctantly received Classical education is disconcertingly frank: the young Hunt was disinclined to evince unquestioning respect for revered authors such as Ovid, Cicero, and Homer. Indeed, the technique of 'artificial memory' that he deployed so imaginatively while conning his Greek extracts is, in effect, a delightfully subtle and adroit form of cultural subversion, a way of disobeying while appearing to conform. The enforced recitation of a description of a prestigious Ancient battle could become merely 'a series of jokes', and even the listening schoolmaster could himself be incorporated into the account, the unwitting target of Hunt's mocking homophonic puns. By destabilising the linguistic component of his traditional Classical education, Hunt was already expressing his dissatisfaction with a prevailing social order, and, in his mature work, he would maintain this kind of provocative stance. Consequently, linguistic and socio-political considerations are necessarily fused.

In the light of the above, it seems as if Turley is correct to emphasise the centrality of linguistic concerns during the Romantic period, and, given this, it is surely obvious that Hazlitt's writings should offer invaluable insights. Apart from his explicit contributions to debates concerning the teaching of English grammar (such as the aforementioned *Atlas* essay), Hazlitt was, of course, a noted literary critic who often incorporated linguistic details into his textual analyses, as well as an essayist who provoked controversy by choosing to write in a unconventionally informal style; therefore, he was well-placed to write about philological matters with a variety of contrasting allegiances. Curiously, though, while his writings about language have sometimes been mentioned by critics who are primarily interested in his philosophical or literary beliefs, his views concerning linguistic theory have received comparatively scant attention in the past. Since this book will attempt to remedy this, it may be helpful, as a prelude, briefly to indicate the range and scope of Hazlitt's writings about this topic.

1.2 Hazlitt on Language and Linguistic Theory

Ignoring for the time-being the useful glimpses that are contained in his letters, Hazlitt's interest in linguistic matters first manifests itself in his earliest publications. For instance, although it does not offer an explicit theory of linguistic function, his *Essay on the Principles of Human Action* (1805), at least indicates the manner in which he rejected certain traditions in eighteenth-century philosophy of mind, an intellectual stance that certainly has implications for linguistic theory. Similarly, early texts such as *The Eloquence of the British Senate* (1807), which Hazlitt edited, testify to his abiding interest in the socio-political dimensions of oratory, rhetoric, and style, though, once again, the discussion of particular grammatical and linguistic structures is minimal. Consequently, Hazlitt's *Grammar* constitutes his first protracted reflection upon the structure of the English language, and this curious little text had a rather odd genesis.[12] The work was commissioned in late 1808 by William Godwin, who intended to sell it as a pedagogical textbook in his 'Juvenile Library' series. Hazlitt managed to complete an initial draft during 1809, and his *Grammar* was published later that year. Hazlitt's grandson later offered a rather melancholic (and not especially well-informed) account of the enterprise:

Mr. and Mrs. Hazlitt settled for the present at Winterslow, in one of the cottages which belonged to the latter in the village. It was there, in the early months of his union, that my grandfather wrote his 'English Grammar', founded on an entirely new principle, and *intended* to supersede Lindley Murray. It was not till 1810, however, that he succeeded in inducing anybody to print it, and it never came to a second edition. 'Murray's Grammar' is still kept in stock; Hazlitt's is only on the shelves of the curious.[13]

As Stanley Jones has shown, there were various reasons why Hazlitt's *Grammar* never reached a second edition. Godwin certainly knew that the text would have to compete with successful existing grammars such as Robert Lowth's *A Short Introduction to English Grammar* (1762) and Lindley Murray's *English Grammar* (1795). Consequently, he had urged Hazlitt to highlight the deficiencies of these publications as often as possible, and Hazlitt had obliged with unflinching precision. Despite this, Godwin quickly became dissatisfied with the project. He seems to have been worried that the *Grammar* would not be accepted by schoolmasters (generally a rather conservative breed), and a negative response from its main target audience would have been disastrous. Matters became even more complex, though, in July 1809, when Godwin received a philological revelation which radically altered his views concerning linguistic pedagogy. As he put it, 'I think I have made an entirely new discovery as to the way of teaching the English language'.[14] Accordingly, he appended to Hazlitt's *Grammar* his own (pseudonymous) *New Guide to the English Tongue* (henceforth *New Guide*), and the type of scheme that he recommended focused upon morphology. Specifically, he noted that many English words can be derived from a root via affixation, and he provided several examples:

Love, substantive.
Love, verb.
Lovely, adjective.
Unlovely, negative adj.
Lover, substantive of the person.
Loveliness, substantive of the thing.[15]

The main point is that, if these words all have to be learned separately, as independent lexical items, then it causes 'superfluity and vexation' for the students.[16] By contrast, if general affixation rules are learnt systematically, then only the root of each derived form need be memorised, since the rules can then be applied mechanically in order to obtain the desired words:

All these meanings are in reality one meaning; all these variations are made by rule; is it not better that the scholar should learn the Rule at once, than that he should repeat a multitude of examples every day, without ever knowing the rule at all.[17]

This observation was not especially original. For instance, eighteenth-century lexicographers had used similar techniques to reduce the number of words that they had to include in their dictionaries.[18] However, Godwin's insight primarily concerned the pedagogical advantages that would accrue if the vocabulary of English were taught to school-children in this manner.

Hazlitt's *Grammar* (supplemented by Godwin's *New Guide*) was finally published in late 1809, and all seemed to be well since it received a favourable notice in the *Critical Review*:

We entirely agree with the author of this useful work, that there is something radically wrong in the common method of teaching English grammar, by transferring the artificial rules o[f] other languages to our own. We also coincide in another opinion of the writer, that 'the grammatical distinctions of words do not relate to the nature of things, or ideas spoken of, but to our manner of speaking them.' This appears to us, on the whole, a more rational, simple, and intelligible English grammar, than most of those in common use; and we think that it may, with great benefit to the scholar, be introduced into our elementary schools.[19]

This anonymous appraisal suggests that Hazlitt's text appealed to those who felt that the teaching of grammar in British schools needed reforming. A less public, but equally encouraging, response was penned by

Hazlitt's friend Charles Lamb in a private letter. Clearly, Lamb did not value Godwin's supplementary treatise highly and, rarely able to resist an inviting pun, he drily observed that

Hazlitt has written a *grammar* for Godwin; Godwin sells it bound up with a treatise of his own on language, but *the grey mare is the better horse*. I don't allude to Mrs. Godwin, but to the word *grammar*, which comes near to *grey mare*, if you observe, in sound. That figure is called paranomasia in Greek. I am sometimes happy in it.[20]

Despite such positive responses, Godwin remained discontent, even with the augmented version of the *Grammar* and, in 1810, he published a revised edition, entitled *Outlines of English Grammar, Partly Abridged from Mr Hazlitt's New and Improved Grammar of the English Language*. Hazlitt was irritated; he declared that he was 'sick of the subject of grammar',[21] and, significantly, when he presented a copy of the textbook to his son, William Hazlitt Jnr, in 1822, he gave him the unabridged version.[22] However, the existence of this modified text accounts for the lack of a second edition of the former, and, therefore, William Carew Hazlitt obfuscated matters somewhat when he claimed that his grandfather's *Grammar* had 'dropped dead from the press'.[23]

If the task of writing his *Grammar* caused Hazlitt to reflect carefully both upon the structure of the English language and upon the best manner of teaching this subject to children, then, in his subsequent work, he was inclined to consider some of the philosophical implications of linguistic analysis in greater detail. For instance, in 1812 he gave a series of *Lectures on English Philosophy* at the Russell Institution, and while this sequence of presentations included detailed discussions of the work of Hobbes, Locke, Berkeley, and others, there was also a lecture concerning John Horne Tooke in which Hazlitt explored the metaphysical implications of Horne Tooke's linguistic theorising. Not surprisingly, Hazlitt's assessment of Horne Tooke's work provides one of the recurrent topics developed in this book, since it is certainly revealing to determine which aspects of the latter's theories Hazlitt accepted and which he rejected.

If Hazlitt's *Grammar* and 1812 lectures provide insights into his thinking about philology, some of his later publications explore linguistic concerns specifically in relation to English literature. Well-known texts such as his *Lectures on the English Poets* (1815-17, printed 1818), *Characters of Shakespear's Plays* (1817), *Lectures on the English Comic Writers* (1819), and *Lectures on the Literature of the Age of Elizabeth* (1820) have

1.2 Hazlitt on Language and Linguistic Theory 11

been frequently discussed, but the passages concerning the status and function of grammatical structures and stylistic registers in literary contexts have not always received the attention they deserve. Predictably, therefore, such details will figure prominently in this book. For instance, while discussing John Arbuthnot, in the *Lectures on the English Poets* Hazlitt observes that

Arbuthnot's style is distinguished from that of his contemporaries, even by a greater degree of terseness and conciseness. He leaves out every superfluous word; is sparing of connecting particles, and introductory phrases; uses always the simplest forms of construction; and is more a master of the idiomatic peculiarities and internal resources of the language than almost any other writer. There is a research in the choice of a plain, as well as of an ornamented or learned style; and, in fact, a great deal more. Among common English words, there may be ten expressing the same thing with different degrees of force and propriety, and only one of them the very word we want, because it is the only one that answers exactly with the idea we have in our minds. Each word in familiar use has a different set of associations and shades of meaning attached to it, and distinguished from each other by inveterate custom; and it is in having the whole of these at our command, and in knowing which to choose, as they are called for by the occasion, that the perfection of a pure conversational prose-style consists. But in writing a florid and artificial style, neither the same range of invention, nor the same quick sense of propriety – nothing but learning is required. If you know the words, and their general meaning, it is sufficient: it is impossible you should know the nicer inflections of signification, depending on an endless variety of application, in expressions borrowed from a foreign or dead language. They all impose upon the ear alike, because they are not familiar to it; the only distinction left is between the pompous and the plain; the *sesquipedalia verba* have this advantage, that they are all of one length; and any words are equally fit for a learned style, so that we have never heard them before.[24]

So, Hazlitt praises Arbuthnot's writing both because his concision avoids superfluity and because his use of idiomatic English precludes artificiality – and it is important to determine which particular linguistic and literary traditions influenced Hazlitt's thinking about such matters. Crucially, in the late eighteenth and early nineteenth centuries, considerations of this sort were unavoidably riddled with socio-political connotations: long accepted social and literary conventions were in a state of transition, and reformers (of many different sorts) were conspicuous. The close association between language, society, and politics is one that will be addressed repeatedly throughout this book since it goes some way towards explaining why Hazlitt responded warmly to some writers (such as Arbuthnot) and coldly to others. It also illuminates the sometimes vitriolic assessments of Hazlitt's own work that were published by certain contemporaneous critics.

Similar reflections upon language and style are sprinkled liberally throughout Hazlitt's various collections of essays. For instance, *The Round Table* (1815-17, printed 1817) contains several pieces, such as 'On Pedantry' and 'On Common-Place Critics', which address a range of linguistic concerns, while *Table Talk, Essays on Men and Manners* (1822) includes such texts as 'On Familiar Style', 'On Criticism', 'On Milton's Sonnets', and 'On Vulgarity and Affectation', all of which probe, in different ways, the social and literary implications of various interconnections that exist between different stylistic and literary registers. Specifically, in 'On Criticism', Hazlitt seeks to sub-classify different kinds of critics, and he attempts to characterise the persistent beliefs to which the members of the different critical sects subscribe. The 'Occult School', for example, champions obfuscation to such an extent that '[i]f an author is utterly unreadable, they can read him for ever: his intricacies are their delight, his mysteries are their study'.[25] By contrast, there are 'the verbal critics', or '*Ultra-Crepidarian* critics', a group that are described as being 'mere word-catchers, fellows that pick out a word in a sentence and a sentence in a volume, and tell you it is wrong'.[26] Clearly, in such classifications, literary judgements and grammatical correctness are brought into close proximity, and this uncomfortable coupling will become the central concern in later chapters. In this context, though, it is worth noting that related issues were addressed at length in Hazlitt's polemical pamphlet 'A Letter to William Gifford, Esq.' (1819), and the linguistic aspects of texts such as this merit close attention. The complexity of the task should not be underestimated, though, and William Gifford (1756-1826) himself, the target of Hazlitt 1819 pamphlet, exemplified the tortuousness of the linguistic and socio-political stratifications. Born in poverty in Devonshire, the son of a house painter, Gifford worked as a plough boy and as a cobbler before becoming a student at Exeter College, Oxford. However, despite his lowly background, he became an embodiment of conservative linguistic and literary values, publishing pro-Tory satires and criticism, and editing *The Quarterly Review*. Since Hazlitt himself was often accused by 'verbal critics' (such as Gifford) of writing in a lowly and debased form of English, it is important to appreciate the cultural and intellectual predilections which prompted both the condemnations of his work and his own robust rebuttals.

Although *The Spirit of the Age* (1825) contains some intriguing passages about linguistic theory, it wasn't until *The Plain Speaker* appeared

1.2 Hazlitt on Language and Linguistic Theory 13

in 1826 that Hazlitt once again gathered together some of his essays that explored familiar language-related preoccupations. Intriguingly, essays such as 'On the Prose-Style of Poets', 'On the Difference between Writing and Speaking', and 'On the Conversation of Authors' indicate the extent to which his interest in such matters had remained largely constant since the early 1800s. For instance, 'On the Difference between Writing and Speaking' assesses various aspects of oratory and eloquence, issues that Hazlitt had foregrounded, albeit in an editorial capacity, in *The Eloquence of the British Senate*, while 'On the Conversation of Authors' once again assesses particular contrasts between speech and writing in different stylistic registers. At one point he observes

> I agree that no style is good that is not fit to be spoken or read aloud with effect. This holds true not only of emphasis and cadence, but also with regard to natural idiom and colloquial freedom. Sterne's was in this respect the best style that ever was written. You fancy that you hear the people talking. For a contrary reason, no college-man writes a good style, or understands it when written. Fine writing is with him all verbiage and monotony – a translation into classical centos or hexameter-lines.[27]

Hazlitt's commendation of Sterne's 'natural idiom' recalls his praise for Arbuthnot's idiomatic style, and suggests that, for Hazlitt, good spoken and written English do not conform to different sets of stylistic criteria. Academic writing, which is far removed from conversational speech, is artificial and stilted, full of mere 'verbiage and monotony'. Obviously, these topics will feature prominently in the ensuing chapters of this book.

The preceeding paragraphs have hopefully provided a brisk catalogue of some of the ways in which linguistic concerns manifest themselves in Hazlitt's published works. Despite this, though, his musings about such topics have been eerily neglected by critics in the past. In particular, comparatively little has been written about the way in which nineteenth-century British, continental, and North American readers responded to his philological ideas. Accordingly, since the reception history of Hazlitt's work has never received sustained attention, it is useful to determine which specific issues have been addressed previously, and, although the following overview cannot be comprehensive, it can at least indicate how attitudes towards Hazlitt's linguistic interests have fluctuated and shifted since his death in 1830.

1.3 Reception and Analysis

Soon after his father's death, Hazlitt's son, William Hazlitt Jnr, gathered together various selected writings for the 1836 collection *Literary Remains of the Late William Hazlitt*, and he mentions the *Grammar* in his introduction:

> Part of the summer of this year (1808) was occupied in the composition of an English Grammar, which was published, soon afterwards, by Mr. Godwin. The principle points in which this Grammar differed from others are four. First, in the definitions of the parts of speech; secondly, the compound and constructive tenses of the verbs are separated from the real inflections, and thrown back into the syntax, to which they properly belong; thirdly, a brief review is given of Horne Tooke's theory of Grammar; and lastly, an endeavour is made to render syntax more perfect than in the prevailing systems. This work was favourably received and was afterwards abridged by Mr. Godwin, under the name of Baldwin.[28]

While the four points mentioned here will all be discussed in greater detail later, the fact that Hazlitt's *Grammar* is described as carefully as this suggests that his grammatical labours had certainly not been forgotten. Indeed, William Hazlitt Jnr explicitly emphasises the way in which his father's work differed from that of other grammarians such as Lowth and Murray – respected authorities whose names were still familiar in the 1830s.

As the nineteenth century advanced, though, Hazlitt gradually became a less distinct figure. Aware of this drift towards obscurity, a later generation of admirers attempted to revivify his reputation, and a number of publications sought to establish his reputation as an acknowledged master of English prose. Most prominent amongst texts of this kind were William Carew Hazlitt's *Memoirs of William Hazlitt; with Portions of his Correspondence* (1867) and Alexander Ireland's two volumes, *List of the Writings of William Hazlitt and Leigh Hunt* (1868) and *William Hazlitt, Essayist and Critic: Selections from his Writings, with a Memoir, Biographical and Critical* (1889). Significantly, these works justify their own existence partly by claiming that they are seeking to popularise Hazlitt's work. William Carew Hazlitt, for instance, suggests (or, at least, hopes) that while the number of living representatives of the Regency generation is gradually dwindling, younger Victorians are nonetheless being drawn to his grandfather's writings: 'while death kept thinning the ranks, new recruits did not cease to enrol themselves'.[29] By contrast, when Ireland assessed the mood of his contemporaries twenty years later, he concluded that Hazlitt was not widely read:

Should the following selections from his writings inspire in some thoughtful minds a desire to become better acquainted with a remarkable writer, too little known to the present generation, I shall feel amply rewarded for my labour of love.[30]

Seemingly, then, although Hazlitt was admired by authors such as Dickens, Thackeray, Bagehot, and Stevenson, the general public was not especially familiar with his work in the 1880s, which suggests that he had become a writer's writer. Not surprisingly, perhaps, as his reputation declined, his writings about linguistic matters received less (and less probing) attention. Although William Carew Hazlitt, for instance, paraphrases (in the third person) Hazlitt's anecdote concerning a woman who had once complained because he used the word 'learneder' rather than 'more learned', he merely summarises the incident and does not comment on the particular stylistic concerns that it raises.[31] Chatty asides of this kind are liberally included in the *Memoirs*, but there are no serious attempts to evalute Hazlitt's views concerning linguistic theory and literary style.

Partly due to the labours of certain late-Victorian memorialists, Hazlitt became better known during the period 1880-1920, and, significantly, his views concerning philology and literary style once again became a topic of interest. Caleb Thomas Winchester's *A Group of Essayists of the Early Nineteenth Century* (1910) exemplifies this tendency, since it provides an assessment of the prose style(s) deployed by writers such as Hazlitt, Lamb, and De Quincey. In particular, Hazlitt is described as being 'one of the most delightful writers', and, although denying him absolute supremacy, Winchester is content to accord him high status in the literary pantheon of the Regency period:

Let me first except Sir Walter's novels and everything of Lamb's, and then I insist that the very best prose written in English between 1800 and 1830 is to be found in the pages of William Hazlitt.[32]

While Winchester's sometimes tiresomely urbane appraisal does not merit close consideration, it is of interest that he attempts to determine the precise nature of Hazlitt's 'eloquence'. Alluding to De Quincey's verdict that Hazlitt's writings lacked this particular quality, Winchester observes, rather mysteriously, that 'there are many passages in his essays that, if not eloquent, are something better'.[33] Although he does not indicate exactly which stylistic qualities are superior to eloquence, attitudes concerning such topics had altered since the mid nineteenth century, and Hazlitt's work appears to have benefited from the change.

The fact that Hazlitt's writings had started to reach a wider audience in the early twentieth century is evidenced by the appearance of Jules Douady's *Vie de William Hazlitt L'essayiste* (1907). The reception history of Hazlitt's work in the French critical tradition has never really been explored in detail, yet given his experiences while living in Paris in 1802-1803 and his 1824 account of his journey through France (and Italy), not to mention his lifelong admiration of Napoleon (which culminated in a vast four volume biography), texts such as Douady's are of considerable importance since they enable Hazlitt to be surveyed from a distinctly Gallic perspective. For instance, Douady states openly that Hazlitt was even less well-known to French readers in the early twentieth century than he had been to English readers in the last decades of the nineteenth century. Indeed, he confesses that Hazlitt is 'à peine connu, même de nom'.[34] It is of interest, therefore, that he discusses Hazlitt's linguistic work at some length, and, curiously, he is rather dismissive, claiming that the latter's interest in this topic was merely a temporary and superficial caprice:

[c]ette passion philologique n'etait chez Hazlitt (nullement spécialiste en la matière) qu'une fantaisie accidentelle et passagère, due biens moins aux attraits de la syntaxe des noms et des verbes, qu'à l'influence d'un philologue amateur, le fameux Horne Tooke, pour la personne duquel Hazlitt avait infiniment de considération [...].[35]

This is a contentious passage. As will be shown in the main chapters of this book, it is as erroneous to assert that Hazlitt's interest in grammar was 'une fantaisie accidentelle et passagère' as it is to claim that Horne Tooke was a person for whom Hazlitt had 'infiniment de considération'. Nonetheless, despite these insufficiencies, Douady's account of Hazlitt's life and work, which inevitably drew heavily upon William Carew Hazlitt's *Memoirs* and other late nineteenth-century publications, places Hazlitt in the context of the continental European tradition, preparing the ground for later studies such as Jules Dechamps's *Hazlitt et Napolèon* (1939).

By the early twentieth century, then, Hazlitt was no longer a forgotten figure, and, consequently, a reliable critical edition of his complete works became desirable. The centenary of Hazlitt's death prompted Percival Presland Howe to prepare his twenty-one volume edition of *The Complete Works of William Hazlitt* (1930-1934), which effectively replaced Alfred Rayney Waller's and Arnold Glover's twelve volume 1902 *Collected Works*. In conformity with its title, Howe's edition brought together all of Hazlitt's writings that were known to exist. Consequently, for the first time in over one hundred years, the text of the original version of his *Grammar* (i.e., the 1809 text) was easily accessible, as were other less well-known works such as the 1812 lectures on British philosophy, and isolated articles such as his 1829 essay on 'English Grammar'. In addition to the texts themselves, though, Howe provided critical, if selective, notes which contextualised Hazlitt's arguments and explained references and allusions which had become obscure with the passing decades. Howe himself seems to to have valued Hazlitt's linguistic writings particularly highly, remarking of the *Grammar* in his 1922 biography that '[i]ts philology only, which he took from Horne Tooke, is outmoded'.[36]

As the twentieth century advanced, Hazlitt's theories concerning the desirable linguistic qualities of a fine prose style began to be considered with greater acuity, and texts such as Emma Chandler's *An Analysis of the Stylistic Technique of Addison, Johnson, Hazlitt, and Pater* (1928) and Stewart Wilcox's probing study *Hazlitt in the Workshop: The Manuscript of The Fight* (1943) are representative of this trend. The latter, in particular, focuses attention on the way in which Hazlitt crafted his 'familiar' style, and therefore relates his theories to his actual practice. By examining the textual revisions to the 'The Fight', which are visible on the existing handwritten sheets of this essay, Wilcox was able to explore the manner in which Hazlitt adapted and modified his own initial grammatical and lexical choices in order to ensure that his essay made more extensive use of common idioms. As Wilcox notes, the main purpose of his study is 'to examine Hazlitt's writing habits in order to illuminate his methods of composition and revision, and his sense of structure and style',[37] and he comments that

[h]e was a direct descendent of the Addisonian style of the eighteenth century, and, like Dryden in the "Defence of the Epilogue," advocated a golden mean in diction and usage that is governed by fashion and custom. Yet this restraint might have robbed even Hazlitt of his liveliness had he not given rein to the familiar elements of style.[38]

While some of Wilcox's ideas will be discussed in detail in chapter 4, it is worth stressing that his study explores the implications of the fact that Hazlitt wrote 'The Fight' soon after completing his essay 'On Familiar Style', and, given this association, it is not surprising that there should be close connections between the stylistic properties advocated in the latter essay, and the characteristic lexical and grammatical structures present in the former.

During the period 1930-1970, Hazlitt's philosophical writings began to be read with real seriousness for the first time, a process that had been facilitated, and to some extent inspired, by the appearance of the *Essay on the Principles of Human Action* in Howe's *Complete Works*. Elisabeth Schneider's *The Aesthetics of William Hazlitt: a Study of the Philosophical Basis of his Criticism* (1933) and William Prince Albrecht's *Hazlitt and the Creative Imagination* (1965) both belong to this general movement, and such studies in turn implied that the conventional view of Hazlitt as merely an impressive early nineteenth-century literary critic required considerable reassessment. As a result, a flurry of biographies appeared during the middle of the twentieth century, with Hesketh Pearson's *The Fool of Love (a Life of William Hazlitt)* (1934), John Boynton Priestley's *William Hazlitt* (1960), Herschel Baker's *William Hazlitt* (1962), and Ralph Wardle's *Hazlitt* (1971) being the most prominent. Given the biographical focus of these studies, it inevitable that assessments of Hazlitt's attitudes towards language and linguistic theory should only occur briefly and sporadically. For instance, Baker states rather bluntly that Hazlitt wrote his *Grammar* merely 'to make money', adding that even Hazlitt's mastery of English prose 'cannot save the little book from dullness', and other comments are equally negative.[39] He maintains, for example, that 'in his own approach to language he [i.e., Hazlitt] had merely followed John Horne Tooke'.[40] Although Baker devotes six full pages (171-177) to a consideration of the influence that Horne Tooke's work exerted upon Hazlitt, he nevertheless fails to recognise the full complexity of the association between these two theorists.

The 1970s continued the revival in Hazlitt scholarship, and Roy Park's *Hazlitt and the Spirit of the Age: Abstraction and Critical Theory* (1971) is still quite rightly deemed to be a seminal contribution to the field. However, while Park's monograph offers profound analyses of (amongst other things) Hazlitt's rejection of empiricism, the relationship between painting and philosophy, and the role of abstraction in literary criticism, it barely addresses the problems raised specifically by his linguistic work. For instance, the *Grammar* is not even mentioned, and some of his important later essays, which elaborately reveal his views concerning various language-related matters, are only briefly discussed. The essay 'On Familiar Style', for example, which, as noted earlier, reveals Hazlitt's awareness of the socio-political and literary implications of different stylistic registers, is only referred to once, when it is described merely as being '[t]he best general introduction to his criticism of individual prose writers'.[41] There is no attempt, however, to situate this essay in the context of (say) either the belletristic rhetoric movement of the late eighteenth century or the contemporaneous grammar textbook tradition, yet, without such contextualisation, this subtle essay remains recondite and strangely disconnected.

If Park's critical study was the most significant work of Hazlitt-related scholarship to emerge from the 1970s, then there is no doubt that David Bromwich's masterly *Hazlitt: The Mind of a Critic* (1983, 2nd ed. 1999) was the most important text to appear in the 1980s. Unfortunately, though, Bromwich also chose not to prioritise Hazlitt's writings about linguistic theory: he does not mention (let alone discuss) the *Grammar*, and while some aspects of literary style are explored, they are not placed in their full historical context. Although he includes a whole chapter entitled 'Familiar Style', for instance, he largely avoids close language-based analysis of Hazlitt's work. First, he compares and contrasts Hazlitt and Montaigne, before considering the way in which 'associative energy' manifests itself in three of the former's essays.[42] While Bromwich states that he wishes to elucidate Hazlitt's 'larger strategy of shifts, transpositions, sudden invasions from or excusions to a far reach of the world, or another mind', his discussion of stylistic properties usually remains merely metaphorial.[43] For example, we are told that 'Hazlitt's "I" can enter the scene like a whirlwind, and leave the whole countenance of things altered by his departure' and while this obviously presents a vivid analogy, it is a shame that there is no detailed discussion of specific passages which exemplify these characteristic pronominal changes.[44] Such considerations, though, are crucial since, in the early nineteenth century, the appearance of a particular part-of-speech in an unconventional sentential context could insinuate (or, at least, be perceived to insinuate) an author's political allegiances. Bromwich was clearly aware of the political dimensions to the literature of the Romantic period; he offers probing reflections upon Hazlitt's responses to such figures as William Gifford and Edmund Burke, and it is simply unfortunate that he never approached these topics from a linguistic perspective.[45]

Partly as a result of the resurgence of interest in Hazlitt's work that was prompted by texts such as Park's and Bromwich's, several new biographies have appeared subsequently, and the most authoritative works of this kind are probably Stanley Jones's *Hazlitt, a Life: from Winterslow to Frith Street* (1989) and A.C. Grayling's *The Quarrel of the Age: the Life and Times of William Hazlitt* (2001). Since these texts both attempt to provide a summary of Hazlitt's life and work, they do not concentrate specifically and exclusively upon his linguistic interests, and the introductory discussions they contain, while useful as an initial guide, are understandably superficial. However, the pervasive neglect of Hazlitt's preoccupation with linguistic theory is perhaps best exemplified in Duncan Wu's 9-volume *The Selected Writings of William Hazlitt* (1998). Since, by self-proclaimed definition, a collection of selected writings cannot be comprehensive, it is always revealing to consider which particular writings have been included and which excluded. In this case, it is symptomatic that Hazlitt's *Grammar* does not appear in Wu's edition, and that later lectures and essays about various linguistic topics have also been omitted. Consequently, if one were to use Wu's volumes, without exploring the additional texts contained in Howe's *Complete Works*, then one would be inclined to conclude (erroneously) that Hazlitt had not been especially interested in the analysis of natural language.

The availability of new biographical studies and freshly edited texts coincided with a renewal of interest specifically in Hazlitt's political and philosophical work, and, as a result, several researchers have attempted to elucidate the arguments that Hazlitt presented in order to motivate his rejection of empiricism, and to identify the particular characteristics of his own brand of philosophical idealism. The most important monographs that have focused on these and related issues are Uttara Natarajan's *Hazlitt and the Reach of Sense: Criticism, Morals, and the Metaphysics of Power* (1998), Tom Paulin's *The Day-Star of Liberty: William Hazlitt's Radical Style* (1998), and Natarajan *et al*'s *Metaphysical Hazlitt: Bicentenary Essays* (2005). This research has encouraged a reassessment of texts such as *An Essay on the Principles of Human Action* and the 1812 *Lectures on English Philosophy*, and, as a consequence, a greater value has been placed upon Hazlitt's contributions to philosophical enquiry. This is a worthwhile development, and one desirable consequence is that it has prompted certain critics to approach his writings about language with greater care. In general, though, when this has occurred, the main intention has been to search through his various discussions of language for clues as to the nature of his critique of empiricism. For example, Natarajan considers such matters in chapter 1 of *Hazlitt and the Reach of Sense*, and during the engaging analysis offered there, Hazlitt's linguistic work is considered in direct relation to that of Horne Tooke. Natarajan's main purpose is to demonstrate how and why Hazlitt rejected the kind of strict empiricist stance that Horne Tooke espoused, and therefore Hazlitt is described as presenting language as 'the manifestation of an innate formative ability in the mind'.[46] Although this attempt to contextualise Hazlitt's philological inclinations is certainly welcome, it is unfortunate that Natarajan does not also discuss Hazlitt's frequently expressed admiration for Horne Tooke's etymological researches into indeclinable function words, since his advocacy for this part of Horne Tooke's theory indicates that he responded to empiricist linguistic theories in a rather complex manner. Given this, it is crucial to determine whether both the admiration and contempt that Hazlitt expressed, at different times, for Horne Tooke's philologising were reconcilable or contradictory. However, such intricacies are only revealed if Hazlitt's views are contextualised in several different ways, and this cannot be accomplished with any completeness if his writings about language are merely positioned in relation to contemporaneous debates concerning empiricism and idealism, crucial those these were to the development of his thought.

Outside the particular tradition of Hazlitt-centred scholarship, a few of the issues mentioned above have sometimes been briefly considered in texts which are primarily concerned with linguistic theory in the eighteenth and early nineteenth centuries. For instance, Hazlitt's views concerning language are mentioned, if only parsimoniously, in Hans Aarsleff's *The Study of Language in England, 1780-1860* (1983), a text in which Hazlitt is condemned (along with such figures as Erasmus Darwin, Thomas Belsham, James Mill, and Jeremy Bentham) for being one of those 'philosophic radicals' that were 'too dazzled by the flash of light to examine its source', where 'the flash of light' refers to the kind of etymological analysis that Horne Tooke had presented in his *Diversions*.[47] Aarsleff's remark suggests that Hazlitt meekly accepted Horne Tooke's conclusions with unquestioning admiration. However, as noted above, the conventional critical stance maintains that Hazlitt completely rejected Horne Tooke's methods and conclusions. For instance, according to Tim Milnes, Hazlitt consistently maintained that 'Tooke's etymological reductivism' was 'ill-conceived', thereby suggesting that, far from being blinded by the lustre of *Diversions*, Hazlitt actually scrutinised it closely and had profound doubts about the advantages of such an approach.[48] It is intriguing, to say the least, that two such contrasting conclusions could be reached. Apparent disjunctions such as these obviously require exploration and, if possible, explanation.

Other studies which concentrate predominantly on eighteenth- and nineteenth-century theories of language include (to specify just a few) Olivia Smith's *The Politics of Language: 1791-1819* (1984), Richard

Turley's *The Politics of Language in Romantic Literature* (2002), and William Keach's *Arbitrary Power: Romanticism, Language, Politics* (2004). While Hazlitt's work is sometimes mentioned in these works, it never provides a main focus. Turley, for instance, notes that Hazlitt 'commented influentially on language throughout his career' – but this is all he says about the matter, and there is no attempt to illuminate the precise nature of Hazlitt's contribution.[49] Such remarks tantalise rather than satisfy, and they certainly suggest that Hazlitt's various reflections upon natural language and linguistic theory have not yet received the critical attention they deserve, especially if, as Turley claims, his statements about such matters were indeed influential.

1.4 The Way Ahead

As the above discussion has hopefully demonstrated, Hazlitt's numerous writings about language and linguistic theory have been treated with scant regard in previous studies, and the following chapters will attempt to rectify this. Accordingly, in order to sketch in the background for the ensuing discussion, chapter 2 presents an overview of a range of eighteenth-century theories concerning the structure and function of natural language. Not surprisingly, the main emphasis falls upon those texts and authors which subsequently exerted a discernable influence over Hazlitt. In particular, the 'philosophical grammar' movement is described and the content and purpose of several major treatises (such as James Harris' *Hermes* (1751), Joseph Priestley's *Course of Lectures on The Theory of Language, and Universal Grammar* (1762), and Horne Tooke's *Diversions*) is summarised. In a similar manner and for similar reasons, belletristic rhetoric, grammar textbooks, and dictionaries are also considered. The main discussion of Hazlitt's work begins with chapter 3, which concentrates upon his response to the eighteenth-century philosophical grammar movement. In particular, his evaluation of the work of Horne Tooke is assessed, and the central task is to demonstrate that, rather than merely rejecting Horne Tooke as a dangerous and unswerving empiricist (as has often been claimed), Hazlitt in fact selectively incorporated ideas developed in *Diversions* into his own philological writings. For example, while he often condemned Horne Tooke's metaphysical beliefs, he consistently responded with enthusiasm to his analyses of indeclinable function words, and in order to understand the rationale behind this seemingly inconsistent stance, Hazlitt's linguistic work must be assessed in relation to his philosophical convictions.

1.4 The Way Ahead

If chapter 3 focuses upon Hazlitt's response to the philosophical grammar movement, then his views concerning more practical guides to natural language are explored in chapter 4. In essence, this chapter situates Hazlitt's writings about language in the context of the eighteenth-century grammar textbook tradition, and in order to accomplish this, it is necessary to consider the relationships that existed between publications such as Murray's *English Grammar* and certain treatises about belletristic rhetoric that appeared during the second half of the eighteenth century. In particular, George Campbell's *The Philosophy of Rhetoric* (1776) and Hugh Blair's *Lectures on Rhetoric and Belles Lettres* (1783) provide the main focus, and it is shown that Murray drew upon such texts (sometimes *verbatim*) when he collated the materials for his influential *English Grammar*. Given this background, this chapter relates Hazlitt's own *Grammar* to Lowth's and Murray's texts, indicating how he attempted to distinguish his work from theirs. In addition, though, Hazlitt's advocacy of the 'familiar style' is assessed, and it is argued that he sought to prove that, far from constituting a low and contemptible literary manner of writing, the familiar style conformed to the kind of stylistic guidelines specified by theorists such as Lowth, Campbell, Blair, and Murray.

Given the various topics addressed in chapters 3 and 4, it is appropriate that chapter 5 should attempt to indicate the extent to which Hazlitt's views concerning linguistic theory influenced his literary criticism. For instance, his negative appraisal of Pope's verse in his *Grammar* is considered in relation to the views expressed in his mature criticism, and it is argued that his later critiques often explore linguistic concerns that were first expressed in his early writings about the English language. In a similar manner, given Hazlitt's advocacy of idioms in the context of general linguistic theory, it is shown that, in his literary critical works, he consistently admired writers who either used existing idioms, or else constructed phrases in such an artful manner that they ultimately became idioms themselves.

As a coda to the main discussion, the final chapter of this book, chapter 6, considers Hazlitt's views concerning natural language, stylistic registers, and linguistic theory in the context of subsequent developments that occurred in the decades following his death. This task is complicated somewhat by the fact that the Victorian grammar textbook tradition has never been studied in exhaustive detail, and, consequently, our understanding of this aspect of Victorian culture is more nebulous than is desirable. However, by considering Hazlitt's work in the context of prose writers, newspapers, and grammar textbooks that were published in the mid to late nineteenth century, it becomes possible to perceive some of the connections that relate the Romantic period to specific cultural changes that occurred from 1830 to 1900. In general, this is an area of historiographical linguistics that awaits more serious consideration, and the observations offered in chapter 6 only provide an initial glimpse of several sprawling and diverse topics.

2
Linguistic Theory in the Eighteenth Century

2.1 Theories and Theorists

It will quickly become apparent that the overview of eighteenth-century linguistic theory offered in this chapter is wilfully idiosyncratic, but this quirkiness is inevitable (indeed desirable) since the central purpose is to explore those works and ideas which influenced Hazlitt's thinking about natural language and linguistic theory. Consequently, the ensuing account is not intended to offer a comprehensive survey of eighteenth-century philology. Indeed, an exhaustive discussion of this beguiling topic could hardly be accomplished in several sizeable tomes. Therefore, in this fragmentary exploration, several notable works will be analysed in detail, while others, no less significant, will be mentioned only in passing, and no doubt this approach will sometimes seem perverse. Nonetheless, it will ensure that the foundations for the discussions that are developed in later chapters are securely in place.

2.2 Philosophy of Language

John Locke's influence upon eighteenth-century language-related philosophy is well-attested. However, as Hazlitt himself repeatedly emphasised, although Locke included only a few explicit references to other texts in his *An Essay Concerning Human Understanding* (1689; henceforth *Essay*), many aspects of his philosophy of mind can be traced back to theories promulgated by earlier theorists – and Thomas Hobbes is perhaps the most obvious antecedent. In fact, for Hazlitt, Locke's dependence on Hobbes was such that many of the plaudits bestowed upon the former rightly belonged to the latter. As he put it in one of his 1812 lectures, 'Mr. Locke was not really the founder of the modern system of philosophy as it respects the human mind' – this accolade, he claimed, should rightly be accorded to Hobbes.[1] Although when substantiating assertions like this Hazlitt sometimes quoted from texts such as *De Corpore Politico, or the Elements of Law, Moral & Politick* (1649), he returned to *Leviathan* (1651) most frequently, and it formed the basis of his critique. In particular, he was keen to demonstrate that eighteenth-century empiricism was rooted firmly in Hobbes' reflections concerning human understanding, and he was struck by the latter's insistence on the fundamental importance of sensory perception which is manifest in observations such as 'there is no conception in a man's mind, which hath not at first, totally, or by parts, been begotten upon the organs of Sense'.[2] Hazlitt was swift to recognise that statements such as this partly anticipated Locke's more fully developed account. As regards language specifically, Hobbes' characteristic logocentrism is made explicit when he contrasts printing and speech, claiming that the latter is 'the most noble and profitable invention of all other',[3] and his literalistic scriptural slant reveals itself when he declares that '[t]he first author of Speech was *God* himself'.[4] If speech had a divine and monogenetic origin, though, then the conspicuous diversity of languages in the modern world requires explanation, and, conventionally, Hobbes accounts for this plurality by referring to the aftermath of the Tower of Babel.[5] Linguistic diversity, then, came to be associated with sinfulness, and, throughout the seventeenth and eighteenth centuries, there was a tendency to view linguistic standardisation as being desirable for moral as well as philological reasons.

While Hobbes' work was certainly familiar to many eighteenth century language theorists, the unavoidable philosophical text to which they were compelled to respond, either overtly or covertly, was Locke's *Essay*. Although the intricacies of Locke's thinking about the structure and purpose of natural language cannot be explored here in their entirety, it is possible to outline a few of his most influential claims – especially those that provoked the ire of Hazlitt. As noted earlier, Hazlitt was not impressed with Locke's *Essay*, and, at his most acerbic, he could be brutal, once denigrating Locke for being '[...] without any exception, the most barefaced, deliberate and bungling plagiarist, that ever appeared in philosophy'.[6] Despite being daringly provocative, statements such as this do not really indicate why Hazlitt was inclined to question the significance of the *Essay*, and, in order to understand his critique, it is important to assess Locke's theory of language in its own terms. For instance, it is well known that Locke philosophy of mind posits a dis-

2.2 Philosophy of Language 27

tinction between 'simple ideas', which are received 'from *sensation* and *reflection*', and 'complex ideas', which are 'made up of several simple ones put together', and his subsequent division of complex ideas into three distinct subtypes – namely, modes, substances, and relations – remains controversial.[7] Significantly, Locke posits this ideational ontology in Book II, thus confining his later discussion of language to this particular analytical framework. Indeed, the dependence of language upon thought (or, more particularly, of words upon ideas) is central to the *Essay*. For example, Locke states clearly that 'Man' produces 'articulate sounds', or spoken words, which 'stand as Marks for the *Ideas* within his own Mind',[8] noting that words are 'sensible Marks of *Ideas*' and that 'the *Ideas* they stand for, are their proper and immediate Signification'.[9] As these quotations indicate, Locke was frequently concerned with semantic theory – in particular, he sought to demonstrate how meaning, or 'Signification', results from the tripartite relationships that exist between ideas, words, and things. Nonetheless, he was certainly not uninterested in grammatical concerns, nor was he unaware of the difficulties which disturb any attempt to classify words into syntactic categories. For instance, fully cognisant of the fact that his discussion of the 'names' of simple and complex ideas in Book III (chapters 4-6) provides no real insight into grammatical concerns, he offers a brief analysis of 'Particles' in chapter 7. For Locke, particles such as prepositions and conjunctions were of considerable importance mainly because they indicate the sorts of connections that exist between different ideas, and he bewailed the fact that 'this part of Grammar has been, perhaps, as much neglected, as some other overly-diligently cultivated'.[10] The following lines help to clarify why words of this type were central to Locke's philosophy of language:

[...] Particles themselves, in some Languages, have been, with great show of exactness, ranked into their several Orders. But though *Prepositions* and *Conjunctions*, &c., are names well known in Grammar, and the Particles contained under them carefully ranked into their distinct subdivisions; yet he who would show the right use of Particles, and what significancy and force they have, must take a little more pains, enter into his own Thoughts, and observe nicely the several Postures of his Mind in discoursing.[11]

The phrase 'the several Postures of his Mind in discoursing' is critical here: in order to understand the manner in which particles operate, superficial analogies between English and, say, Latin are unhelpful. Instead, the philosopher of language must reply upon finely discriminative introspection in order to determine the manner in which such words are deployed – a task which constitutes a type of stylistic analysis.

Locke's interest in stylistic matters manifests itself elsewhere in the *Essay* – especially when he reflects upon the nature of linguistic imperfection. He notes, for example, that words are often problematic because of the '*doubtfulness* and uncertainty *of their signification*',[12] and he adds that the 'imperfection' which results from words being associated with certain kinds of complex ideas (e.g., mixed modes) cannot be avoided:

'Tis true, *common Use*, that is, the Rule of Propriety may be supposed here to afford some aid, to settle the signification of Language; and it cannot be denied but that in some measure it does. Common use *regulates the meaning of Words* pretty well for common Conversation; but nobody having an Authority to establish the precise signification of Words, nor determine to what *Ideas* any one shall annex them, common Use is not sufficient to adjust them to philosophical Discourses; there being scarce any Name of any very complex *Idea* (to say nothing of others) which, in common Use, has not a great latitude, and which, keeping within the bounds of Propriety, may not be made the sign of far different *Ideas*. Besides, the rule and measure of Propriety its self being nowhere established, it is often matter of dispute, whether this or that way of using a Word, be Propriety of Speech, or no.[13]

In passages such as this, the relationship between language and society is foregrounded: semantic ambiguity cannot be avoided even if 'common Use' is adopted, since the conventions of 'Propriety' can never be established irrefutably, and although common conversation can occur despite this uncertainty, 'philosophical Discourse' requires greater precision. Intriguingly, as described in section 2.6, the term 'Propriety' became increasingly central to linguistic theory during the eighteenth century, eventually being incorporated into the complex schemes proposed by the belletristic rhetoricians.

While Locke identifies certain linguistic imperfections which are inherent and unavoidable, he later catalogues a number of 'abuses' which could be eliminated from all discourse if only the participants were minded to eradicate these 'wilful Faults and Neglects'.[14] Offences of this kind include such things as using words without a clear understanding of their meaning (Locke offers the intentionally provocative examples '*Wisdom*','*Glory*', and '*Grace*') and generating 'affected obscurity' by devising new connotations for old words.[15] By enumerating these abuses, Locke identifies areas of linguistic communication which could be rendered less opaque, and, he proposes a number of remedies for these

2.2 Philosophy of Language 29

problems. For example, he suggests that one should 'take care *to use no word without a signification*, no name without an *Idea*',[16] and he indicates that this sort of conversational discipline could greatly ameliorate linguistic communication.

The above overview has sketched a few of Locke's linguistic concerns, and such was his influence that all who wrote about natural language during the eighteenth century felt obliged to respond. Some, like David Hume in his *A Treatise of Human Nature* (1739) confronted Locke directly by reconsidering some of the topics that he had broached, while others, like Adam Smith and Lord Monboddo, chose to concentrate instead on the origin and development of language, both topics about which Locke had little to say.[17] This latter subject intrigued another philosopher who has already been mentioned in relation to Hazlitt – namely, William Godwin – and although Godwin cannot be classified as a linguist of particular distinction, his *Enquiry Concerning Political Justice* (1793; henceforth *Political Justice*) merits attention in this context since the view of language offered there draws upon theories of origins and evolution in order to provide a sharp contrast with Locke's ultimately pessimistic assessment of the imperfections of linguistic communication. In chapter 6, for instance, Godwin writes about the 'Perfectibility of Man', and one of the topics that he addresses is linguistic communication.[18] Viewing natural languages in relation to a hypothetical account of the crude communication systems that human beings must have used initially, Godwin notes that modern languages manifest various 'improvements'.[19] While the first spoken words must have been like 'those involuntary cries, which infants for example are found to utter in the earliest stages of their existence', languages now enjoy 'the copiousness of lexicography or the regularity of grammar'.[20] Godwin's assertion is that natural language is one of the 'human inventions' that is continually improving and which is, indeed, ultimately perfectible,[21] and this assessment certainly implies that natural language is constantly evolving towards an ideal state. Clearly, for Godwin, linguistic developments were inextricably associated with socio-political advances, and his views concerning social progress can be related to his understanding of linguistic improvments. As will be demonstrated in this book, Godwin was not unusual in identifying similarities between linguistic and political structures.

2.3 Philosophical Grammars

The philosophical interest in natural language, which became an insistent concern in the eighteenth century, is apparent also in other genres. For instance, from the mid century onwards, rather than merely focusing upon specific structures and categories associated with a given language, certain theorists sought to identify those properties that were common to *all* languages, an approach that became know as 'universal' or 'philosophical' grammar. With a few exceptions, the philosophical grammars can be distinguished from the 'textbook' grammars that are discussed in section 2.4, since, although the former often provided analyses of linguistic structures, they were not intended to be used in classrooms. Indeed, in order to understand the function and purpose of the philosophical grammars, it is necessary to view them in the context of earlier traditions.

The second half of the seventeenth century witnessed a remarkable proliferation of linguistic exploration. While these investigations were prompted by a startlingly diverse range of intellectual and cultural concerns, certain dominant patterns emerge with reasonable distinctness. For instance, a profound theological awareness of the (perceived) imperfections of natural languages motivated particular theorists to attempt to create artificial 'philosophical' languages which were designed to eradicate (or at least to minimise) arbitrary ambiguity. Perhaps the most celebrated work of this kind was John Wilkins' *An Essay towards a Real Character and a Philosophical Language* (1668). In this text, Wilkins attempted to provide a graphemic encoding which would enable every possible thought to have a unique expression such that it could be read and understood perfectly by anyone familiar with his system, irrespective of their native language. The resulting scheme, he claimed, defined a universal language which would allow communication to occur with greater exactness. Although Wilkins' work was particularly influential, many other 'universal language' schemes were constructed – the most important being devised by people such as Cave Beck, George Dalgarno, and Francis Lodwick – and these systems, which all intricately combined philosophical and grammatical concerns, were usually underpinned by Aristotelian taxonomological ontologies.[22] By the middle of the eighteenth century, though, the creation of artificial languages was no longer a dominant focus of linguistic research, and, rather than seeking to construct a new coding scheme that would facilitate communication, philosophers and philologers alike attempted instead to identify those linguistic categories that were common to all natural languages. This shift from the seventeenth-century language planning endeavour to the eighteenth-century philosophical grammar movement is not well understood, and the reasons for this gradual change of emphasis appear to have been multifarious and convoluted.[23] For instance, schemes such as the one that Wilkins proposed are dependent upon the validity of the taxonomical system they presuppose to such an extent that, if this system fails, then the whole linguistic scheme is inevitably undermined. Not surprisingly, an awareness of vulnerabilities of this kind certainly seems to have quelled the enthusiasm of later linguists. In addition, though, Locke's well-known scepticism concerning artifical languages was certainly persuasive. For instance, as discussed in the previous section, Locke examined both imperfections in, and abuses of, language, and he stated bluntly in his *Essay* that

I am not so vain to think, that anyone can pretend to attempt the perfect *Reforming* the *Languages* of the world, no not so much as that of his own Country, without rendering himself ridiculous. To require that Men should use their words constantly in the same sense, and for none but determined and uniform *Ideas*, would be to think that all Men should have the same Notions, and should talk of nothing but what they have clear and distinct *Ideas* of. Which is not to be expected by anyone, who hath not vanity enough to imagine he can prevail with Men to be very knowing or very silent. And he must be very little skilled in the world who thinks that a voluble Tongue shall accompany only a good Understanding; or that Men's talking much or little should hold proportion only to their Knowledge.[24]

This implies that any attempt to devise a language that is free from all ambiguity is patently absurd. Although they present a contestable view of the matter, as the eighteenth century progressed, comments of this sort gathered validity as Locke's reputation burgeoned. However, another factor which seems to have triggered the shift from artificial languages to philosophical grammars was the dominance of the kind of scientific methodology that Newton had used so convincingly in his *Philosophiae Naturalis Principia Mathematica* (1687). The mid eighteenth-century philological preoccupation with the task of identifying hidden regularities which underlie the seemingly irregular structure of natural languages is, in essence, a search for linguistic universals, and therefore it can be associated with the contemporaneous search for physical laws. Some of these concerns are manifest in the entry on 'Universal Grammar' which appeared in the first edition of the *Encyclopedia Britannica* (1771):

[...] grammar considered as a *Science*, views language in itself: neglecting particular modifications, or the analogy which *words* may bear to *each other*, it examines the analogy and relation between *words* and *things*; distinguishes between those particulars which are *essential* to language, and those which are only *accidental*; and thus furnishes a certain standard by which different languages may be compared, and their several excellencies or defects pointed out. This is what is called PHILOSOPHIC or UNIVERSAL Grammar.[25]

The proposed research programme, then, seeks to distinguish between '*essential*' and '*accidental*' properties of languages; the basic assumption is that regularities can be identified and analysed, and therefore universal linguistic laws can be proposed. As will become apparent, the various definitions of '*PHILOSOPHIC* or *UNIVERSAL* Grammar' that were offered during the eighteenth century sometimes differ in fundamental respects. For instance, in the above definition, the relationship between words and things is prioritised over the Lockean preoccupation with the connections between words and ideas – though, as will be shown, other theorists adopted approaches that were based on the basic framework that Locke had introduced.

Having summarised a few of the intellectual and cultural concerns that influenced the writers of philosophical grammars, it is necessary now to discuss several texts which shaped Hazlitt's thinking about such matters – and an obvious place to start is James Harris' *Hermes: or, a Philosophical Inquiry concerning Language and Universal Grammar* (1751).[26] Harris was born in 1709, and educated at the Salisbury Grammar School, in the Cathedral Close, from whence he proceeded to Wadham College, Oxford. Although he initially pursued a career in law, he became independently wealthy when his father died, and he returned to Salisbury where he served as a Justice of the Peace and as Member for Parliament until his death in 1761.[27] His treatise on philosophical grammar, *Hermes*, was begun in 1747, and, in the Introduction, he states simply that his intention was to identify the 'constituent Parts' of natural language.[28] Indeed, according to Harris, the study of the manner in which the basic elements of language are analysed 'constitute what we call, PHILOSOPHICAL GRAMMAR, or UNIVERSAL GRAMMAR',[29] and, from the outset of his investigation, he asserts that, rather than merely seeking to explore the structure of any particular natural language, he intends to identify '*those Principles, that are essential to them all*'.[30]

This, then, was Harris' intention, and the methodology he adopted was both distinctive and revealing. Although he appears to have been

2.3 Philosophical Grammars 33

familiar with contemporaneous writings about philosophy and linguistic analysis, *Hermes* contains very few references to such texts. Instead, he purposefully sought to trace antecedents for the various arguments he developed in the work of Classical authors such as Plato, Aristotle, and Cicero, as well as neo-Aristotelians such as Ammonius and Scaliger. In fact, Harris actually claimed that his theory of universal grammar had been inspired by Franciscus Sanctius' *Minerva, seu de Causis Linguae Latinae* (1587), though, characteristically, he does not refer to Sanctius in *Hermes*. This distinctive tendency to present only Classical antecedents arose from Harris' conviction that, in focusing on the work of modern philosophers such as Locke, contemporaneous thinkers were neglecting the glorious Classical heritage.[31] As a result, it becomes extremely difficult to determine how he reacted to contemporaneous linguistic theory. For instance, the Newtonian context of Harris' project appears to reveal itself when he makes an explicit comparison between his linguistic research and the scientific exploration of the solar system. Having discussed the relationship between '*Causes*' and '*Effects*', and having stated that mankind is forced to work backwards from effects to causes, Harris adds that

Often had Mankind seen the Sun in Eclipse, before they knew its Cause to be the Moon's Interposition ; and much oftner had they seen those unceasing Revolutions of Summer and Winter, before they knew the Cause to be the Earth's double Motion. Even in Matters of Art and *human* Creation, if we except a few Artists and critical Observers, the rest look no higher than to the *Practice* and mere *Work*, knowing nothing of those Principles, on which the whole depends.[32]

So, works of 'Art and *human* Creation' can be analysed in terms of the essential principles that guide their construction, and, in the next paragraph he notes that this is true particularly of 'SPEECH'.[33] The implications of this are apparent: natural language is not part of the natural world in the same way that the sun, the earth, and the moon are natural phenomena, and therefore it must be bundled together with 'Art' and the products of human creation. However, although such reflections may have been inspired by Newton's *Principia*, they could just as easily have been prompted by a familiarity with Ptolemaic epicycles, and either Classical or modern sources could have been cited. Despite these complexities, though, perhaps the greatest difficulties occur when one attempts to situate Harris in the context of the various types of empiricism that had become prevalent by the mid eighteenth century. For instance, it is often assumed that he was profoundly sceptical about the validity of Locke's work, yet there are very few explicit references to Locke in Harris' writings, and therefore his views can generally only be inferred.[34] As a result, while it has sometimes been claimed that his theories of language and mind were 'shaped by idealism', it has also been asserted that his position concerning empiricism was 'ambiguous', and some of the complexities arising from this uncertainty will be considered later.[35]

As noted above, Harris wished to explore the fundamental universal principles which underlie linguistic structure, and *Hermes* is divided into three books which outline a progression from linguistic particulars to general reflections upon the purpose of language in human society. The first book considers those types of words, such as 'substantives' (e.g., nouns) and 'attributives' (e.g., adjectives) which are 'significant by themselves', while, in the second book, he analyses those words, such as 'articles' and 'conjunctions', which are 'significant by relation'.[36] This basic bipartite distinction is fundamental to his theory, and it is similar to the modern distinction between content and function words.[37] This discussion of the primary lexical categories is presented in terms of linguistic universals, and Harris seeks to identify the categorial similarities that exist between languages such as Greek, Latin, French, and English. Through a consideration of particular structures (e.g., sentences, noun phrases, verb phrases), he is often inclined to sub-classify specific parts-of-speech into smaller sub-categories, thus establishing a taxonomical hierarchy, and, in this respect, his approach is certainly reminiscent of the elaborate classificatory schemes that had been adopted by the seventeenth-century language planners. His discussion of 'connectives', for instance, exemplifies his approach. Having noted that conjunctions and prepositions both function as connectives, he concentrates on the clausal level, and he considers structures such as the following:[38]

(1) Rome was enslaved BECAUSE Caesar was ambitious
(2) Manners must be reformed, OR Liberty will be lost

According to Harris, in (1) above, 'the *Meanings* as well as the *Sentences*, appear to be connected', while in (2) although the word 'OR' joins the two clauses 'yet as to their respective *Meanings*, [it] is a perfect *Disjunctive*.'[39] Consequently, he is compelled to divide the category 'conjunction' into two sub-types – namely, 'CONJUNCTIVE' conjunctions and 'DISJUNCTIVE' conjunctions.[40] In a similar manner, having presented yet more sentences as examples, he further sub-divides conjunctions into 'COPULATIVES, or CONTINUATIVES', stating that

2.3 Philosophical Grammars

while 'and' is an example of the former, words such as *if, because, therefore*, and *that* are instances of the latter. He does not stop here though, and continuatives are further sub-divided into 'SUPPOSITIVE' and 'POSITIVE' sub-types[41] – and so it goes on, with each distinct type of conjunction being associated with a distinct category. In section 3.2, it will be shown that this classificatory complexity irritated Hazlitt tremendously, to the extent that he fundamentally rejected the type of linguistic theory that Harris expounded. Further, it is worth noting that, by classifying 'connectives' in this manner, Harris was echoing exactly the kind of approach that Locke had recommended for particles – that is, modifying his analytical system as a result of introspective reflection.

Harris' *Hermes* was widely admired by philosophers and philologers from different traditions, and it inspired more intensive research into philosophical grammar. Indeed, such was the charm of this emerging field that it even appealed to intellectuals who were generally more closely associated with other domains of knowledge. For instance, Joseph Priestley delivered *A Course of Lectures on the Theory of Language and Universal Grammar* while he was teaching at the Warrington academy in the 1750s (the text was eventually published in 1762) and, not surprisingly, Priestley mentions *Hermes* as one of the sources upon which he drew.[42] Although it was never recognised as a master work, Priestley's text is of interest not least because it seeks to introduce some of the concerns of the philosophical grammarians to a students of language, and therefore it exists in the twilight zone which separates the philosophical grammars from the grammar textbooks. Also, Priestley's text illustrates the continuing influence of the seventeenth-century language planners: he describes the task of creating a perfect artificial language as 'one of the last and greatest achievements of human genius', and he writes at length about Wilkins' system, describing it as a 'noble project'.[43] Although comments such as these were becoming outmoded by the 1760s, they certainly suggest that the seventeenth-century linguistic schemes had not been entirely forgotten by the mid eighteenth century.

Although Harris's *Hermes* inspired an interest in grammatical universals, it had its detractors and, without doubt, its most provocative and idiosyncratic critic was John Horne Tooke. Born simply 'John Horne' in 1736, the son of a Westminster poultry merchant, Horne Tooke was educated at Westminster School and, subsequently, Eton College, before being admitted, in 1754, as a sizar at St John's College, Cambridge. Although, after graduating, he began a career in law, he took holy orders at his father's behest and was ordained priest in 1760. Eventually he became perpetual curate of New Brentford, but he resigned this position in 1773 and began to study law and philology more intensely. During this period he became closely associated with William Tooke, who had acquired a considerable estate, which included Purley Lodge, and which was situated near Croydon in Surrey. As a result of services rendered, William Tooke stated his intention to make John Horne the heir to his estate, and he provided him with financial assistance during his lifetime. Consequently, John Horne eventually added 'Tooke' to his name, as a tribute to his friend and patron. In the 1780s, Horne Tooke was a vibrant political activist, and his activities were certainly noted by the government. Along with Thomas Hardy and John Thelwall, he was accused of High Treason, and imprisoned in the Tower of London during the notorious 'Treason Trials' of 1794. All men were eventually acquitted, and these events were an unfortunate but perhaps inevitable outcome of the nervousness towards the British reform movement that had started to characterise William Pitt's administration during the 1790s. As the new century began, Horne Tooke's revolutionary fervour remained undimmed, and, when he died in 1812 he was still recognised as an unrepentant radical.[44]

Although *Diversions* is Horne Tooke's most famous work concerning linguistic theory, certain key ideas that he elaborated in that treatise were initially presented in his 1778 'A Letter to John Dunning, Esq.'. This tract simply discusses the implications of a legal judgement in which Horne Tooke himself had been involved, and the basic problem concerns statements of the form[45]

(3a) She knowing that Crooke had been indicted for forgery, did so and so
(3b) Crooke had been indicted for forgery – she, knowing that, did so and so

The question raised was whether sentences such as these affirm, or do not affirm, the state of affairs described in the clause 'Crooke had been indicted for forgery'. Horne Tooke argued against the view that, in the case of (3a), the fact that Crooke was indicted is not 'positively averred', and he rejected the conclusion that, in this sentence, the indictment is only conjectured rather than stated as a fact.[46] He attempted to demonstrate that such a conclusion was fallacious by arguing that, if the etymology of the word *that* is taken into account, then it should be classified as a pronoun (rather than a conjunction) in both cases, and that therefore structures such as (3a) do indeed contain an affirmation of the initial clause, which means that, semantically, they are equivalent to structures such as (3b). The most characteristic feature of Horne

Tooke's argument is that it depends upon an etymological analysis, and it seeks to demonstrate that two seemingly different uses of a word (i.e., *that* as a conjunction and *that* as a pronoun) are underlyingly the same. This basic idea was elaborated into a whole philosophy of language in *Diversions*.

The first volume of *Diversions* appeared in 1786, while the second volume was published in 1806, and, taken together, they constitute a sustained meditation upon the structure and purpose of natural language. In the Platonic tradition, the work is written in the form of a conversation involving several interlocuters, and it is set in William Tooke's Purley Lodge. Therefore the treatise is presented as if it recorded some of the discussions at Purley, and this accounts for the subtitle of the work, which, without this contextualisation, baffles rather than clarifies. Indeed, as Hazlitt noted, on the basis of its subtitle alone '[m]any people have taken it up as a description of a game, others supposing it to be a novel'.[47] The participants in the dialogue are only indicated in the text by single letters, but the codes used are the following: 'H' is Horne Tooke, 'B' is Richard Beadon, 'F' is Sir Francis Burdett, and 'T' is William Tooke. At the start of the Introduction, the discussion swiftly moves to linguistic matters, and Horne Tooke is called upon to defend his belief that 'though Grammar be usually amongst the first things taught, it is always one of the last understood'.[48] In the ensuing exchanges, he explicitly states his view that the study of grammar is 'absolutely necessary in the search after philosophical truth',[49] so, once again, philosophy and grammar are brought into close proximity. Although Horne Tooke's theory of language will be discussed at length in chapter 3, it is worth mentioning here that he gave especial prominence to the role of abbreviation in natural language – in particular, he was concerned with the kind of abbreviation that enables a word which is associated with a particular part-of-speech to take on a different grammatical role in order to facilitate communication. For Horne Tooke, natural language is littered with abbreviations of this kind, they are 'the *wheels* of language',[50] and, since they are so central, linguistic structure must be analysed in terms of 'dispatch' – that is, with an awareness of the manner in which abbreviations permit communication to take place swiftly.[51]

In certain respects, the linguistic theory that Horne Tooke propounded can be viewed as a direct reaction against dominant trends in both the philosophy of language and philology that had characterised the first half of the eighteenth century. While he stridently asserted, for example, the strict empiricism that he had encountered in Locke's writings ('[t]he business of the mind [...] extends no further than to receive impressions'[52]), yet, he openly rejected the manner in which Locke had analysed particles, mainly because he felt that the latter had not recognised the way in which they facilitate linguistic abbreviation. Similarly, Horne Tooke's work can be viewed as an attempt to destabilise the kind of philosophical grammatical theory that Harris and Priestley had presented in their philological work. For instance, while discussing the relationship between grammatical and biological gender, Horne Tooke notes that Harris had been 'particularly unfortunate' in claiming that the sun is naturally masculine while the moon is naturally feminine, adding in a footnote that '[i]t can only have been Mr. Harris's authority, and the ill-founded praises lavished upon it' that caused Priestley to claim that '*[a]ll nations*' recognise this distinction. In order to demonstrate his greater learning, Horne Tooke notes rather grandly that '[i]n the Gothic, Anglo-Saxon, German, Dutch, Danish and Swedish, SUN is *feminine*: In modern Russian it is *neuter*'.[53] *Diversions* is riddled with such quibbles, corrections, and rejections – and these are often intended to indicate the frailty of the theoretical structures that prior philosophical grammarians had erected.

2.4 Grammar Textbooks

As noted above, treatises concerning philosophical grammar were usually aimed at a sophisticated, intellectual audience, and they standardly presupposed a familiarity with philosophical and linguistic texts, both ancient and modern. By contrast, grammar textbooks were generally less exulted publications, since they were usually intended to be used by people (generally children) who were studying the English language in a pedagogical context. Although the existence of different kinds of educational environments means that it is difficult to devise a comprehensive definition of the grammar textbook genre, as it is used here the phrase is intended to have roughly the same scope that Ian Michael specifies in *The Teaching of English: From the Sixteenth Century to 1870*:

By textbook I mean a book used by pupils in class; or a book read out of school in preparation for work to be done in class; or a book used by a teacher or parent for practical guidance; or a manual of self-instruction.[54]

This definition usefully captures something of the diversity of the educative situations in which these books were used during this period. However, despite this heterogeneity, the texts themselves were usually written with a clear pedagogical agenda in mind, and it is this that enables them to be grouped together as a single genre.

The general resurgence of interest in texts which introduced the elements of English grammar can be broadly associated with a gradual shift towards linguistic standardisation of various kinds (e.g., orthographical, lexical, syntactic) which came to characterise eighteenth-century linguistic theorising.[55] However, it was certainly not the case that grammarians active during the period 1750 to 1800 presented a uniform view of the English language. Indeed, one of the most startling aspects of the eighteenth-century grammar textbook tradition is simply its heterogeneity. Different grammar books specified different essential parts-of-speech and proposed different (sometimes opposed) syntactic rules.[56] Nonetheless, despite this confusing and pervasive lack of uniformity, a small number of texts eventually emerged which, as a result of their distinctive clarity and practical utility, remained unquenchably popular well into the nineteenth century. Of these, by far the most influential were Robert Lowth's *A Short Introduction to English Grammar* and Lindley Murray's *English Grammar*.

Robert Lowth was born in 1710, and, as a boy, he attended Winchester College, where he revealed his early interest in literature by writing a poem about the genealogy of Christ which was inspired by the east window of the college chapel. He entered New College, Oxford, as a scholar, in 1729, graduating with his M.A. eight years later. While still a student, he was ordained into the Anglican church, and, after a brief period as vicar of the parish of Overton in Hampshire, he was appointed Professor of Poetry at Oxford. During the following years he rose swiftly through the ranks of the ecclesiastical hierarchy, being appointed archdeacon of Winchester in 1750, bishop of Oxford in 1766, and bishop of London in 1777. At the grand old age of 73, he was offered the Archbishopric of Canterbury, an opportunity he declined due to the increasing frailty of his health. He died in 1787.[57]

In an age of remarkable intellectual endeavours, Lowth's academic achievements were conspicuous. His treatise on Hebrew poetry, *De Sacra Poesi Hebraeorum* (1753) prompted a reconsideration of the manner in which Biblical Hebrew verse was read and interpreted, and his Biblical translations were greatly admired. However, it was his grammar textbook, which was first published in 1762, that would prove to be his most influential accomplishment. In writing this work, Lowth was self-professedly responding to Jonathan Swift's plea for greater linguistic regulation which had appeared in print in 1712. Swift's text, 'A Proposal for Correcting, Improving, and Ascertaining the English Tongue' was addressed to Robert Harley, the Earl of Oxford, and it depicted the English language as being in a parlous state:

> My Lord; I do here in the Name of all the Learned and Polite Persons of the Nation, complain to your Lordship [...] that our Language is extremely imperfect; that its daily Improvements are by no means in proportion to its daily Corruptions; and the Pretenders to polish and refine it, have chiefly multiplied Abuses and Absurdities; and, that in many Instances, it offends against every Part of Grammar.[58]

In order to remedy this disastrous state of affairs, Swift suggested that a government 'Ministry' should provide 'some effectual method for Correcting, Improving, and Ascertaining' the English Language in order to achieve 'the Improvement of Knowledge and Politeness'.[59] In other words, a regulatory body fashioned after the model of the greatly admired l'Académie française was required (so Swift argued) in order to correct the imperfections which marred the English tongue.[60] In essence, then, Swift argued that criteria for standard usage should be established for English, and Lowth agreed with this recommendation, explicitly associating his textbook with the very reforms that Swift had envisaged half a century earlier:

> It is now about fifty years since Doctor Swift made a public remonstrance, addressed to the Earl of Oxford, then Lord Treasurer, of the imperfect State of our Language; alleging in particular, "that in many instances it offended against every part of Grammar." Swift must be allowed to have been a good judge of this matter. [...] Indeed the justness of this complaint, as far as I can find, hath never been questioned; and yet no effective method hath hitherto been taken to redress the grievance of which he complains.[61]

After considering the implications of Swift's critique, Lowth concludes that, while the most refined speakers of English, and the finest authors, do indeed write ungrammatically from time to time, the language itself is not so 'irregular and capricious' that it prohibits rational analysis.[62] Accordingly, Lowth's self-imposed task was to try to present the rudiments of English grammar in a simple and approachable manner, so that they could be taught with greater precision.

Although his textbook was aimed at 'the Learner even of the lowest class', Lowth certainly related his work to the philosophical grammar tradition, discussed in the previous section.[63] In particular, he wanted his more educated readers to recognise that his account of the English language was in complete accordance with the more general analytical

2.4 Grammar Textbooks

framework that Harris had propounded in *Hermes*. For instance, concerning the study of grammar, Lowth remarked that

[t]hose, who would enter more deeply into this Subject, will find it fully and accurately handled, with the greatest acuteness of investigation, perspicuity of explication, and elegance of method, in a Treatise intitled Hermes, by James Harris Esq; the most beautiful and perfect example of Analysis that has been exhibited since the days of Aristotle.[64]

As will be discussed at length later (especially in chapter 4), Lowth's unqualified admiration for Harris' *Hermes* irritated Hazlitt inordinately since he personally had profound reservations about the kind of analytical methodology that both men had adopted.

Having indicated his general intention in the Preface, Lowth approaches the task of introducing the rudiments of English grammar by starting with the smallest elements, namely the 'Letters' and then proceeding to 'Syllables'. Having defined these categories, and having illuminated them by presenting specific examples, he then discusses in turn each of the nine 'Sorts of Words, or, as they are commonly called, Parts of Speech'.[65] The specific classes Lowth identifies are articles, substantives, pronouns, adjectives, verbs, adverbs, prepositions, conjunctions, and interjections, and, initially, he is simply concerned with the task of defining these and identifying sub-categories. For example, 'verb' is 'a word which signifies to be, to do, or to suffer' (a definition that Hazlitt would later reject), and he then immediately introduces three different types of verb – namely, 'Active, Passive, and Neuter'.[66] With the basic parts-of-speech introduced in this manner, Lowth then considers 'Sentences', and he attempts to provide guidance concerning the manner in which words can be combined in order to create larger linguistic structures. For instance, he defines a 'phrase' as 'two or more words rightly put together in order to make a part of a Sentence; and sometimes making the whole sentence',[67] and he subsequently describes the 'most common' phrases that are used in 'simple sentences'.[68] For example, the '1st Phrase' is defined as '[t]he substantive before a Verb Active, Passive, or Neuter', and this is exemplified in sentences such as 'I am' and 'Thou writest'.[69] It is in expository sections of this sort that Lowth often makes use of passages extracted from works of literature in order either to reinforce the point that he is making, or else to provide an example of incorrect construction. Having noted, for instance, that, in phrases of type 1, the verb should agree with the nominative subject in number and person, he includes in a footnote the following line from Dryden:

"Scotland and *Thee* did each in other live".
Dryden, Poems, Vol.II. 220.[70]

and adds, rather laconically, 'It ought to be *Thou*'.[71] Lowth's point here is that Dryden has used the object pronoun *Thee* when he should have used the subject pronoun *Thou*, and therefore the phrase is ill-formed.

A Short Introduction was revised several times, and it swiftly became the most influential grammar textbook of the last forty years of the eighteenth century. However, although Lowth was still generally recognised as a venerable authority well after his death in 1787, it was Lindley Murray's *English Grammar* that became the most popular guide to the English language during the first decades of the nineteenth century. Like Lowth (and many other eighteenth-century grammarians) Murray was a profoundly religious man, and his understanding of linguistic theory was partly influenced by his North American upbringing. Born in Pennsylvania in 1745, the son of a Quaker merchant, he rejected mercantile pursuits, and trained for the bar instead, to which he was admitted in 1767. He practised as a lawyer in New York until the Revolution began, and he then moved to Islip on Long Island where he managed to earn a considerable amount of money. During the War of Independence, he became a fervant loyalist, and, in 1784, he emigrated to England, eventually settling in York. His *English Grammar* was written for The Mount School for girls, where he taught English for many years.[72]

In his Introduction, Murray stated clearly that, rather than being an original work, his *English Grammar* was 'a new compilation' that was intended to facilitate 'the instruction of youth',[73] and it is a characteristic feature of his work that, from the very beginning, he associates the study of grammar with the pursuit of virtue:

The author has no interest in the present publication, but that of endeavouring to promote the cause of learning and virtue; and, with this in view, he has been studious, through the whole of the work, not only to avoid all examples and illustrations which might have an improper effect on the minds of youth; but also to introduce, on many occasions, such as have a moral and religious tendency. This, he conceives to be a point of no small importance; and which, if scrupulously regarded in all books of education, would essentially advance the best interests of society, by cherishing the innocence and virtue of the rising generation.[74]

Seemingly, those tasked with the humble chore of teaching grammar to children were responsible for far more than merely the linguistic well-being of their charges. Evangelisation (of a kind) could be accomplished via the process of grammatical analysis if well-chosen quotations were selected. As will be discussed at length later, the close association that was believed to exist between grammar and morality in the early nineteenth century is often manifest in the vitriolic criticism that was directed against writers such as Hazlitt, Leigh Hunt, Percy Shelley, and other figures associated with radical politics.

Murray's textbook was divided into five main sections. First, a section on 'Orthography' introduced the letters of the alphabet, and specified rules for pronouncing them, for dividing words into syllables, and for spelling words of different kinds. The second section, which discussed 'Etymology', provided an overview of the nine parts-of-speech, and Murray used the same basic categories as Lowth. The word 'Etymology' requires careful consideration in this context: throughout the eighteenth century, it could be used to refer either to core syntactic categories or to the linguistic origins of the words concerned, though, significantly, the former was a usage which John Horne Tooke and Hazlitt (amongst others) rejected. During this section of his textbook, Murray used both examples derived from simple English sentences, and unattributed quotations from works of English literature in order to exemplify both correct and incorrect usage. In section 5.1 it will be argued that the deployment of such passages in grammar textbooks can be viewed as a form of language-focused literary criticism.

The longest section of the *English Grammar* was the third section, 'Syntax'. This part of the work introduced the rules that regulate the manner in which words can be combined in order to create grammatical sentences, and the educational intention behind Murray's text can be seen most clearly in these expository sections. For instance, in the page layout that he adopts, the rules of syntax are numbered and stated in large type with simple examples to illustrate the point being made:

Rule II

Two or more nouns, &c. in the singular number, joined together by one or more copulative conjunctions, have verbs, nouns, and pronouns agreeing with them in the plural numbers; as, "Socrates and Plato *were* wise; *they* were the most eminent philosophers of Greece;" "The sun that rolls over our heads, the food that we receive, the rest that we enjoy, daily admonish us of a superior and superintending Power."[75]

Here core grammatical principles are exemplified in sentences which present an explicitly religious perspective, in accordance with Murray's declared educative purpose. However, beneath these sections, in a smaller font, a more detailed consideration of the grammatical structures is developed, and this is where difficult cases, dubious counter-examples, and permissable exceptions are described. For instance, in the above case, we learn that

> This rule is often violated. [...] When the nouns are nearly related, or scarcely distinguishable in sense, and sometimes when they are very different, some authors have thought it allowable to put the verbs, nouns, and pronouns, in the singular number; as "Ignorance and negligence has produced the effect" [...][76]

Consequently, in many cases, it is the passages in a smaller font which contain the most insightful reflections upon the form and structure of English, and which indicate that Murray was not an unbending prescriptivist. Indeed, he was fully aware of the idiosyncracies and irregularities of the English language, and, although he offered specific rules as useful guidelines, he certainly did not think that they should never be broken.

The impact that Murray's text had upon linguistic pedagogy is incalculably profound. His highly successful *English Grammar* was followed in 1797 by two tremendously popular sets of grammatical exercises, *English Exercises* and *A Key to the Exercises*, as well as an *Abridgement* of the *English Grammar*. Subsequently, Murray published a sequence of other textbooks, including an anthology called *The English Reader* in 1799, the *Sequel* to the anthology in the following year, the *Introduction to the English Reader* in 1801, and, three years later, an *English Spelling Book*. These texts were all widely used is classrooms throughout the country, and the *English Grammar* itself ran to sixty-four numbered editions in Britain alone, while the *Abridgement* achieved almost twice that number. However, Murray's success was not confined only to Britain; his grammar textbooks were accepted as authoritative sources of guidance in his native America; they were translated into various European languages, and they even influenced linguistic pedagogy in such places as Japan and New Zealand.[77]

2.5 Lexicography

If the practical tendency of eighteenth-century philology is manifest in the textbook grammar tradition, then it is also visible in the contemporaneous lexicographical tradition, and a few distinctive aspects of this branch of linguistic research must be mentioned here. In particular, it is important to appreciate the manner in which the basic purpose and function of (English) dictionaries has changed over the centuries. While small bilingual collections of 'hard words', such as Galfridus Grammaticus' *Promptorium Parvulorum* (1440, printed 1499), appeared in the fifteenth and sixteenth centuries, publications of this kind certainly did not seek to provide a *comprehensive* catalogue of the English lexicon. Consequently, during the sixteenth and seventeenth centuries, English dictionaries gradually increased in scope and coverage, providing a greater amount of information about a larger set of words. Texts such as Robert Cawdrey's *A Table Alphabetical Of Hard Usual English Words* (1604) and Thomas Blount's *Glossographia* (1656) set new standards of rigour, precision, and ambition, and this progression continued into the early eighteenth century. Indeed, one of the most important dictionaries of this period was John Kersey's *A New English Dictionary* (1702), and, as with the textbook grammars discussed earlier, the educational purpose of Kersey's work is clearly stated in his Preface when he notes that he wishes

to instruct Youth, and even adult Persons, who are ignorant of the learned language, in the Orthography, or the true and most accurate manner of Spelling, Reading and Writing the genuine Words of their own Mother-tongue [...] the usefulness of this Manual to all Persons not perfectly Masters of the English Tongue, and the assistance it gives to young Scholars, Tradesmen, Artificers and others, and particularly, the more ingenious Practitioners of the Female Sex, in attaining to the true manner of Spelling of such Words, as from time to time they have occasion to make use of, will, we hope procure it a favourable Reception.[78]

As with all lexicographical projects, there are illuminating self-referential details, and it is rewarding here to search for some of the words in the above quotation amongst the entries that Kersey includes within his *New English Dictionary*. For instance, 'Artificer' is defined as 'a handy-craft man'; 'ingenious' is said to mean 'quick-witted, shrewd, or cunning', while 'shrewd' implies 'subtil, smart, or ingenious'.[79] It is also worth noting his use of the word 'genuine', since his desire to include only 'the genuine Words' of the language suggests that he is consciously and systematically seeking to identify an appropriate subset of the available lexicon. Indeed, Kersey was explicit about both the kinds of words, and the sorts of supplementary information, that he wished to incorporate into, and (perhaps more revealingly) exclude from, his dictionary. For instance, he does not include lexical items that are 'obsolete, barbarous, foreign or peculiar to the Counties of England',[80] which suggests that he considered particular sub-types of words to fall outside the scope of his lexicographical project, and dialect terms are also excluded. However, he does include words that are associated with 'Divinity, Ecclesiastical Affairs, Plants, Gardening, Husbandry, Mechanics; Handicrafts, Hunting, Fowling, Fishing &c'.[81] As ever, lists of this kind provide intriguing insights into the socio-political contexts in which the eighteenth-century lexicographers operated, identifying some of the knowledge domains that were associated with the intended market. In addition to these things, Kersey does not offer 'derivatives' in his dictionary[82] – that is, although he gives the verb *to love*, he gives neither the past participle (i.e., loved) nor the present participle (i.e., loving) since he felt that these forms could be obtained 'with a very little application'.[83] This stance should seem familiar since it is very close to the approach that Godwin would later advocate in his 1810 *New Guide*. As mentioned in section 1.2, although Godwin placed more emphasis on the pedagogical implications of this approach, he may well have encountered the central idea in dictionaries such as Kersey's.

Despite Kersey's desire to be as comprehensive as possible (within his self-proscribed limits), certain definitions that appear in his dictionary suggest that he was still influenced by the prior 'hard word' tradition. For instance, his definition of the the word *work* is given as 'to work (in all senses)', and his guidance concerning the word *house* is even less helpful, consisting as it does merely of the parenthetical phrase '(in several senses)'.[84] These renderings do not merit being referred to as 'definitions' at all, and they suggest that Kersey was content to presuppose a considerable familiarity with commonly used vocabulary. Sometimes, though, even when he does supply a definition in an attempt to clarify the several senses of a given word, he makes curious decisions when prioritising possible meanings. For instance, the word *table* is defined as

A Table, *for meat, to write upon*, &c; also an index, or collection of the Chapters, or principle matters in a book.[85]

While the first definition of *table* offered here is typically abrupt and incomplete, merely specifying two possible practical purposes for which a table of this kind could be used, the main emphasis of the entry clearly falls upon the second definition which supplies the more technical bibliographical sense of the term. Seemingly, Kersey desires to clarify this sense rather than the former, and the entry has been devised in accordance with this intention.

2.5 Lexicography

While Kersey's dictionary was one of the most popular dictionaries of the first half of the eighteenth century, Samuel Johnson's *A Dictionary of the English Language* (1755) was undoubtedly one of the most conspicuous lexicographical works of the second half of the century, and the reforming tendency of Johnson's work is stated explicitly in his Preface:[86]

> When I took the first survey of my undertaking, I found our speech copious without order, and energetick without rules: wherever I turned my view, there was perplexity to be disentangled, and confusion to be regulated; choice was to be made out of boundless variety, without any established principle of selection; adulterations were to be detected, without a settled test of purity; and modes of expression to be rejected or received, without the suffrages of any writers of classical reputation or acknowledged authority.[87]

Johnson here presents himself as standing in an unweeded garden, and, as will become apparent, horticultural analogies were not uncommon in eighteenth-century tracts concerning linguistic reform. The position Johnson adopts – namely, the view that the English language was largely unregulated – anticipates Lowth's profound dissatisfaction with the state of English grammar. Johnson's awareness of linguistic irregularity may be well-know, but the subtlety of his assessment is not always appreciated. For instance, he distinguishes between orthographical irregularities that are 'inherent' and those that are due to 'ignorance or negligence':

> In adjusting the ORTHOGRAPHY, which has been to this time unsettled and fortuitous, I found it necessary to distinguish those irregularities that are inherent in our tongue, and perhaps coeval with it, from others which the ignorance or negligence of later writers has produced. Every language has its anomalies, which, though inconvenient, and in themselves once unnecessary, must be tolerated among the imperfections of human things, and which require only to be registered; that they may not be increased, and ascertained, that they may not be confounded: but every language has likewise its improprieties and absurdities, which it is the duty of the lexicographer to correct or proscribe.[88]

This distinction juxtaposes orthographical irregularities which have always been present in the language, and which must simply therefore be identified and catalogued, with orthographical irregularities which are avoidable and which arise solely from ignorance and negligence – an analysis that recalls Locke's distinction between linguistic imperfections (which are unavoidable) and abuses (which can be prevented). In practice, though, this fine distinction is difficult to maintain, and Johnson himself seems willing to tolerate a certain amount of graphemic variance: although he uses the word 'stile' in his Preface, this lexical item only appears in the *Dictionary* under the entry 'style'. Presumably, this kind of irregularity is avoidable, yet Johnson has permitted it to exist – possibly to amuse the attentive.

Like Kersey, Johnson explicitly specifies the kinds of words he has included and excluded. He declares openly that he has not provided information for 'words which have a relation to proper names' (e.g., 'Calvinist'), technical terms 'which are supported by a single authority', 'compounded or double words' if the meaning of the whole is the sum of the parts (e.g., 'coachdriver'), words derived from other by means of suffixes such as '-ly' and '-ish' (e.g., 'greenish'), words that begin with prefixes such as 're-' or 'un-' and so on, and morphological variants of verbs (e.g., present participles).[89] However, he does include foreign words 'though commonly only to censure' the authors that use them,[90] and some information concerning etymology of the words is included since 'ETYMOLOGY was necessarily to be considered'.[91] Strategies such as these, which Johnson adopted in order to deal with particular morphological and lexical phenomena, reveal the fundamental principles that regulate the kind of analytical approach that he advocated, and therefore (conveniently) they enable his lexicographical work to be associated with dominant trends in eighteenth-century linguistic theory.

As mentioned in the previous section, the use of literary examples in eighteenth-century grammar books is a complex and beguiling topic, and the manner in which Johnson made use of quotations from literature in his *Dictionary* is of particular interest. He states openly that he has attempted to use literary examples drawn from '*the wells of English undefiled*, as the pure sources of English diction',[92] adding that this has been done in order to provide a corrective for a general stylistic shift that had been taking place since the mid seventeenth century:

Our language, for almost a century, has, by the concurrence of many causes, been gradually departing from its original *Teutonick* character, and deviating towards a *Gallick* structure and phraseology, from which it ought to be our endeavour to recall it, by making our ancient volumes the ground-work of stile, admitting among the additions of later times, only such as may supply real deficiencies, such as are readily adopted by the genius of our tongue, and incorporate easily with our native idioms.[93]

The influence of French language and literature, then, was to be counteracted in the *Dictionary* by the inclusion of literary examples which manifest the Germanic aspects of the English language, and the political implications of this declaration are resonant. The period of English literature that Johnson surveyed was severely truncated, though, and he himself tightly proscribed the epochal limits. He determined that Philip Sidney would provide a lower boundary 'beyond which I make few excursions', while (with only a few exceptions) the upper boundary was marked by 'living authors [...] that I might not be misled by partiality and that none of my contemporaries might have reason to complain'.[94] Occasionally, he admits, he was forced to include passages from texts that could not be considered to be examples of great literature:

Some of the examples have been taken from writers who were never mentioned as masters of elegance or models of stile ; but words must be sought where they are used ; and in what pages, eminent for purity, can terms for manufacture or agriculture be found?[95]

This observation makes a cogent sociolinguistic point: certain social groups make extensive use of distinctive technical vocabulary, and therefore passages exemplifying the usage of such words must be sought in the writings of the groups concerned, even if they are not generally recognised as masters of prose style.

Johnson's *Dictionary* was well-known and greatly admired throughout the second half of the eighteenth century, but there were other lexicographical texts which influenced Hazlitt's views concerning linguistic theory. One such text was David Booth's *Introduction to an Analytical Dictionary of the English Language* (1806; from henceforth *Introduction*). Booth was born in Kennetles, Forfarshire, in 1766, and although as a young man he had business interests in the brewing industry, he eventually became a schoolmaster in Newburgh, Fifeshire, where he remained for many years. He published his *Introduction* in order to present the plan for a proposed *Analytical Dictionary*, a scheme to which he returned throughout his life. In 1820 Booth moved to London where he tackled various literary projects, and where he supervised the publication of works prepared by the Society for the Diffusion of Useful Knowledge. In the following years, he wrote some articles on brewing and printed several texts about English grammar. The first (and only) volume of the *Analytical Dictionary* appeared in 1835, and Booth died, back in Fifeshire, in 1846.

In the summary that he provided in his *Introduction*, Booth stated that, at the highest level, his intention in his dictionary was 'to arrange the vocables into classes : beginning with the explanation of the Root, and proceeding with its compounds'.[96] This rather vague sketch already emphasises the focus on morphology that was such a distinctive aspect of his work. Indeed, he notes specifically that English morphology 'presents a considerable degree of regularity', and he claims that his dictionary would reveal the patterns lurking beneath the apparent chaos of English word formation. Predictably, therefore, a large part of the discussion in the *Introduction* is concerned with the different '*Prefixes* and *Terminations*' (i.e., prefixes and suffixes) that are used in English.[97] The Lockean character of Booth's proposal is signalled by his description of the relationship between words and ideas, and the following passage is typical:

Ideas are the reflected image of nature. Words are the pictures of ideas. Simplicity of thought will produce simplicity of expression ; and hence the individual impulses of the mind will be marked by monosyllabic sounds. Two or more simple impressions form what is termed a complex idea, which is expressed by as many primitive words.[98]

Booth appears not to have questioned the rather simplistic relationship between 'ideas' and 'words' that he had extracted from Locke, and the general empirical thrust of his work is apparent when he states that ideas are derived from 'impressions' and that there is a direct association between the 'impulses of the mind' and the words that are used to express them. It is reasonable to suggest that Locke himself would probably have found Booth's analytical framework rather parsimonious and lacking in subtlety.

Eventually, Booth's discussion turns to the 'divisions of Words'[99] – that is, the parts-of-speech – and, yet again, another classificatory scheme is presented. He specifies three basic lexical categories – Names, Qualities, and Actions – and then associates the traditional parts-of-speech with these. For instance, nouns are obviously Names, while adjectives and adverbs are both different types of Qualities.[100] Like Horne Tooke before him, Booth was keen to reduce the traditional parts-of-speech to a smaller set of linguistic types, and the precise nature of the relationship between their views will be discussed in section 3.4. As his *Introduction* progresses, Booth simply attempts to analyse specific prefixes, suffixes, cases, and so on, indicating how they function in English, and he gives prominence to etymological arguments. For example, the prefix *dia* is considered in relation to the 'Saxon' word 'thruh', before its Greek origins are discussed:

The Greek *dia* (probably from *dis*) signifies *passage* from one end of a space or period to the other. Words formed with this prefix are directly from the language, and are generally confined to scientific terms. Thus *diameter* is the measure across or *through* any thing : the *diameter* of a circle is the measure of its breadth.[101]

This gives a flavour of the analysis that Booth offered in his *Introduction*, and, although prefixes such as *dia* were well-understood, he certainly felt that many of the structures he was compelled to confront had been neglected by linguists in the past. Indeed, he seems to have viewed his task as being akin to that of an explorer in the New World. He speaks of the 'pathless plain' that stretches before him; he describes etymology as being 'one of the tractless wilds of Nature',[102] and the language of bush-whacking returns from time to time. Revealingly, though, Booth views himself as a linguist-botanist, rather than as a mere pioneer, and, while apologising for his own prolixity, he comments (metaphorically) as follows:

> [...] while we stray we are allured by the charms of novelty : we wander from shrub to shrub, and from tree to tree, till we can no longer recover the beaten path which surrounds without entering the forest.[103]

The analytical lexicographer, it seems, is an explorer-scientist, a philolgical Joseph Banks – a person who wanders into unknown regions, who identifies new species, and who risks becoming lost in the surrounding wilderness. Significantly, the unweeded garden that Johnson had sought to regulate is here represented as a forest, an environment that is altogether more extensive and threatening.

2.6 Language and Style

The various trends in linguistic theory that have been discussed so far can all be associated, in distinct ways, with 'belletristic rhetoric', which emerged in the mid eighteenth century and which can be viewed as a linguistic and literary response to a changing socio-economic environment. In essence, the elaborate rhetorical tropes and schemes which had dominated the discourse of aristocratic Europe during the Renaissance were deemed to be inadequate for the types of communication that were necessitated by the cultural conditions of eighteenth-century Britain, and therefore new conventions were proposed which sought to redefine notions of effective and desirable rhetorical style.[104] As David Kaufer and Kathleen Carley have argued, this shift was also prompted partly by the increasing availability of print culture which meant that literacy was no longer uniquely within the purview of the more privileged members of society.[105] Significantly, in Britain, these changing attitudes were initially manifest most explicitly in the lectures and writings of certain Scottish intellectuals in the mid to late 1700s, and many of the core ideas propounded in their works were subsequently received with favour in other parts of the country. In a recent summary, Linda Ferreria-Buckley and Michael Halloran have emphasised the impact that this reconfiguration and transference had specifically upon the study of English literature during this period:

> The Scots – through their texts and the graduates of educational institutions – shaped the study of English language and literature in England, and in doing so, they gave it a traditional rhetorical shape that transferred to English studies some offices formerly entrusted to Greek and Latin rhetoric and their sister arts in the trivium.[106]

One consequence of the new rhetorical treatises, then, was that English literature began to receive more critical attention, thereby partly usurping a position that had traditionally been occupied by Classical texts and languages. Given the existing social and educational structures, this development had extensive ramifications, and, as will be shown later, by the early nineteenth century, writers from low prestige backgrounds and radical tendencies, such as Leigh Hunt and Hazlitt, were being repeatedly twitted by Tory critics for their (alleged) lack of Classical learning.

Although different theorists proposed different kinds of belletristic rhetorical systems, they generally advocated a synthesis of ideas extracted from Classical, French, and British sources. For instance, Aristotle's *Rhetoric* and *Poetics*, Isocrates' *Antidosis*, Longinus' *On the Sublime*, Quintilian's *Institutio Oratoria* and Horace's *Ars Poetica* were often cited, as were works by neo-classical French rhetoricians such as Dominique Bonhours, François de Salignac de La Mothe-Fénelon, René Rapin, and Charles Rollin. In addition, influential figures such as Lord Kames (a.k.a. Henry Home) and Adam Smith, both of whom wrote about rhetorical and linguistic matters from time to time, provided indigenous texts that could be incorporated into the mixture. Indeed, Lord Kames' *Elements of Criticism* (1762) is sometimes considered to be the first publication that can be attributed specifically to the Scottish school of rhetoric, but later authors were responsible for writing treatises which came to define the belletristic rhetoric tradition more particularly. While various examples could be usefully considered here, since this overview is primarily intended to provide the background that is required to appreciate Hazlitt's writings about language and literary style, the main emphasis will fall, suitably enough, upon those authors whom Hazlitt acknowledged as having had a significant impact on his own thinking about such matters. Therefore the focus will fall on the work of George Campbell and Hugh Blair.

George Campbell was born in 1719, the son of a Calvinist minister. He entered Marischal College, in his native Aberdeen, at the age of fifteen, where he studied logic, metaphysics, pneumatology, ethics, and natural philosophy, eventually graduating in 1738. After a short period in which he considered a career in Law, he turned instead to Divinity and was licensed to preach in 1746. Once ensconced in the parish of Banchory Ternan, Campbell was able to devote more time to his academical interests, drafting the first two chapters of *The Philosophy of Rhetoric* at some time around 1750. In 1759 he became principal of Marischal College, an appointment which brought him to greater prominence as a figure in the Scottish Enlightenment. In the following years, he was one of the joint founders of the The Aberdeen Philosophical Society, and many of his ideas concerning rhetoric were first presented during meetings of this Society. In 1770 he became Professor of Divinity at Marischal, and *The Philosophy of Rhetoric* was published six years later. He retired in 1795, and died the following year.

In the Introduction to *The Philosophy of Rhetoric*, Campbell seeks to justify the kind of study that he has undertaken, and he does this by emphasising the centrality of 'eloquence' as an art-form:[107]

[...] there is no art whatever that hath so close a connexion with all the faculties and powers of the mind, as eloquence, or the art of speaking, in the extensive sense in which I employ the term. For in the first place, that it ought to be ranked among the polite or fine arts, is manifest from this, that in all its exertions, with little or no exception, (as will appear afterwards), it requires the aid of the imagination. Thereby it not only pleases, but by pleasing commands attention, rouses the passions, and often at last subdues the most stubborn resolution. It is also a useful art. This is certainly the case if the power of speech be a useful faculty, as it professedly teaches us how to employ that faculty with the greatest probability of success. Further, if the logical art, and the ethical, be useful, eloquence is useful, as it instructs us how these arts must be applied for the conviction and the persuasion of others. It is indeed the grand art of communication, not of ideas only, but of sentiments, passions, dispositions, and purposes. Nay, without this, the greatest talents, even wisdom itself, lose much of their lustre, and still more of their usefulness.[108]

The emphasis on practical utility is prominent: eloquence enables us to persuade others, and therefore it engenders useful activity. Book I of the treatise is concerned with '[t]he Nature and Foundations of Eloquence',[109] and, in chapter 1, Campbell offers a rather general definition of eloquence by adapting several ideas gathered from Quintilian: '[t]he word eloquence in its greatest latitude denotes, "That art or talent by which the discourse is adapted to its end."'[110] Having considered the implications of this definition, he then presents a detailed discussion of various kinds of discourse including 'wit, humour, and ridicule' (chapters 2-3), the relationship between eloquence and both logic and grammar (chapter 4), and the connections that exist between 'Speakers' and 'hearers' (chapters 7-9). Book II focuses on 'The Foundations and essential Properties of Elocution'[111] and it deals with such matters as 'the nature and use of verbal criticism' (chapter 2) and 'grammatical purity' (chapter 3). The final part of the treatise, Book III, elaborates '[t]he discriminating Properties of Elocution'[112] by considering the property of 'vivacity' in relation to such things as 'the choice of words' (chapter 1), 'the number of words' (chapter 2), and 'the arrangement of words' (chapter 3). Many of these topics will be explored at greater length when Hazlitt's views concerning such matters are considered. However, while Campbell attempted to achieve a bold reconfiguration of rhetorical teaching, it was Hugh Blair's *Lectures on Rhetoric and Belles Lettres* (1783; 1785; henceforth *Lectures*) that exerted the most potent influence over subsequent generations.

Born in 1718, Blair was educated at the High School of Edinburgh, a civic institution, where he excelled at the Classical curriculum.[113] When he graduated, in 1730, he enrolled at the University of Edinburgh, and it was while a student there that he seems to have first started to reflect upon rhetoric in relation to the English language. In particular, John Stevenson, the professor of logic and metaphysics, lectured on rhetoric (in English) and, in addition to the Classical texts such as those mentioned above, he also analysed the contemporary prose of Addison, Dryden, and Pope.[114] The thesis that Blair submitted as part of his M.A. was *De Fundamentis et Obligatione Legis Naturae*, a wide-ranging discussion of the principles of morality and virtue which anticipated some of the themes that he would explore in his mature sermons. Having graduated from the University, Blair was licensed to preach as a Presbyterian, and he was ordained in 1742. His sermons seem to have been popular, and certainly the experience of having to prepare regular discourses which were aimed at lay, rather than academic or ecclesiastical audiences, influenced the manner in which he thought about both English composition and the desirable qualities of prose style. During the 1750s, he began to acquire a reputation as an acute editor of texts; his eight-volume *Works of Shakespeare* appeared in 1753, and his burgeoning reputation as an arbiter of literary taste caused him to be considered an authority on matters of style. Eventually, in 1759, he began to deliver lectures on rhetoric and belles lettres at the University of Edinburgh, a post which initially brought him no remuneration. However, in the following year, his situation changed when he was officially appointed to the salaried position of Professor of Rhetoric, while, in 1762, he was awarded the title of the first Regius Professor of Rhetoric and Belles Lettres. He continued to deliver his lectures annually until his retirement in 1783, an event that prompted him to prepare the text of his lectures for publication.

The first edition of Blair's *Lectures* appeared (in two-volumes) in 1783, and clearly his printers, William Strahan and Thomas Cadell, were confident that the text would prove to be successful since they paid Blair the unusually large sum of £1,500 for the copyright.[115] However, Blair published a three-volume second edition in 1785, which incorporated many minor corrections and revisions, and numerous other unofficial abridged versions of the text appeared during the period 1783 to 1820. The existence of these truncated and edited versions helped both to distribute and to distort several of Blair's core ideas.[116] Ironically, in his Preface to the 1785 edition, Blair states that he was prompted to publish his *Lectures* partly as a result of the existence of 'Imperfect Copies' which had been produced by his students. In the event, publication aggravated rather than alleviated this undesirable state of affairs. It is revealing also that, in his Introduction, he stresses the fact that his *Lectures* contain his own thoughts about the subject, even though he makes extensive use of existing sources:

> The Author gives them [the lectures] to the world, neither as a Work wholly original, nor as a Compilation from the Writings of others. On every subject contained in them, he has thought for himself. He consulted his own ideas and reflections; and a great part of what is found in these Lectures is entirely his own. At the same time, he availed himself of the ideas and reflections of others, as far as he thought them proper to be adopted. To proceed in this manner, was his duty as a Public Professor.[117]

This humbly self-assertive summary reveals Blair's awareness of the complex synthesis that he had achieved, drawing upon various existing sources, and yet reformulating and repositioning the ideas that he encountered so that he could present a unified system.

Although a detailed discussion of Blair's text is well beyond the scope of this introductory summary, it is possible to give some ideas as to the range of topics that he addresses. For instance, he devotes a whole lecture to 'Taste', which he defines as '[t]he power of receiving pleasure from the beauties of nature and art',[118] before considering such issues as 'The Sublime in Writing' (lecture 4), the 'Structure of Language' (lecture 8), 'Style' (lecture 10), 'Metaphor' (lecture 15), 'Figurative Language' (lecture 18), various aspects of 'Eloquence' (lectures 35-38), and different kinds of poetry such as 'Pastoral' (lecture 39), 'Didactic' (lecture 40) and 'Epic' (lecture 42). As this meagre list indicates, the scope of Blair's *Lectures* was vast, and this no doubt partly accounts for its popularity: his treatise concerns itself with such a wide range of linguistic usages that all practitioners of language, whether they were professional authors, politicians, or simply aspiring members of the mercantile classes, could find something in the text that impinged upon their daily encounters with the English language.

As mentioned above, Blair's work has been discussed here primarily because it subsequently exerted a potent influence on Hazlitt. Although the particular nature of that influence will be discussed in chapter 4 (and elsewhere), it is worth anticipating the ensuing analysis slightly by indicating that it was the advice Blair offered concerning 'Style' which Hazlitt seems to have valued most highly. Blair initially defines 'Style' rather blandly, as being 'the peculiar manner in which a man expresses his conceptions, by means of Language'[119] However, when he returns to the topic in lectures 18 and 19, he attempts to distinguish between different styles such as 'Diffuse, Concise – Feeble, Nervous – Dry, Plain, Neat, Elegant, Flowery'.[120] More importantly, though, he emphasises the importance of 'Simplicity' and the need to form 'a Proper Style'.[121] In particular, he claims that 'Perspicuity' is a desirable stylistic quality which constitutes a 'positive beauty', and he suggests that if the stylistic qualities of '*Purity, Propriety,* and *Precision*' are present in a work of literature, then it will also possess the desirable quality of 'Perspicuity'.[122] These ideas will be explored extensively in section 4.4, where it will be shown how they influenced Hazlitt's appreciation of the literary validity of different stylistic registers – especially the so-called 'familiar' style.

It is not really possible to overstate the extent of the influence that Blair's *Lectures* exerted in Britain and, more widely, throughout Western Europe. The text was translated into German (1785-1789), French (1796), Spanish (1798), Italian (1801), and Russian (1837), and its impact in more distant regions, such as Asia and Central and South America, has only recently started to be explored. However, the fact that the text was known in such places indicates the potency of its attractiveness. Intriguingly, though, a consideration of the reception history in such comparatively exotic locations may be somewhat premature since, as the discussion in chapter 4 will demonstrate, even the manner in which English intellectuals responded to Blair's work during the first decades of the nineteenth century is, at present, insufficiently understood.

2.7 Tories and Radicals

As promised, this chapter has presented an eclectic survey of linguistic theory in the eighteenth century. From language-focused philosophers, to philosophical grammars, to grammar textbooks and lexicographical endeavours, to belletristic rhetoricians systematically reflecting upon stylistic registers, a wide range of theories and theorists has been glimpsed, and many of the authors and texts considered above will reappear in the remaining chapters, providing a foundation for a detailed analysis of linguistic theory during the Romantic period. Before turning again towards Hazlitt's work, though, it is worth pausing to reflect upon a few words that will appear quite frequently in the ensuing discussion, and, given the close connection between language and politics that was so typical of the Romantic period, it should be no surprise that the lexical items concerned relate to these topics.

Studies of writers such as Hunt, Hazlitt, Shelley, Byron, and others, sometimes seek to contextualise and account for the negative contemporaneous reviews which appeared in publications such as *The Quarterly Review* or *The Anti-Jacobin Review and Magazine* by attributing such responses to 'Tory' critics such as William Gifford and John Gibson Lockhart. The word 'Tory', though, is more nebulous than this customary, casual usage suggests. Indeed, as Robert Harris has recently argued, in the mid eighteenth century, the term could indicate a range of political allegiences:

Toryism is, in fact, a slippery quarry [...] What is difficult is to determine exactly what the Tories stood for as a national force. A significant minority of Tories had Jacobite connections [...] and, in several cases these continued even after the crushing defeat of Culloden. Yet in parliamentary terms, Toryism meant little more than 'country' politics by this period. [...] What Tories sought was to protect landed independence and interest in Parliament and in local government – which meant their admission to the ranks of county Justices of the Peace – and to eliminate corruption from politics.[123]

Certainly, by the 1780s and 1790s, political views throughout the country had started to become polarised more obviously along ideological lines, and William Pitt the Younger's government adopted an increasingly conservative stance as the fear of revolution grew. This gradual shift, combined with the fact that certain factions within the Whig opposition began to associate themselves more explicitly with the proponents of reform, meant that the word 'Tory' started to accrue reactionary connotations. Consequently, during the first decades of the nineteenth century, a stereotypical Tory was associated with anti-Jacobin views, loyalty towards Church and State, a respect for existing institutions, and a desire for social stability in the future. Linguistically, this world-view frequently expressed itself in an advocacy of the grammatical rules that had been propounded by eighteenth-century theorists such as Lowth, Murray, Campbell, and Blair. As a result, young writers who used innovative vocabulary and unconventional syntactic structures were not infrequently suspected of being subversively in league with the advocates of reform. As Jeffrey Cox has noted

[...] there was the general assumption that there was a link between poetic vision and political debate [...] poetry was judged on political grounds; put simply, one's reception was dependent upon one's view of the government of Castlereagh, Sidmouth, and Eldon.[124]

Although Cox is concerned here primary with poetry, the same was also true of other literary forms, and, as will be discussed later, Hazlitt recognised the way in which political concerns would frequently inform literary reviews which did not explicitly address political matters.

If 'Tory' is one word that requires careful consideration, then terms such as 'radical' and 'reformer' also merit delicate handling. Critical studies of the Romantic literature often refer to 'radicals' and 'reformers' without always distinguishing too finely between the many different sub-groupings that were prevalent during this period. Although these words acquired their distinctive political connotations only in the mid eighteenth century, they were soon being widely used, and individuals from different social classes with such diverse political agendas as electoral, parliamentary, and economic reform, the abolition of the monarchy, the disestablishment of the Church, the redistribution of property, the freedom of the press, and the abolition of the slave trade have all been subsequently classified as 'radicals' and/or 'reformers'. Indeed, during the past twenty years, the diversity of the reform movement has become a topic of focused scholarly consideration. In the early 1990s, for instance, Mark Philp observed (perhaps somewhat ruefully) that

[r]eformism and radicalism in the 1790s is protean stuff. It resists simple

definitive classification of its nature and objectives, and it demands a more complex understanding of its ideology and political objectives than is often offered. To treat reformism or radicalism (or indeed loyalism) as a single, consistent, continuous programme throughout the decade is to ignore at the very least, the extent to which reformist and loyalist movements shaped and conditioned each other's objectives and tactics, the way that government and judicial action against reformers helped to focus and narrow the range of strategies open to them, and the manner in which events in France fed into each group's understanding of the danger of and potential for reform in Britain.[125]

The ideological fragmentation that Philp's explores certainly reveals the underlying heterogeneity that characterised the reformism and radicalism of the period. In addition, to this prevalent heterongeneity, though, the situation was further complicated by inconsistencies and ambiguities that could be associated with even apparently distinct sub-types of reformism/radicalism. As J. Ann Hone has argued,

[...] years of training in the hard school of politics made many radicals adept at ambiguity and at keeping their political options open; of others, it can be shown that they changed their minds and their interests in response to changing situations; of others again, that their careers demonstrated the wide range of alternative possibilities – political, philanthropic, educative, and educational (in the widest sense) – open to those who in this period wished to change the world for the better.[126]

Once again, the convolutions of these socio-political movements prove to be bafflingly intricate, and, in general, the more minutely one scrutinises a particular manifestation of reformism or radicalism, the more complex the picture becomes. Thankfully, it is not the task of this book to document this complexity accurately, in its entirety, and therefore words such as 'reformer' and 'radical' will be used from time to time in the following chapters without elaborate attempts at definition in each case. Hopefully, the context of the discussion should largely disambiguate the usage. Nonetheless, such vocabulary remains problematical and should always provoke a sense of unease.

Having offered these cautionary words, it is appropriate now to begin to explore Hazlitt's views concerning natural language in more detail, and it is convenient to start by considering the manner in which he responded to the philosophical grammar movement.

3
Philology and Philosophical Grammar

3.1 Hazlitt and Philosophical Grammar

In order to begin the process of situating Hazlitt's linguistic work in the context of eighteenth-century philology, his response(s) to the philosophical grammar movement will be considered, with particular emphasis falling upon his complex reaction to Horne Tooke. As noted earlier, even though Hazlitt's assessment of Horne Tooke's theorising has sometimes been evaluated in the past, the critical tradition has usually focused primarily (and often exclusively) upon the former's rejection of the latter's empiricism, and Park, Bromwich, Natarajan and others have all attempted to elucidate Hazlitt's distinctive brand of philosophical idealism. This requires an understanding of the way in which his philosophical preoccupations developed in direct response to dominant trends in seventeenth- and eighteenth-century thought, and, accordingly, his writings have been juxtaposed with those of Thomas Hobbes, John Locke, David Hume, George Berkeley, Jeremy Bentham, to name just a few. However, since Hazlitt's interest in the interconnections between philology and philosophy was both acute and abiding, his linguistic work is rather more intricate than is generally supposed. For instance, rather than merely revealing the nature of his idealism, it also manifests his concern for the methodology of grammatical analysis – and, although these issues are closely related, they are certainly not identical.

Before turning to Hazlitt's writings about such matters, though, it is worth briefly summarising the manner in which he is likely to have encountered certain key works of philosophical grammar. This task is of some importance since, by the time he came to write his 1809 *Grammar*, he was already familiar with a wide range of linguistic theories which had been developed largely during the eighteenth century.[1] Indeed, his

3.1 Hazlitt and Philosophical Grammar

dissenter upbringing had prepared him well for such pursuits. In particular, it can be safely assumed that Hazlitt had been taught the rudiments of English grammar at his school in Wem, and it is known that, subsequently, while a student at New College in Hackney, he studied Hebrew, Greek, and Latin variously with Thomas Belsham, John Corrie, and Joseph Priestley.[2] Indeed, one of the letters that he wrote to his father in November 1793 indicates the extent to which grammatical studies of different kinds provided a focus for the New College syllabus:

I will here give you an account of my studies, etc. On Monday I am preparing Damien's lectures from seven until half-past eight, except the quarter of an hour in which I say Corrie's grammar lecture, and from nine till ten. From ten till twelve we are with him. His lectures are Simpson's elements of gram[mar]. and Bonnycastle's algebra. By the bye, the Ass's bridge is the tenth proposition of the geometry. From twelve to two I am preparing Belsham['s] lectures in shorthand, and the Hebrew grammar, which I am saying till then. The shorthand is to write out eight verses, [of the] Bible. From half-past three till five I walk. From five to six, I have my g[reek] grammar for the morning. At liberty from six to seven. From seven to eight, preparing Belsham's evening lectures in L[atin] and Heb[rew]. With them from eight to nine. And from half after nine till eleven I am reading Dr. Price's lecture for the next day. On Tuesday I am from seven till h[alf].p[ast]. eight preparing Corrie's classical lecture, only the time that I am saying my grammar.[3]

If this describes a typical day, then it indicates the extent to which close linguistic analysis, in a range of different languages, was a dominant part of the regieme. Hebrew, Greek, and Latin were all obligatory subjects, and this course of study necessarily prioritised grammatical analysis. Incidentally, it is of interest that Hazlitt learnt shorthand while he was at New College, and no doubt he made good use of these skills later in life when he began to work as a parliamentary reporter for the *Morning Chronicle* in 1812.

In addition to these studies, since New College also offered the topic of 'Universal Grammar' as part of its syllabus, it is likely that Hazlitt was able to consider the implications of this distinctive approach to the study of language while he was still a student. Whether that is the case or not, though, his own writings indicate that, at some point before he published his *Grammar*, he had become familiar with such texts as Harris' *Hermes*, Priestley's *The Rudiments of English Grammar* and *Course of Lectures on The Theory of Language, and Universal Grammar*, Lowth's *A Short Introduction*, Murray's *English Grammar*, and Horne Tooke's *Diversions* – and his familiarity with such texts is attested repeatedly by the frequent references and citations which he incorporated into his later essays and lectures.

In the light of Hazlitt's educational experiences at New College, the following extract from his *Table Talk* essay 'On the Ignorance of the Learned', provides insights into his views concerning the validity of such educational techniques:

Any one who has passed through the regular gradation of a classical education, and is not made a fool of by it, may consider himself as having had a very narrow escape. It is an old remark, that boys who shine at school do not make the greatest figure when they grow up and come out into the world. The things, in fact, which a boy is set to learn at school, and on which his success depends, are things which do not require the exercise either of the highest or the most useful faculties of the mind. Memory (and that of the lowest kind) is the chief faculty called into play in conning over and repeating lessons by rote in grammar, in languages, in geography, arithmetic, etc., so that he who has the most of this technical memory, with the least turn for other things, which have a stronger and more natural claim upon his childish attention, will make the most forward school-boy. The jargon containing the definitions of the parts-of-speech, the rules for casting up an account, or the inflections of a Greek verb, can have no attraction to the tyro of ten years old, except as they are imposed as a task upon him by others, or from his feeling the want of sufficient relish or amusement in other things. A lad with a sickly constitution and no very active mind, who can just retain what is pointed out to him, and has neither sagacity to distinguish, nor spirit to enjoy for himself, will generally be at the head of his form. An idler at school, on the other hand, is one who has high health and spirits, who has the free use of his limbs, with all his wits about him, who feels the circulation of his blood and the motion of his heart, who is ready to laugh and cry in a breath, and who had rather chase a ball or a butterfly, feel the open air in his face, look at the fields or the sky, follow a winding path, or enter with eagerness into all the little conflicts and interests of his acquaintances and friends, than doze over a musty spelling-book, repeat barbarous distichs, after his master, sit so many hours pinioned to a writing-desk, and receive his reward for the loss of time and pleasure in paltry prize-medals at Christmas and Midsummer. There is indeed a degree of stupidity which prevents children from learning the usual lessons, or ever arriving at these puny academic honours. But what passes for stupidity is much oftener a want of interest, of a sufficient motive to fix the attention and force a reluctant application of the dry and unmeaning pursuits of school learning. The best capacities are as much above this drudgery as the dullest are beneath it. Our men of the greatest genius have not been most distinguished for their acquirements at school or at the university.[4]

It is hard not to believe that Hazlitt is here partly recollecting his days as a student at New College. The topics covered and the emphasis on grammatical analysis are certainly reminiscent of the account he gave in his 1793 letter to his father. Seemingly then, in his maturity, he was convinced that there was a disconnection between academic ability in the classroom and accomplishments in later life. He associates 'an idler at school' with physicality, with 'high health and spirits', and he suggests that such people are not necessarily content to be 'pinioned' to a desk and forced to work through 'a musty spelling-book' in order to master various arcane linguistic and literary skills. Despite subsequent reservations of this kind, though, Hazlitt certainly encountered a wide range of texts concerning different kinds of linguistic theory during the 1780s and 1790s, and his knowledge of works such as those listed earlier was extensive. Nonetheless, although he read widely, he returned with particular avidity to Horne Tooke's theories, especially his influential and controversial *Diversions*.

3.2 Nonsense and Redemption

In theory, it should be straightforward to evaluate Hazlitt's assessment of Horne Tooke, since he discussed the latter's work explicitly on various occasions. For instance, in his 1825 *Spirit of the Age* essay 'The Late Mr Horne Tooke', he noted that:

The great thing which Mr. Horne Tooke has done, and which he has left behind him to posterity, is his work on Grammar, oddly enough entitled THE DIVERSIONS OF PURLEY. Many people have taken it up as a description of a game - others supposing it to be a novel. It is, in truth, one of the few philosophical works on Grammar that were ever written [...] Mr. Tooke's work is truly elementary. Dr. Lowth described Mr. Harris's *Hermes* as 'the finest specimen of analysis since the days of Aristotle' – a work in which there is no analysis at all, for analysis consists in reducing things to their principles, and not in endless details and subdivisions. Mr. Harris multiplies distinctions, and confounds his readers. Mr. Tooke clears away the rubbish of school-boy technicalities, and strikes at the root of his subject.[5]

While revealing Hazlitt's admiration for certain aspects of Horne Tooke's *Diversions*, this passage effectively establishes the perspective from which he viewed the work: specifically, it is here situated in the eighteenth-century philosophical grammar tradition, and the explicit condemnation of 'Mr. Harris' – that is, of course, James Harris, the author of *Hermes* – indicates the extent of Hazlitt's scepticism concerning the analytical methodology generally deployed by eighteenth-century philosophical grammarians. In *A Short Introduction*, Lowth had praised Harris' *Hermes* using the very words that Hazlitt quotes above, and, in doing this,

Lowth was seeking to align his own textbook overtly with the philosophical grammar movement. However, Harris had been condemned by Horne Tooke for failing to provide a sufficiently parsimonious framework for linguistic analysis, and the latter had particularly derided the use of a needlessly vast panoply of grammatical categories and subcategories, or, as he put it (with characteristic inventiveness) 'that farrago of useless distinctions'.[6] Possibly prompted by Horne Tooke's criticism, Hazlitt was equally unimpressed with the kind of analytical system that Harris had proposed, specifically mocking, for instance, the many 'frivolous varieties' of conjunction that Harris had identified.[7] By contrast, Hazlitt was persuaded that Horne Tooke had advantageously rejected such an absurdly elaborate approach in favour of an unremitting reductivist analysis which truly revealed 'the principles' of certain linguistic phenomena.

So, Hazlitt certainly appears to be an enthusiastic advocate of Horne Tooke's linguistic speculations. However, the true complexity of his reaction to *Diversions* manifests itself when favourable assessments such as these are juxtaposed with other extracts in which the analytical methodology outlined by Horne Tooke is referred to as being 'to the last degree despicable', and 'downright unqualified, unredeemed nonsense'.[8] The central critical query here is as obvious as it is insistent: why, in these and other passages, did Hazlitt express such seemingly divergent opinions concerning the validity of Horne Tooke's linguistic speculations?

Given these apparent contradictions, it is not surprising that the critical tradition has often attributed to Hazlitt conflicting views concerning linguistic matters. For instance, as mentioned in section 1.3, Hans Aarsleff and Tim Milnes (to name but two) have disagreed profoundly concerning Hazlitt's intellectual allegiance to Horne Tooke. For Aarsleff, Hazlitt was an unquestioning devotee of *Diversions*, while, for Milnes, Hazlitt entirely rejected Horne Tooke's methods. At different times, then, Hazlitt has been presented as being either *pro* or *anti* Horne Tooke, and even discussions which focus explicitly on the intellectual connections that relate the two men, tend to overlook the intricacy of Hazlitt's stance. For example, Uttara Natarajan explores such matters in *Hazlitt and the Reach of Sense*, and, after the empirical tendency of Horne Tooke's work has been stressed, Hazlitt's position is described as follows:

By contrast, in Hazlitt's own account of language as the manifestation of an innate formative ability in the mind, we begin to perceive the concept, central to his epistemology, of an active and empowered mind.[9]

Statements such as this appear to be entirely transparent and irrefutably conclusive. Unfortunately, though, Natarajan does not discuss Hazlitt's frequently expressed admiration for Horne Tooke's etymological researches into indeclinable function words (e.g., *if*, *that*), and therefore no attempt is made to indicate whether the admiration and contempt that Hazlitt expressed at different times for Horne Tooke's work were reconcilable or contradictory. As a result, critical analyses such as Natarajan's generally avoid several troublesome and provoking issues which should be acknowledged. While Natarajan's essential conclusion is certainly in keeping with the long-established critical tradition which classifies Hazlitt as a proponent of a particular type of philosophical idealism – that is, (crudely) as a thinker who constantly stressed the mind's creative and formative power over its passive receptivity – it nevertheless fails to acknowledge the delicacy of his philological views. Although there is absolutely no doubt that Hazlitt did advocate (a certain kind of) idealism and that this philosophical inclination manifested itself in such writings as his *Essay on the Principles of Human Action* and his *Lectures on English Philosophy*, it is equally clear that his linguistic work often synthesises and assimilates techniques and assumptions that he had encountered in treatises written by unwavering empiricists. Since a reconsideration of Hazlitt's understanding of Horne Tooke's *Diversions* may help to delineate the precise nature of his reaction to eighteenth-century philology and philosophy, the remaining sections of this chapter will attempt to elaborate a reappraisal of this kind.

3.3 Horne Tooke's Theory of Language

The swift rise to prominence of John Wilkes in the 1760s fuelled Horne Tooke's interest in politics, and, even though his linguistic work will provide the main focus of this section, it is crucial to recognise that his political and philological ideas were closely related. Like Wilkes, Horne Tooke was part of an emerging generation of reformers who challenged the existing monarchical and parliamentary power structures, and his radical views informed his numerous writings in a range of different ways. In 1765, for instance, he published a trenchant attack on John Stuart, 3rd Earl of Bute and William Murray, 1st Earl of Mansfield that was entitled 'The Petition of an Englishman', and the patriotic nationalism apparent both in the title and the content of this pamphlet is typical of his robust approach.

Given the close associations between linguistic theories and political ideologies, it is certainly convenient that Horne Tooke actively sought to position his text explicitly in the context of the various language debates that had raged since the seventeenth century. For example, as mentioned in chapter 2, Horne Tooke unambiguously associated his own philosophy of language with Lockean empiricism, and this association partly accounts for the conspicuously reductivist tendency of his work. The clearest expression of his tenaciously empirical stance is contained in chapter 3 of *Diversions*:

The business of the mind, as far as it concerns Language, appears to me to be very simple. It extends no further than to receive impressions, that is, to have Sensations or Feelings. What are called its operations, are merely the operations of Language.[10]

Although this claim necessarily associates *Diversions* closely with the eighteenth-century British empiricist tradition, as manifest in such influential texts as George Berkeley's *A Treatise Concerning the Principles of Human Knowledge* (1710) and David Hume's *Philosophical Essays Concerning Human Understanding* (1748), Horne Tooke clearly takes Locke as his starting point. He devotes a whole chapter to a reassessment of the theory of language developed in the *Essay*. He maintains, for example, that, without realising it, Locke was primarily concerned with the manner in which words (or 'terms') are used to refer to disparate groups of entities that constitute a 'complex idea'.[11] To demonstrate that this was the case, Horne Tooke focused on linguistic abbreviation, and, drawing upon such sources as the Port-Royal *Grammaire* (1660) and Charles de Brosse's *Traité de la Formation Mèchanique des Langues et des Principes Physiques de l'Etymologie* (1765), he distinguished three distinct types:[12]

(i) abbreviation 'in terms'
(ii) abbreviation 'in sorts of words'
(iii) abbreviation 'in construction'

Type (i) refers to abbreviations which occur when pluralities are denoted by single words (e.g., the word *constellation* enables a collection of stars to be indicated without having to specify all the stars individually); type (ii) indicates those in which words that belong to a specific part-of-speech seemingly take on a different grammatical role in order to allow a given construction to be more concise (examples of this type are discussed at length below), while type (iii) indicates those in which

3.3 Horne Tooke's Theory of Language

single words convey the same semantic content as an equivalent phrase or clause (e.g., the adverb *slowly* is a shorter way of conveying the idea contained in the prepositional phrase *in a slow manner*). Given these three sub-categories, Horne Tooke provocatively asserted that Locke's *Essay* provided the 'best guide' to type (i), and, to justify this claim, he cited those passages where Locke had emphasised the manner in which words serve to unify complex ideas.[13] Consequently, he considered such sections as chapter 5 of Book 3, in which Locke had observed that, although 'complex ideas' are sometimes 'loose enough, and have as little union in themselves [...] yet they are always made for the convenience of Communication'.[14] From Horne Tooke's perspective, since the words 'term' and 'idea' are interchangeable in Locke's work, the whole of the *Essay* can therefore reasonably be described as an attempt to elucidate those instances of abbreviation in natural language that are mediated by 'terms'.[15]

Despite this emphasis on type (i) abbreviations, though, Horne Tooke acknowledged that Locke did indeed provide a preliminary overview of type (ii), since, having discussed the ways in which nouns and verbs come to be associated with external objects, Locke had briefly considered the problem caused by 'particles' (e.g., closed-class function words such as prepositions and conjunctions). Associating himself with the Aristotelian tradition (as mediated by Scholasticism), which had distinguished between categorematic and syncategorematic words, Locke had declared that particles appear to exist primarily in order 'to signify the *connexion* that the Mind gives to *Ideas*, or *Propositions*, *one with another*', and this statement suggests that such words have a distinct grammatical role.[16] However, Locke also described particles as being '*Marks of some Action or Intimation of the Mind*', and he attempted to indicate the range of analytical problems associated with such words by discussing five different nuances of meaning that could be associated with the disjunctive conjunction *but*, concluding that '[t]o these, I doubt not, might be added a great many other significations of this Particle'.[17] However, Locke did not explore these interpretative possibilities in detail, and he terminated his discussion having raised, but not resolved, some of the analytical problems caused by troublesome elements such as conjunctions.

Given the above, it is understandable that Horne Tooke was not satisfied with Locke's account of particles. It is no surprise, then, when, in the second chapter of *Diversions*, Locke's division of words into 'Names of Ideas and Particles' is described as being accomplished in 'a very cautious, doubting, loose, uncertain manner', with the result that the whole chapter is 'vague'.[18] Indeed, in Horne Tooke's assessment, Locke's discussion of particles constitutes 'a full confession and proof that he [Locke] had not settled his own opinion concerning the manner of signification of Words'.[19] The central problem that Horne Tooke identifies is primarily classificatory: if particles are indeed '*Marks of some Action or Intimation of the Mind*', then should verbs also be included in the 'particle' category?[20] If not, then how is one to distinguish between the actions associated with particles, and the actions associated with verbs? His dissatisfaction with this aspect of Locke's theory provided him with a starting point for his own grammatical work, and therefore he pronounces robustly in *Diversions* that, unlike Locke, he will be primarily concerned with abbreviation 'in sorts of words' – that is, abbreviations of type (ii).[21]

Since Horne Tooke's etymological analysis of abbreviations has been discussed in detail on numerous occasions, the main characteristics of his approach will only be summarised here.[22] In short, then, he argued that a significant number of frequently occurring words in natural language 'are merely abbreviations employed for dispatch, and are the signs of other words', and, significantly given the foregoing discussion, he claimed that particles, such as the conjunctions that Locke has discussed, fall into this category.[23] He further maintained that the etymological origins of such abbreviations could reveal their fundamental meaning. Therefore, throughout the two volumes of *Diversions* that were first published in 1786 and 1798 respectively (and, presumably, throughout the third volume, which he destroyed before he died), he attempted to develop a reductivist work of philosophical grammar which stressed the centrality of etymology to linguistic theory. For instance, he suggested that grammarians such as James Harris had erred when they had classified the word *that* as being sometimes a pronoun (e.g., I saw **that**) and sometimes a conjunction (e.g., I think **that** I saw it), and, in Horne Tooke's system, *that* 'retains always one and the same signification' in all contexts.[24] Specifically, taking a sentence such as[25]

I wish you to believe THAT I would not wilfully hurt a fly

it is possible to rearrange its constituent elements as follows:

I would not wilfully hurt a fly, I wish you to believe THAT

a 'resolution' which indicates (at least, according to Horne Tooke) that the conjunction *that* should be classified as a pronoun in both sentences.[26]

3.3 Horne Tooke's Theory of Language

As he develops his argument, he discusses a wide range of English conjunctions and attempts to demonstrate (amongst other things) that *if*, *unless*, and *yet* are actually imperative verbs, while *lest* and *since* are participle forms.[27]

Significantly, having applied his etymological method to conjunctions, prepositions, and adverbs in Volume 1 of *Diversions*, Horne Tooke extended his analysis to other parts-of-speech in Volume 2. As he elaborated his approach, he introduced the notion of 'subaudition', and argued that certain abstract nouns should be reanalysed as participles and adjectives, since it could be shown that they were etymologically derived from such roots. Accordingly, he provided a long list of nouns which included such words as 'Fate, Destiny, Luck, Lot, Chance, Accident, Heaven, Hell', and he concluded that they are all 'merely Participles poetically embodied, and substantiated by those who use them'.[28] To consider only a few examples, he claimed that the noun 'Church' is actually an adjective, derived from Greek, 'whose misinterpretation caused more slaughter and pillage of mankind than all the other cheats together', while 'Fate' and 'Destiny' are 'sham deities' that are actually past participles derived from the Latin verbs *Fari* and *Destiner* respectively.[29] However, rather than merely tracing the etymology of these words, Horne Tooke went further and stated that, since abstract nouns such as 'Truth' were originally derived from participle forms, the entities that they appeared to denote had no ontological validity. In the case of 'Truth', he sought to demonstrate that this abstract noun was derived from the past participle of the Old English verb *treothan*, and since this verb meant 'to consider, To Think, To Believe firmly, To be thoroughly persuaded of, To Trow', he concluded that:

There is therefore no such thing as eternal, immutable, everlasting TRUTH; unless mankind, *such as they are at present*, be also eternal, immutable, and everlasting. Two persons may contradict each other, and yet both speak TRUTH: for the TRUTH of one person may be opposite to the TRUTH of another. To speak TRUTH may be a vice as well as a virtue: for there are many occasions where it ought not to be spoken.[30]

The radical implications of this theory are transparent: if etymological analysis can demonstrate that certain abstract nouns are actually participles or adjectives, then it is possible to eradicate the 'metaphysical jargon' and 'false morality' which have arisen as a result of their mistaken classification as nominals – at least, this is the conclusion that Horne Tooke reached.[31]

It was suggested earlier that it is misleading to consider Horne Tooke's writings about natural language without also considering his political views, and the etymologies he derived certainly provide clues as to his understanding of the relationship between language and society. His repeated use of 'Anglo-Saxon' roots ensures that *Diversions* can be considered in relation to other antiquarian endeavours which sought to revive an awareness of English culture as it had existed (or, at least, as it was perceived to have existed) before the Norman Conquest. While seeking lexical origins, for instance, Horne Tooke drew upon such sources as Stephen Skinner's *Etymologicon Linguae Anglicanae* (1671) and Edward Lye's *Dictionarium Saxonico et Gothico-Latinum* (1772), and he attempted to show that certain words once possessed pure meanings which, as a result of successive invasions and subsequent political subordination during the intervening centuries, had become distorted and unrecognisable in modern English. Inevitably any exploration of this kind has overt socio-political implications, and it is no mere coincidence that several of Horne Tooke's associates were involved in comparable projects. For example, John Cartwright and John Jebb both created persuasive narratives about the constitutional history of England, thereby inculcating a belief in a remote (but reclaimable) idyllic age.[32] In certain reformer circles, then, there was a desire to revive mythical political and linguistic systems that were believed to have been available to all subjects in the 'Anglo-Saxon' period, but which had vanished after the imposition of a feudal system under the Normans. In this sense, such activists were quite literally *reformers* – that is, they advocated a return to a previous state rather than the adoption of an entirely new political system. Although in much modern scholarship, the theories of eighteenth-century nationalists such as Horne Tooke, Cartwright, and Jebb are often dismissed as patently absurd, Gerald Newman has argued convincingly that they should be viewed in a more sympathetic manner:

[...] the ethnographical ideas of Horne and his friends, far from signalling a "quite extreme naivety," far from being the ridiculous antiquarianism which conventional scholarship imagines them to have been, were nothing less than the pivot on which the radicals attempted to overturn and democratise the whole political structure they confronted. Like all nationalists they posited an egalitarian paradise in the past, demanded that this be 'recovered' in the present, and held the current system up to it as damning proof of modern corruption, unconstitutionality and illegitimacy.[33]

Therefore, although Horne Tooke's etymological arguments may seem to be manifestly and unavoidably problematical, there is no doubt that they exerted a potent influence over a whole generation of intellectuals

3.3 Horne Tooke's Theory of Language

who came to prominence in the late eighteenth and early nineteenth centuries. For instance, it is well-known that Coleridge was influenced by Horne Tooke's etymological theories. In a 1800 letter, Coleridge proposed the following project to William Godwin:

> I wish you to write a book on the power of words, and the processes by which human feelings form affinities with them – in short, I wish you to "philosophize" Horne Tooke's system, and to solve the great questions – whether there be reason to hold that an action bearing the semblance of predesigning consciousness may yet be simply organic, and whether a series of such actions are possible – and close on the heels of this question would follow the old, "Is logic the essence of thinking?" – in other words, "Is thinking possible without arbitrary signs? or how far is the word arbitrary a misnomer? are not words, etc., parts and germinations of the plant, and what is the law of their growth?" In something of this order I would endeavour to destroy the old antithesis of Words and Things, elevating, as it were, Words into Things, and living things too. All the nonsense of vibrations, etc., you would, of course, dismiss.[34]

It is characteristic that Coleridge should move seamlessly from an exhortation aimed at Godwin ('I wish you to write a book...I wish you to "philosophize"...') towards a statement of his own projected intentions ('...I would endeavor to destroy...'). Nonetheless, this extract suggests that Coleridge was personally inspired by the linguistic arguments that he had encountered in *Diversions*, and that he considered them to provide a foundation for more extensive philosophical reflections. However, as ever with Coleridge, it is perilous to assume that his advocacy of one approach necessarily implies a dismissal of all alternative strategies. In this case, James McKusick has shown that Coleridge actively sought to combine certain aspects of the work of both Horne Tooke and Harris in order to create a philosophical linguistic theory that avoided an extreme empirical stance by incorporating both moral and metaphysical aspects. As McKusick puts it,

> In his mature theory of language, Coleridge never fully rejects the materialism of Horne Tooke; instead, he retains it as a methodology held strictly subordinate to the idealism derived in part from James Harris. Coleridge finds that this dual methodology is necessary because language itself contains two kinds of words: some denote perceptual objects, while others denote mental activities.[35]

As will be shown later, Hazlitt also attempted to incorporate certain aspects of Horne Tooke's empiricist linguistic theory into his own idealistic theories of language and mind. Consequently, like Coleridge, his mature theories drew upon several different traditions within eighteenth-century philology and philosophy, and it is appropriate now to explore some of these interconnections.

3.4 Indeclinable Words

There is no doubt that Horne Tooke was a conspicuous social figure in London throughout the 1790s, and it was during this period that Hazlitt became an established member of his network of acquaintance. Although it is not known exactly when and where the two men met for the first time, Horne Tooke had certainly befriended John Thelwall by the early 1790s and, since Thelwall was a friend of Hazlitt's, it is likely that he introduced them. In 1792, Horne Tooke moved to a large house on the west side of Wimbledon Common (overlooking Rushworth pond), and this residence became a meeting place for the many people who were invited to enjoy Sunday dinners there.[36] In their detailed biography of Horne Tooke, Christina and David Bewley describe these occasions as follows:

> A motley collection of his acquaintances from all walks of life would stream out from London, arriving between two and four and leaving between seven and eight. Politicians who might dislike his political views but enjoyed his brilliant conversation, artists, distinguished authors and scientists, journalists, bankers, classical scholars, men about town, artisans with little education and rough country manners, would mix happily together, due to Tooke's gifts as a host, genial and exuding *bonhomie*.[37]

Given Horne Tooke's well-attested linguistic interests, it is highly likely that philological and philosophical topics were often addressed during these dinners, and consequently it is possible that Hazlitt was able to discuss language-related matters with his host in person. However that may be, it is clear that Hazlitt was greatly impressed by the conversational skills on display. In his *Spirit of the Age* essay, he observes that Horne Tooke was 'without a rival (almost) in private conversation', adding that

> Mr. Horne Tooke was in private company, and among his friends, the finished gentleman of the last age. His manners were as fascinating as his conversation was spirited and delightful. He put one in mind of the burden of the song of '*The King's Old Courtier, and an old Courtier of the King's.*' He was, however, of the opposite party. It was curious to hear our modern sciolist advancing opinions of the most radical kind without any mixture of radical heat or violence, in a tone of fashionable *nonchalance*, with elegance of gesture and attitude, and with the most perfect good-humour.[38]

3.4 Indeclinable Words

Presumably, this description draws upon Hazlitt's own recollections of Horne Tooke's conversational manner, and it is clear that Hazlitt associates the latter strongly with late eighteenth-century social conventions. Indeed, as well as personal recollections, Hazlitt appears to have cherished anecdotal accounts of Horne Tooke's prowess in debates. In his essay 'On the Conversation of Authors', for example, he refers to the latter's 'ingenious absurdities', adding that

A person who knew him well, and greatly admired his talents, said of him that he never (to his recollection) heard him defend an opinion which he thought right, or in which he believed him to be himself sincere. He indeed provoked his antagonists into the toils by the very extravagance of his assertions, and the teasing sophistry by which he rendered them plausible. His temper was prompter to his skill. He had the manners of a man of the world, with great scholastic resources. He flung every one else off his guard, and was himself immovable. I never knew any one who did not admit his superiority in this kind of warfare. He put a full-stop to one of Coleridge's long-winded prefatory apologies for his youth and inexperience, by saying abruptly, 'Speak up, young man!' and, at another time, silenced a learned professor by desiring an explanation of a word which the other frequently used, and which, he said, he had been many years trying to get at the meaning of, – the copulative Is! He was the best intellectual fencer of his day. He made strange havoc of Fuseli's fantastic hieroglyphics, violent humours, and oddity of dialect.[39]

Hazlitt's admiration of Horne Tooke's multi-faceted oratorical versatility is apparent, and he obviously took great delight in recalling the manner in which the latter disconcerted Coleridge and Fuseli. However, although these personal and anecdotal associations are of considerable interest, it is perhaps more illuminating specifically to explore his response to Horne Tooke's philological research.

As indicated earlier, Hazlitt repeatedly praised particular aspects of Horne Tooke's *Diversions*, and his appreciation was first extensively articulated in his *Grammar*. Indeed, the full title of this publication overtly aligns it with Horne Tooke's linguistic theories:

A New and Improved Grammar of the English Tongue: for the Use of Schools. In which the Genius of our Speech is especially attended to, And the Discoveries of Mr. Horne Tooke and other Modern Writers on the Formation of the Language are, for the first time, Incorporated.

Hazlitt's textbook *Grammar*, then, was specifically designed to introduce some of the 'recent discoveries' associated with Horne Tooke (and others) to its target audience of school-children, and, in the Preface, Hazlitt claims that *Diversions* had produced 'a very important change in the theory of language', adding that his own text attempted 'to take advantage of the discussion contained in that work, without adopting its errors'.[40] This deceptively nonchalant aside indicates that Hazlitt viewed Horne Tooke's work with considerable ambivalence. Nonetheless, it is reasonable to characterise the *Grammar* as a text which presents Horne Tooke's perceived philosophical linguistic insights in a form that made them accessible to those who were learning the rudiments of English grammar, and therefore it is crucial both to determine precisely which aspects of Horne Tooke's work Hazlitt enthusiastically adopted, and to identify those elements which he classified as 'errors'.

Since Horne Tooke's etymological investigations were the most characteristic aspects of *Diversions*, it is helpful to consider how Hazlitt presents etymology in his *Grammar* – and, it is important to recall that the word 'etymology' could refer either to the origins of words or else to different parts-of-speech. Influenced by Horne Tooke, no doubt, Hazlitt objected to the latter practice, referring to 'that branch of grammar which usurps the name of Etymology', and noting that:

Etymology properly signifies tracing the origins of words. In this sense it has been very little attended to, in that part of grammar which bears its name; though it would be of great use in explaining the true properties and nature of language. The neglect of it hitherto only seems to render an attention to this branch of the subject the more necessary.[41]

For Hazlitt, then, word origins are 'of great use' when the various parts-of-speech are considered, and therefore, it would be better if grammar textbooks actually discussed such matters when introducing different classes of words such as nouns, verbs, adjectives, and so on. It is no surprise, therefore, that word origins are considered in his own *Grammar*. In chapter 11, for example, he discusses 'indeclinable words' and acknowledges that the etymological derivations presented there were '[c]ompiled from Mr. H. Tooke's 'Diversions of Purley', Salmon, Booth, &c'.[42] The 'Salmon' referred to here is Nicholas Salmon who had published his *The First Principles of English Grammar* in 1798, while the 'Booth' is David Booth, whose *Introduction* had appeared in 1806. Unfortunately, the work of both Salmon and Booth has been neglected in the past when the influence of Horne Tooke has been considered, despite the fact that they both drew extensively upon *Diversions*. For instance, neither author is discussed in detail in such studies as Aarsleff's authoritative chapter concerning 'Horne Tooke's Influence and Reputation', and this neglect means that their contributions have been generally overlooked.[43] Hazlitt, however, responded to their work directly, in a complex manner, and their arguments certainly exerted a lasting influence upon his own thinking about language and linguistic analysis. For instance, although he criticised Booth for claiming that verbs are always associated with actions, he accepted some of his etymological derivations, and used them almost *verbatim* in his own *Grammar*.[44]

If some of the associations that relate Hazlitt's work to that of Booth are obvious, then, in a similar manner, many of the connections that relate his grammatical theorising to Horne Tooke's *Diversions* are often so transparent that they do not require extensive discussion. For example, while introducing the word *that*, Hazlitt states that this lexical item is 'sometimes a conjunction and sometimes a demonstrative pronoun', before adding in a recognisably Horne Tookeian manner, that 'the differences arise only from the differences of application and construction'.[45] Other words that he considers in this context include a range of function words such as *if, unless, yet, still, though, but*, and, in each case, he provides information about putative etymological origins in order to demonstrate that such words all ultimately derived from other parts-of-speech. Crucially, the words which he considers in this section are all 'indeclinable words' – that is, function words that are not subject to morphological change of any kind – and those words that Locke had classified as 'particles' certainly fall into this set.

There are various reasons why Hazlitt was inclined to present etymological derivations when he considered indeclinable words. For instance, it was mentioned earlier that Hazlitt traduced Harris' *Hermes* for presenting an analytical framework that was almost as complex as the phenomenon (i.e., natural language) that it was designed to analyse, and this concern seems to have compelled him, in his own work, to adopt analytical methods that achieved meaningful simplifications. If such a distinction can be consistently maintained, then this concern is predominantly philological rather than primarily philosophical – that is, it is prompted mainly by his interest in the categories posited for textbook grammatical analysis. Specifically, etymological derivations for 'indeclinable words', which associate these particular lexical items with nominal or verbal roots, considerably simplify the task of grammatical analysis since they enable the number of parts-of-speech to be reduced: if all prepositions and conjunctions can be shown to be ultimately derived from either verbs or nouns, then two categories can be eliminated from the grammatical system. However, Hazlitt seems also to have believed that word origins can be used to resolve seemingly insoluble semantic difficulties. For example, if it is assumed that all words are associated with specific meanings (or 'significations', or 'ideas'), then, as mentioned previously, prepositions and conjunctions cause tiresome problems since they indicate a range of abstract relationships between entities, clauses, or sentences. Consequently, less recalcitrant parts-of-speech (e.g., nouns and verbs) can neither be easily associated with a clear set of meanings nor related to specific actions or entities in the external world. Uncertainty concerning the grammatical status of function words was not new. Indeed, it had prevailed since at least the seventeenth century. For example, in his 1668 *Essay Towards A Real Character and a Philosophical Language*, John Wilkins incorporated particles into the language system that he expounded, yet his irresolution was apparent. As Stephen Land has noted,

> Particles are clearly a lesser order of substantives, less amenable to organisation, perhaps something of a mystery, and therefore rather a nuisance. The bewilderment with respect to particles is not peculiar to Wilkins but common to most of the philosophers of the period who try to take linguistic research beyond the discussion of the name relation.[46]

If particles are 'a mystery' and 'a nuisance', then this suggests that they are not susceptible to the same kinds of analytical methodology as, say, nouns and verbs. As a result, particles (in Locke's sense) continued to perplex philosophers and language theorists throughout the eighteenth century.

Anxiety concerning these matters was widespread when Hazlitt was writing his *Grammar*, and Horne Tooke's unswervingly empiricist attempt to demonstrate that certain conjunctions and prepositions could be reanalysed as verbal forms sought to provide a secure explanation for these otherwise seemingly inexplicable linguistic phenomena. Other theorists, though, offered interpretations that were similarly constrained by fundamental empiricist assumptions. For instance, in his *Introduction*, Booth adopted a distinctly empiricist stance. He stated that '[i]deas are the reflected image of nature. Words are the pictures of ideas', and he lavishly praised Horne Tooke's linguistic work:[47]

> It was reserved for a Linnaeus, a Lavoisier, and a Tooke, to build anew the temple of Science, and to replace the Gothic arches and gloomy vaults by the elegant and cheerful structures of modern taste. It is sometime, however, before the rising fane can attract the worship of the crowd. The spirit of prejudice, like the ghosts of the departed, love to linger near the mouldering walls, under the covert of the night.[48]

In Booth's ornate description, Horne Tooke is grouped together with scientists such as Carolus Linnaeus and Antoine Lavoisier, and these

3.4 Indeclinable Words 77

researchers are associated with the eradication of outmoded analytical methods which are only retained by some members of 'the crowd' as a result of the 'spirit of prejudice'. In Booth's analogy, Horne Tooke is envisioned as a neo-classical architect who replaces Gothic ruins with superior modern structures. More specifically, though, concerning Horne Tooke's treatment of prepositions and conjunctions, Booth elsewhere emphasised the fact that an etymological approach has advantages when semantic concerns are addressed. For instance, he praises Horne Tooke's methodology when, having referred to the 'fifty or sixty' words that are either prepositions or conjunctions, he adds:

All these have been examined, by Mr. Horne Tooke, in his *Diversions of Purley*, and shewn to be merely Verbs, or Nouns, whose other parts, or compounds, are, in general, not to be found in the language; for which reason the task of fixing their accurate signification becomes the more laborious: *and, but, yet; – from, to, with*, and the like, have a significance of their own, independent of their connections in the sentences where they are found.[49]

Booth was keen to determine the 'signification' of these particular function words, and he recognised that their meanings were independent of the specific grammatical contexts in which they can be embedded – in other words, he realised that they have 'a signification of their own'. The task of determining the 'significance' of a given preposition or conjunction may be 'laborious', but, according to Booth, it can be simplified if Horne Tooke's etymological methodology is deployed:

If, then, each have a *meaning*, and is capable of raising an idea in the mind, that idea must have its prototype in nature. It must either denote *an exertion*, and is, therefore, a *verb*; or *a quality*, and is, in that case, *an Adjective*; or it must express *an assemblage of qualities*, such as is observed to belong to *some individual object*, and is, in this supposition, the *name* of said *object*, or a *Noun*.[50]

The suggestion that it was desirable to provide etymological derivations for a given function word so that it could be associated with a clear 'idea in the mind' which corresponded to 'its prototype in nature', a development that would enable the word concerned to be incorporated into a coherent analytical semantic theory. Since Hazlitt was happy to acknowledge in his *Grammar* that he had drawn heavily upon Booth's *Introduction*, it is possible that he was influenced by the latter's distinctive approach to the semantic problems created by function words, and his discussion of such matters certainly implies that this was the case.

Given the above, it is important to consider the manner in which Hazlitt's linguistic work has been presented by critics who are primarily concerned with the task of determining his philosophical position. For instance, there have been numerous attempts to indicate that Hazlitt rejected empiricism in favour of a certain kind of idealism, and passages such as the following (which is taken from his *Grammar*) are standardly adduced as evidence:

> We have endeavoured to show [...] that the grammatical distinctions of words do not relate to the nature of the things or ideas spoken of, but to our manner of speaking of them, i.e., to the particular point of view in which we have occasion to consider them, or combine them with others in the same discourse. [...] The things themselves do not change, but it is we who view them in a different connection with other things, and who accordingly use different sorts of words to show the difference of the situation which they occupy in our thoughts and discourse.[51]

This extract is often quoted specifically in order to demonstrate that Hazlitt rejected entirely a strongly empiricist approach to linguistic analysis. Paul Hamilton, for one, has recently observed that 'Hazlitt is here primarily refuting empiricist theories of grammar, claiming that individual parts-of-speech gain their meaning from what they are used to refer to and not from what they refer to', while Natarajan quotes from the same passage when arguing that Hazlitt 'uses grammatical distinctions to dissever linguistic classifications from immediate correspondence to an absolute reality'.[52] However, in the light of the foregoing discussion, these conclusions seem rather too extreme. Although Hazlitt certainly rejected particular aspects of unremittingly empiricist grammatical analyses (and more will be said about this later), he nevertheless explicitly and unashamedly incorporated aspects of such theories into his own *Grammar*. In the above quotation, for instance, he dismisses the notion that the parts-of-speech used in a grammatical analysis are determined simply by 'the nature of things or ideas spoken of', and argues instead that they are determined by 'our manner of speaking of them'. This somewhat opaque proto-pragmatical usage-based perspective effectively nullifies an extreme empiricist position. Nonetheless, although Hazlitt seeks to emphasise the centrality of usage as opposed to inescapable empirical connections, he accepts that the words are necessarily associated (albeit temporarily) with those things or ideas they are used to refer to, and this causes problems when function words such as prepositions and conjunctions are considered, since, as mentioned previously, these words cannot be simply and transparently associated with either 'things' or 'ideas'. Consequently, it is not surprising that Hazlitt should have been persuaded by the analyses of indeclinable words that Horne Tooke,

Booth, and other empiricist philosophers of language had proposed. In short, any approach that enables indeclinable syncategorematic lexical items to be derived from verbs or nouns ensures that such words can be trivially associated (even if only temporarily, during actual discourse) either with actions, states or entities, thus resolving perplexing semantic difficulties. Seemingly, by adopting a reductivist etymological analysis of 'indeclinable' words, Hazlitt was willing to incorporate into his own theoretical stance certain etymological arguments that had been proposed by empiricist philosophers of language.

3.5 Winged Words

If Hazlitt felt that etymological analyses of indeclinable words were helpful both because they greatly simplified the grammatical scheme adopted and because they resolve certain semantic difficulties, then later passages of his *Grammar* suggest that, in addition, he was also convinced by Horne Tooke's arguments concerning the role of abbreviation in natural language. During a discussion in which the 'syntax' of adjectives is considered, for instance, Hazlitt discusses a number of ungrammatical idiomatic expressions and observes that:

The idioms of every language are in general the most valuable parts of it, because they express ideas which cannot be expressed so well in any other way. And the reason of this is, that they are either abbreviated methods of expressing things of constant recurrence, or have been invented to supply the defects of the general structure of language. To decide on the propriety of every phrase from a principle of abstract reasoning, besides unsettling the only acknowledged standard of propriety, would also be to cramp and mutilate the language, and render it unfit for the real purposes of life.[53]

For Hazlitt, then, 'idioms' are 'the most valuable parts' of any given language, and his justification of this stance partly reveals the intellectual allegiances that characterise his thinking about language. He states that idioms either constitute 'abbreviated methods' which facilitate the discussion of things that are referred to frequently, or else they 'supply [...] defects' which would otherwise manifest themselves in certain non-idiomatic linguistic structures – and these observations both recall similar claims made in Horne Tooke's *Diversions*. In order to appreciate the implications of this, it is essential to reflect upon the various connotations that were associated with the word 'idioms' in the eighteenth century. For instance, for Johnson, an 'idiom' was merely '[a] mode of speaking peculiar to a language or dialect; the particular cast of a tongue; a phrase; phraseology', and he offered a few lines from Dryden and Prior, including the following couplet:[54]

And to just *idioms* fix our doubtful speech.

In this context, 'idiom' simply indicates a specific modality of spoken communication, and there are identifiable degrees of respectability. By contrast, in his *A Course of Lectures on the Theory of Language and Universal Grammar*, Priestley observes that, when 'idioms' are used,

[...] intire words resemble single letters in other words: that is, they have no meaning in themselves, but the phrase composed out of them is the least significant part into which the sentence it helps to form can be divided; as, in general, single words are the least significant parts of a sentence. [...] These complex kinds of idioms are little attended to by those who speak a language because, from their infancy, they learn to affix single ideas to those whole sentences, in the same manner as they usually do to single words: for instance how few *English* people are aware that *to give over a thing* is an idiom of this kind, or a phrase, of which the ideas of the parts do not compose the idea of the whole; yet it requires but little reflection to make them sensible of it.[55]

In this formulation, 'idioms' are specifically identified as being irreducible units of meaning, phrases which effectively function as single lexical items since they cannot be broken down into smaller syntactic units. In short, idioms amount to more than the sum of their semantic parts. It should be obvious that this definition differs markedly from Johnson's and, given this divergence, it is necessary to consider the manner in which Hazlitt uses this term. The fact that, in the extract quoted above, he refers to idioms as being units of meaning which 'cannot be expressed so well in any other way' suggests that he is indeed thinking of the same sorts of structures as Priestley – that is, indivisible phrases which convey an established idea.

Since Hazlitt considered his own *Grammar* to be an attempt to produce a school textbook which introduced certain ideas expounded in *Diversions*, it seems highly likely that his description of idioms as 'abbreviated methods' derives in part from Horne Tooke's notion of 'EPEA PTEROENTA', or 'winged words' which abbreviate in order to accelerate communication.[56] This association suggests that Horne Tooke's distinctive and politically-charged advocacy of common idioms had encouraged Hazlitt to recognise the linguistic merits of such structures, and this realisation in turn prompted a reassessment of the status of those idiomatic constructions that appear in literary contexts – a task that Hazlitt undertook more extensively in some of his later writings.

3.5 Winged Words

In a similar manner, though, Hazlitt's second claim – namely, that idioms 'supply the defects of the general structure of language' – may also reveal Horne Tooke's influence since the latter had robustly dismissed the prevailing Lockean notion that natural language was inherently and unavoidably imperfect, observing that 'the perfections of Language, not properly understood, have been one of the chief causes of the imperfections of our philosophy'.[57] More specifically, he had argued that an etymological analysis of problematical parts-of-speech was a powerful way of demonstrating that language was closer to perfection than was generally supposed, since it could reveal an underlying order beneath the apparent irregularity.[58] For Hazlitt, then, the avoidance of 'idioms' for reasons of abstract grammatical principles (often derived from non-English grammars) could only serve to 'cramp and mutilate the language', rendering it unfit for 'the real purposes of life', and he retained this view throughout his life, consistently stressing the social function of linguistic communication, and championing 'common' usage.[59]

So, from 1809 onwards, Hazlitt appears to have believed that linguistic analysis should focus on etymology and abbreviation. In the aforementioned *Spirit of the Age* essay (which he wrote sixteen years after his *Grammar*), he observed that '[t]he whole of his [i.e., Horne Tooke's] reasoning turns upon showing that the Conjunction That is the pronoun That', remarking that

[t]here is a web of old associations wound round language, that is a kind of veil over its natural features; and custom puts on the mask of ignorance. But this veil, this mask, the author of *The Diversions of Purley* threw aside, and penetrated to the naked truth of things, by the literal, matter-of-fact, unimaginative nature of his understanding, and because he was not subject to prejudices or illusions of any kind. Words may be said to 'bear a charmed life, that must not yield to one of woman born' – with womanish weaknesses and confused apprehensions. But this charm was broken in the case of Mr. Tooke, whose mind was the reverse of effeminate – hard, unbending, concrete, physical, half-savage – and who saw language stripped of the clothing of habit or sentiment, or the disguises of doting pedantry, naked in its cradle, and in its primitive state. Our author tells us that he found his discovery on *Grammar* among a number of papers on other subjects, which he had thrown aside and forgotten.[60]

There is much that can be unpicked here. Horne Tooke is figured as one who seeks to eradicate all imposture and disguise, removing deceptive intervening barriers so that 'the naked truth' can be perceived, and this description should cause us to pause. In the light of the analysis of abstract nouns proposed in *Diversions*, it is intriguing that Hazlitt should associate Horne Tooke specifically with the task of seeking 'the naked truth of things', since, as indicated earlier, the fully-developed linguistic theory outlined in Volume 2 of *Diversions* seeks particularly to eradicate the notion of immutable Truth. Consequently, Hazlitt's enthusiastic appraisal queries the validity of the very methodology advocated by Horne Tooke, thereby insinuating an ironic scepticism. Discordant details of this kind reveal Hazlitt's underlying dissatisfaction with *Diversions*, and the precise nature of his disquiet will be considered at length later. In addition, though, it is of interest that, in Hazlitt's description, Horne Tooke's mental characteristics are described in distinctly masculine terms in order to emphasise the fact that his mind is 'the reverse of effeminate'. His understanding is 'hard, unbending, concrete', and, since his methodology does not utilise the imagination in any way, there is no place in his system for 'illusions', and consequently words are no longer associated with 'womanish weakness'. As Tom Paulin (and others) have noted, it was common practice in dissenter circles to refer to female qualities as constituting weaknesses, and therefore the language used here can be considered in the context of Hazlitt's Wem and New College upbringing.[61] Once again, though, it is revealing that, after referring to the 'literal' and 'matter-of-fact' characteristics of Horne Tooke's thinking, Hazlitt immediately introduces a Shakespearean analogy that draws a parallel between the 'charmed life' of both Macbeth and the words of natural language.[62] Apparently, the naked truth concerning Horne Tooke's linguistic work can only be fully described indirectly via an allusion to a literary text. Analogical asides of this sort are in clear contrast to the unimaginative, literal exactness of the method of enquiry being ostensibly celebrated in this extract.

In addition to these points, the primitivism manifest in Hazlitt's description also merits comment. He describes Horne Tooke's mind as being 'half-savage', suggesting that it was not restricted by the cultured refinements that had led previous grammarians astray, and therefore, rather than succumbing to custom, Horne Tooke (at least in Hazlitt's portrayal) saw language as it had been, 'in its primitive state'. Later in the same essay, Hazlitt summarises Horne Tooke's etymological approach to indeclinable words, commenting that

[t]his is getting at a solution of words into their component parts, not glossing over one difficulty by bringing another to parallel it, nor like saying with Mr. Harris, when it is asked, 'what a Conjunction is?' that there are conjunctions copulative, conjunctions disjunctive, and as many other frivolous varieties of the species as any one chooses to hunt out 'with laborious foolery.' [...]

All was, to his determined mind, either complete light or complete darkness. There was no hazy, doubtful *chiaro-scuro* in his understanding. He wanted something 'palpable to feeling as to sight. 'What,' he would say to himself, 'do I mean when I use the conjunction *that*? Is it an anomaly, a class by itself, a word sealed against all inquisitive attempts? Is it enough to call it a *copula*, a bridge, a link, a word connecting sentences? That is undoubtedly its use; but what is its origin?'[63]

The initial concern here is familiar: works of philosophical grammar, such as Harris' *Hermes*, present analyses that are roughly comparable in complexity to the phenomena that they purport to analyse – and it is likely that Hazlitt had borrowed this general methodological criticism directly from Horne Tooke himself since *Diversions* contains passages such as the following:

By such means alone can we clear away the obscurity and errors in which Grammarians and Philosophers have been involved by the corruption of some common words, and the useful Abbreviations of Construction. And at the same time we shall get rid of that farrago of useless distinctions into Conjunctive, Adjunctive, Disjunctive, Subdisjunctive, Copulative, Negative Copulative, Continuative, Subcontinuative, Positive, Suppositive, Casual, Collective, Effective, Approbative, Discretive, Ablative, Presumptive, Abnegative, Completive, Augmentative, Alternative, Hypothetical, Extensive, Periodical, Motival, Conclusive, Explicative, Transitive, Interrogative, Comparative, Diminuative, Preventive, Adequate Preventive, Adversative, Conditional, Suspensive, Illative, Conductive, Declarative, &c.[64]

Presumably, a mind that is 'half-savage' and which has seen language in the purity and simplicity of 'its primitive state' would naturally reject such a pernickety and gratuitously theory-driven list of grammatical distinctions. Indeed, these remarks must be considered in relation to the contemporaneous belief that a sophisticated language (such as Latin, Greek, or even English) was characterised by a wide range of complex classificatory distinctions, while a simple, primitive language (like the recently encountered indigenous languages spoken in North America, New Zealand, and Australia) were less complex.[65] In numerous texts from the late eighteenth and early nineteenth centuries, such grammatical sophistication was often used to indicate the intellectual superiority of the colonial powers when compared to the indigenous populations of the territories that were being annexed, but Horne Tooke rejected this socio-politically motivated conclusion. Hazlitt too inverts this assumption by suggesting both that syntactic simplicity is actually a desirable attribute, and that even seemingly complex languages such as English can be shown to be underlyingly simple – a truly radical assertion at the time. Even as late as 1829, in his aforementioned essay on 'English Grammar', Hazlitt was still arguing passionately that popular and successful grammar textbooks misanalyse and distort the English language:

> What appears most extraordinary is that notwithstanding the complete exposure of the fallacy and nonsense by Horne Tooke and others, the same system and method of instruction should be persisted in; and that grammar succeeds grammar and edition edition, re-echoing the same point-blank contradiction and shallow terms.[66]

For Hazlitt, then, the overly elaborate grammatical analyses adopted by writers of both philosophical and textbook grammars alike were mistaken and worthy only of plangent disapprobation. Accordingly, since *Diversions* avoided a needlessly ornate analytical framework, Hazlitt was persuaded that Horne Tooke's linguistic research was more scientific than that presented in other grammatical treatises:

> Mr. Tooke, in fact, treated words, as the chemists do substances; he separated those which are compounded of others from those which are not decompoundable. He did not explain the obscure by the more obscure, but the difficult by the plain, the complex by the simple. This alone is proceeding upon the true principles of science: the rest is pedantry and *petit-maitreship*.[67]

In this summary, Horne Tooke's work is considered to have been conducted in accordance with 'the true principles of science', and therefore its conclusions are more secure. While Hazlitt's commendatory remarks concerning Horne Tooke are sometimes laced with irony, there is no doubt that his scepticism exists alongside true admiration. He consistently championed Horne Tooke's analyses of indeclinable words, abbreviations, and idioms, and he repeatedly praised the grammatical framework that Horne Tooke had proposed for its simplicity, comparing it favourably to the more elaborate systems adopted by Harris, Lowth, and other celebrated grammarians. Indeed, if considered in isolation, details such as these could even inspire the belief that Hazlitt was merely a devoted and enthusiastic advocate of Horne Tookeian linguistics, and, as mentioned earlier, Aarsleff (for one) whole-heartedly adopted this view. The task now, however, is to counterbalance this stance by delineating as clearly as possible the boundaries that circumscribed and delimited Hazlitt's advocacy of the methodology presented in *Diversions*.

3.6 Rejecting Metaphysics

Although Hazlitt's admiration for certain aspects of Horne Tooke's linguistic research was deep and abiding, there are numerous passages in his writings which have prompted the now conventional critical view which presents Hazlitt as being an 'anti-empirical, anti-materialist' philosopher who, as a direct result of his scepticism concerning Horne Tooke's metaphysical doctrines, dismissed the latter's entire theory of language.[68] Once again, Hazlitt's *Spirit of the Age* essay about Horne Tooke is a useful place to start:

It is [...] a pity that Mr. Tooke spun out his great work with prolix and dogmatical dissertations on irrelevant matters, and after denying the old metaphysical theories of language, should attempt to found a metaphysical theory of his own on the nature and mechanism of language. The nature of words, he contended (it was the basis of his whole system), had no connection with the nature of things or the objects of thought; yet he afterwards strove to limit the nature of things and of the human mind by the technical structure of language. Thus he endeavours to show that there are no abstract ideas, by enumerating two thousand instances of words, expressing abstract ideas, that are the past participles of certain verbs. It is difficult to know what he means by this. On the other hand, he maintains that 'a complex idea is as great an absurdity as a complex star,' and that words only are complex. He also makes out a triumphant list of metaphysical and moral non-entities, proved to be so on the pure principle that the names of these non-entities are participles, not nouns or names of things. That is strange in so close a reasoner, and in one who maintained that all language was a masquerade of words, and that the class to which they grammatically belonged had nothing to do with the class of ideas they represented.[69]

Hazlitt here indicates unambiguously that he rejected what he refers to as Horne Tooke's 'metaphysical theory', and, in particular, that he objects to the inconsistency which characterised the attempts in Volume 2 of *Diversions* to extend the methodology of etymological analysis from indeclinable words to nouns. Hazlitt is swift to note that Horne Tooke had himself dismissed those 'metaphysical' linguistic theories which had sought to determine either the number of parts-of-speech from the different types of 'things', or the different types of 'things' from the given parts-of-speech. Therefore he castigates Horne Tooke for erecting his own metaphysical theory of language upon the rubble of the philosophical systems he had himself so effectively dismantled.[70] As Hazlitt summarises it, the 'metaphysical' aspect of Horne Tooke's theory manifests itself predominantly in his empiricist desire to demonstrate that there are no such things as abstract ideas. Once again, it is necessary to view these claims in relation to Locke. As is well known, Locke had controversially distinguished between 'simple' and 'complex' ideas, and he had subdivided the latter into three categories: 'Modes', 'Substances', and Relations'.[71] Horne Tooke was dissatisfied with these distinctions, and he attempted to demonstrate that it was 'as improper to speak of *a complex idea* as it would be to call a constellation a complex star'.[72] Consequently, he concluded that 'they are not ideas, but merely terms, which are *general* and *abstract*'.[73] Obviously, this is the very passage that Hazlitt had in mind when he condemned Horne Tooke's 'metaphysical theory' in the extract quoted above. It is worth emphasising that Hazlitt repeatedly argued that all ideas are abstract, in effect inverting Horne Tooke's position. Over thirty years ago, Roy Park summarised Hazlitt's stance in the context of eighteenth-century philosophy as follows:

> Hazlitt is in complete agreement with Berkeley's nominalist criticism of Locke that we do not have abstract ideas corresponding to general terms. He does not, however, argue for this on the grounds that all our ideas are particular. He agrees with Locke that we do possess abstract ideas, but for Hazlitt *all* our ideas are abstract. This radical solution of the problem of universals rules out any meaningful agreement with either of the opposing theories of the eighteenth century.[74]

This analysis acutely highlights the manner in which Hazlitt's philosophical position was developed partly in reaction to prevailing theories concerning abstract ideas. As Park notes, Hazlitt synthesised approaches that he had encountered in the work of both Berkeley and Locke, combining them to fashion a 'radical solution' to the problem of universals, and thereby avoiding either of the undesirable extremes.

Although Hazlitt mentions the weaknesses of Horne Tooke's philosophical and philological work in in his *Spirit of the Age* essay, these issues do not constitute the main focus of his discussion there. However, he had considered these issues extensively many years earlier in his 1812 lecture on 'On Tooke's 'Diversions''. In this lecture, Hazlitt concentrated on the limitations and absurdities which (in his view) undermined Horne Tooke's theory, and therefore the tone of the piece is often uncompromisingly dismissive. At the outset, Hazlitt states that *Diversions* can be viewed from three perspectives – namely, the etymological, the grammatical, and the philosophical – and he adds that, while the etymological part is 'excellent' and the grammatical part is 'indifferent', the philosophical part of the text is 'to the last degree despicable. It is down right, unqualified, unredeemed nonsense'.[75] This three-fold distinction is central to Hazlitt's interpretative response to *Diversions*: although the etymological, grammatical, and philosophical aspects of the work are inevitably closely associated, he maintains that it

3.6 Rejecting Metaphysics

is possible to separate them in order to estimate their respective worth. Accepting this tripartite division, it is possible (at least in theory) for Hazlitt to concentrate on Horne Tooke's 'philosophical' stance without having to refer to the 'etymological' and 'grammatical' aspects of his position. Restricting his discussion in this manner, Hazlitt mocks Horne Tooke for supposing both that his etymological analysis could establish the 'metaphysical principle' that 'the mind has neither complex nor abstract ideas', and that this principle would 'overturn the established notions of law, morality, philosophy, and divinity'.[76] Inevitably, this kind of dual criticism indicates that, rather than being neatly separable, the etymological, grammatical, and philosophical parts of Horne Tooke's treatise are in fact deeply interconnected, and, as will be shown later, despite his best endeavours, Hazlitt was simply unable keep them apart.

The 'metaphysical principle' to which Hazlitt refers is Horne Tooke's belief that abstract concepts such as 'Fate' or 'Truth' could be eradicated by the construction of derivations which demonstrated that such words were originally generated from a verbal base-form of some kind (e.g., a past participle, or an infinitive). In his lecture, Hazlitt repeatedly ridicules this claim without mercy:

While any or all of those metaphysical beings enumerated by Mr. Tooke do or do not exist, what their nature or qualities are, whether modes, relations, substances, I shall not here undertake to determine, but I do conceive that none of these qualities can be resolved in any way by inquiring whether the names denoting them are not the past participles of certain verbs. A shorter method would I think be to say that all metaphysical and moral terms, whether participles or not, are but names, that names are not things, and that therefore the things themselves have no existence.[77]

The central distinction here is that between words and the things they denote, and Hazlitt is effectively elaborating an idea that he had first propounded in his *Grammar* – namely, that verbs can be viewed as nouns since they are effectively the names of certain actions or states. The unarguable absurdity of an analysis which claimed that because names are not things, then the things to which they refer do not exist, is clearly intended to indicate the commensurate absurdity of Horne Tooke's equivalent assertion. Indeed, early on in his lecture, Hazlitt states that '[t]his farcical mummery, this inexplicable dumb show, this emphatical insignificance, neither admits nor deserves any answer', and this passage provides a jarring contrast with the *Spirit of the Age* extract in which Horne Tooke was praised for removing a veil from the face of language.[78] In that instance, Horne Tooke was associated with the elimination of deception and disguise, while in his 1812 lecture Hazlitt repeatedly emphasises misleading and fictional aspects of *Diversions*, depicting its author as being a mummer or a participant in a dumb show. Clearly, then, there are apparent and actual concealments, and the ability to distinguish between them is key.

The preceding paragraphs have sketched an overview of Hazlitt's main criticisms of the philosophical aspects of *Diversions*, and, despite the neat tripartite analysis which he recommends at the start of his lecture, these criticisms provide insights into his understanding of the kinds of etymological explorations that Horne Tooke had introduced. Since (as noted earlier) Hazlitt had enthusiastically adopted Horne Tooke's etymological arguments for indeclinable words in his *Grammar*, it seems likely that he valued this analytical methodology highly. However, as already mentioned, he did not present similar derivations for nouns and verbs, which implies that he considered etymologies of this kind to be of a different order of significance. First, it should be noted that Hazlitt never explicitly rejected as facile the etymologies of abstract nouns that Horne Tooke had presented. Rather, he rejected the metaphysical conclusions that had been reached on the basis of these derivations. For example, he refers to Horne Tooke's presentation of abstract noun etymologies as being a 'tiresome catalogue of derivations', and although 'tiresome' does not indicate invalidity, this description hardly suggests reverential admiration.[79] Why, therefore, did Hazlitt view etymological derivations for abstract nouns and indeclinable words so differently? The answer to this query seems to lie in his understanding of the general methodology and purpose of linguistic analysis. Hazlitt accepted that Horne Tooke's etymological derivations for function words (such as prepositions and conjunctions) greatly facilitated the task of grammatical analysis since they associated these problematical and seemingly unclassifiable words with comparatively well-established and well-understood parts-of-speech (e.g., verbs). However, when the same reductive method is applied to abstract nouns, no considerable simplification of the analytical system results since no part-of-speech categories have been eliminated, and therefore no obvious benefits (in the form of methodological simplifications) accrue.

Once again, then, Hazlitt's position seems to be close to that of Booth: he is preoccupied particularly with the problems created by the controversial function and status of indeclinable words, and therefore he is inclined to reject as 'tiresome' the etymological derivations that Horne Tooke had proposed for content words such as abstract nouns. How-

3.6 Rejecting Metaphysics

ever, it is also the case that he was eager to demonstrate the invalidity of strongly empiricist theories of language which presented the mind as being merely a passive receiver of sense perceptions. Quoting from Anthony Willich's translation of Kant, Hazlitt frequently asserted that 'the mind alone is formative',[80] and, as noted above, rather than accepting the extreme empiricist claim that 'we have neither complex nor abstract ideas', Hazlitt maintained (*contra* Horne Tooke, and others) that 'we have no others' – that is, that all ideas are abstract, even those associated with such seemingly concrete objects as 'a table, a chair, a blade of grass, or a grain of sand', since these all contain 'a certain configuration, hardness, colour, &c', which, without the 'cementing power of the mind [..] would be necessarily decomposed and crumbled down into their original elements and fluxional parts'.[81] Given this conviction, it is inevitable that Hazlitt should have resisted Horne Tooke's efforts to deny the existence of abstract ideas, and therefore that he should have scorned Horne Tooke's use of etymological arguments to show that certain abstract nouns do not exist.

Seemingly, Hazlitt's philosophy of language was predominantly characterised and directed by his response to empiricism, and Roy Park's description of Hazlitt's position is still illuminating:

Hazlitt's own revolutionary solution was in terms of a theory of abstract ideas. By means of this theory he attempted in all his writings to counter not only the claims made on behalf of empiricism in philosophy, moral theory and aesthetics, but to prevent those who shared his anti-empirical outlook from adopting at the opposite extreme a retaliatory idealism.[82]

Hazlitt may have adopted an 'anti-empirical outlook', but, as Park shows, he refused simply to adopt an extreme idealist position in mere retaliation. In recent work, Tim Milnes, in particular, has further explored the beguiling complexity of this aspect of Hazlitt's work, summarising his views as follows:

Revoking the epistemological perspective, yet tied by habit and tradition to empiricism's demand for a criterion of (factual) truth, Hazlitt's thought oscillates between the need for a foundation, and the attraction of a theory of human psychological activity based upon the paradigm of intellectual energy as a field of power.[83]

Milnes states, in addition, that one consequence of this indeterminate oscillation is that Hazlitt 'remained epistemologically empiricist while appearing to be metaphysically idealist'.[84] Although Hazlitt had not developed his mature ideas concerning the philosophy of 'power' by 1812, his views concerning empiricism and the methodology of epistemological enquiry are potently manifest in the lectures he delivered in that year. While debunking Horne Tooke's metaphysics, for instance, he was swift to dismiss the claim that, since there is no such thing as external, objective truth (or '(factual) truth', to use Milnes' phrase), 'two people may contradict each other and yet both speak true':

> Whether Mr. Locke would have been satisfied with Mr. Tooke's account of these words, I cannot say. I know that I am not. I do not think that it is the true one. It is therefore not the true one. Mr. Tooke thinks it is, and therefore it is the true one. Which of us is right?[85]

For Hazlitt, the inescapable relativism that would follow from Horne Tooke's position is intolerable: if two people adopt contrary views concerning a particular matter of demonstrable fact, then one of the individuals concerned must be right and the other must be wrong. Such assumptions reveal the depth of Hazlitt's commitment to (at least) an objectivist perspective, despite his refusal to accept the strong empiricist conclusions that Horne Tooke and others had reached. Passages such as the above suggest that he was inclined to accept both that objective, factual, external truth exists, and that it can be determined in an unambiguous, verifiable manner, since, if the truth of a particular matter could not be determined in a demonstrable fashion, then his concluding question – 'Which of us is right?' – would be irredeemably pointless.

Since the role of 'factual truth' has been problematised above, it should also be noted that, when deliberating concerning such issues and, specifically, when condemning Horne Tooke's metaphysics, Hazlitt's occasional appeals to 'common sense' lodge uncomfortably in his discussion. He observes, for example, that 'Mr. Tooke has on all possible occasions sacrificed common sense to a false philosophy and epigrammatical logic'.[86] However, the placement of the notion of common sense within Hazlitt's philosophy of mind is profoundly disconcerting since this 'sense' appears to function independently of deductive inference or any other identifiable cognitive process. Indeed, it is presented as being a feeling, an inarticulable non-rational hunch, and yet it is of the greatest importance since, if one neglects it (as Horne Tooke had allegedly neglected it) then one is led unavoidably into error and misunderstanding. The opening words of Hazlitt's 1821 *Table Talk* essay 'On Genius and Common Sense' are relevant here:

> We hear it maintained by people of more gravity than understanding, that genius and taste are strictly reducible to rules, and that there is a rule for

everything. So far is it from being true that the finest breath of fancy is a definable thing, that the plainest common sense is only what Mr. Locke would have called *a mixed mode*, subject to a particular sort of acquired and definable tact. It is asked, 'If you do not know the rule by which a thing is done, how can you be sure of doing it a second time?' And the answer is, 'If you do not know the muscles by the help of which you walk, how is it you do not fall down at every step you take?' In art, in taste, in life, in speech, you decide from feeling, and not from reason; that is, from the impression of a number of things on the mind, which impression is true and well founded, though you may not be able to analyze or account for it in the several particulars.[87]

Apparently, common sense contrasts with the kind of deductive procedures that are associated with logical inference in that it cannot be reduced to a procedural rule-based method, manifesting itself instead as an unanalysable 'feeling' which results from 'the impression of a number of things on the mind' – and since Horne Tooke relied upon rational and deductive techniques alone, neglecting the intuitive and the common-sensical, his theory of language is inevitably impoverished, at least in Hazlitt's eyes, as is Locke's theory, upon which Horne Tooke's was erected. Intriguingly, though, common sense is here presented as an accumulated empirical 'impression', caused by the impact of 'a number of things' on the mind, which cannot be analysed or accounted for, but which is nonetheless 'true'. Unfortunately (or perhaps fortunately) there is no attempt to indicate precisely how the veracity of an undecomposable impression is to be determined. Therefore, Hazlitt only provides a creakingly precarious account of common sense, and many of the difficulties contained in this extract arise as a result of his various reflections upon the nature of English grammar and the philosophy of language.[88]

3.7 A Light in the Darkness

It is fair to say that Hazlitt responded in a complex manner to the eighteenth-century philosophical grammar movement, and that his reaction was characteristically bespoke. While consistently criticising the work of theorists such as Harris for being gratuitously elaborate, he was willing to accept other manifestations of the philosophical grammar endeavour as being significant contributions to language study – and the full complexity of his position is exemplified most clearly in his various discussions of Horne Tooke's distinctive brand of (quasi-) philosophical philology. In particular, his contrasting, and seemingly conflicting, observations concerning the etymology-based methodology that Horne Tooke had propounded in his *Diversions* were, in fact, part of a consistent response to the latter's work, and, in general, his reflective evaluation was far more subtle and more selective than is usually supposed. Indeed, in his principled (if convoluted) reaction, he sometimes appears to anticipate the kind of etymology-based argumentation that would later be incorporated into some of the most distinctive and influential linguistic theories and lexicographical projects of the later nineteenth century. Consequently, Hazlitt can perhaps be most usefully classified as a transitional figure who certainly assimilated specific trends in linguistic theory that had been propounded during the previous century, but who also sought to free philological research from the type of language-centred metaphysical speculation that Horne Tooke (and others) had actively encouraged during the second half of the eighteenth century.

Significantly, there is one passsage in Hazlitt's 1812 lecture concerning *Diversions*, which succinctly presents his attitude towards Horne Tookeian etymological analysis. Having rejected the claim that etymological derivations of abstract nouns can provide profound metaphysical insights, Hazlitt observes that

[t]he new-invented patent-lamp of etymology goes out as it is beginning to grow dark, and so the path becomes intricate.[89]

Horne Tooke's etymological approach is characterised as a 'patent-lamp', an object of considerable utility that is associated with the scientific advances of the eighteenth century, and which generally clarifies by illuminating. However, in the realm of Hazlitt's metaphor, the light of the 'patent-lamp' fails just as the darkness approaches, suggesting that Horne Tooke's method ceases to be of assistance as soon as the analysis of anything other than indeclinable function words becomes a central concern – in other words, as soon as the more general task of constructing a coherent linguistic theory for language in its entirety is attempted. Nevertheless, although the metaphorical 'patent-lamp' ceases to be of assistance at this crucial juncture, Hazlitt certainly remained optimistic concerning the possibility of eventually developing a true account of natural language: the dark path may be 'intricate', but it is not impossible.

4
The Implications of Style

4.1 The Influence of Pedagogy

Having explored various aspects of Hazlitt's complex response to the eighteenth-century philosophical grammar tradition, it is important now to focus specifically upon his knowledge of grammar textbooks, since, although there were close associations between the two genres, it was often the case that the textbook writers had distinctive concerns. For instance, they frequently associated grammar with morality and they attempted to identify and classify different stylistic registers, and topics such as these rarely provided the main focus for philosophical grammars.

Although it was suggested in section 3.1 that Hazlitt may have encountered treatises in philosophical grammar in the mid 1790s, it is clear that he had used practical grammar textbooks (in one form or another) long before he joined Hackney New College. Even though Murray's *English Grammar* did not appear until 1795, texts such as Lowth's *A Short Introduction* were widely available in the 1780s, and it is possible that Hazlitt used such books while still a schoolboy at Wem. Indeed, in his earliest extant letter, written in November 1786, the eight-year-old Hazlitt notes that 'I have got a little of my grammar' which presumably suggests that he had already started to study the subject formally. Similarly, in March 1788, he records that he has been using William Enfield's *Speaker, or Miscellaneous Pieces Selected from the Best English Writers* (1774), a text that was designed to inculcate an awareness of good literary style.[1] Indeed, as Grayling, and others, have noted, Hazlitt was deeply influenced by Enfield's text, and works such as *The Eloquence of the British Senate* were 'informed by what he had learned from Enfield'.[2]

While it may seem trivial to focus upon Hazlitt's familiarity with the grammar textbook tradition – an area of pedagogy that was mainly intended to benefit children and the uneducated – it is nonetheless profoundly worthwhile to examine the way in which such texts influenced his own writings about language. As noted earlier, it has been demonstrated repeatedly over the past thirty years or so, that our understanding of Romanticism as a complex socio-political, intellectual, and artistic movement necessitates a clear understanding of the various relationships between linguistic theory and literature during this period. Therefore, it is essential to consider the connections that associate, say, early nineteenth-century attitudes towards certain linguistic registers with the types of stylistic guidelines that were presented in influential eighteenth-century grammar textbooks such as Lowth's and Murray's. Consequently, in this chapter, the discussion will eventually focus on one particular stylistic register – namely, 'the familiar style' – in an attempt to clarify the complex cultural reactions that arose when this style was used. The deployment of the familiar style for literary purposes provoked acrimonious debate in the first decades of the nineteenth century, and it will be shown that Hazlitt (along with certain other writers) was keen to demonstrate that, far from being a disreputable and contemptible medium, it actually conformed fully to standardly assumed requirements of stylistic respectability that had been promulgated by noted theorists and grammarians during the late eighteenth century. The basic task is to probe Hazlitt's belief that the familiar style constituted a valid medium for literary expression, and therefore it is necessary first to review the beguiling range of socio-political implications associated with different stylistic registers in the early nineteenth century.

4.2 Vulgarisms and Broken English

Although the controversial relationship between literary style and linguistic register had been discussed at various points throughout the eighteenth century, the topic necessarily came into unavoidable prominence when the Advertisement to the first edition of *Lyrical Ballads* stated that the poems in the collection 'were written chiefly with a view to ascertain how far the language of conversation in the middle and lower classes of society is adapted to the purposes of poetic pleasure'.[3] The 1800 edition of the text only emphasised the centrality of this theoretical preoccupation by providing a 'systematic defence' of the whole project.[4] As part of this defence, Wordsworth referred to 'the real language of men', and opined that the use of 'simple and unelaborated expressions' could create 'a more permanent, and a far more philosophical language, than that which is frequently substituted for it by Poets'.[5] Although Wordsworth and Coleridge may have been primarily concerned with stylistic experimentation in the context of poetry, later writers encouraged a broader reconsideration of the sorts of linguistic registers that were appropriate for literary expression, and, in chapter 4 of *Arbitrary Power*, William Keach explores a range of ways in which writers from contrasting sociopolitical groups responded to notions of linguistic 'vulgarity' in the first decades of the nineteenth century.[6] Appropriately enough, Keach takes as his starting point Percy Shelley's remark, in an 1819 letter to Leigh Hunt, that his poem 'Julian and Maddalo' is characterised by 'a certain familiar style of language' that can be associated with people 'whom education and a certain refinement of sentiment have placed above the use of vulgar idioms'.[7] The focus of Keach's discussion is (in part) on contemporaneous notions of social and linguistic vulgarity, identifying the difficulties encountered both by writers who championed the cause of the unrepresented lower classes (while often seeking to avoid the intellectual and linguistic mannerisms popularly associated with such groups), and by writers who were keen to demonstrate that 'vulgarity' is a quality that can distinguish the idioms and manners of people from all social strata. Inevitably, after considering different types of linguistic vulgarity in relation to Shelley, Byron, and Keats, Keach turns towards Hazlitt and reflects primarily upon the linguistic distinctions that are proposed in the *Table Talk* essays 'On Vulgarity and Affectation' and 'On Familiar Style'. In the latter, Hazlitt self-referentially observes that 'I endeavour to employ plain words and popular modes of construction, as, were I a chapman and dealer, I should common and vulgar measure', and Keach suggests that Hazlitt's central 'problem' can be expressed as follows: 'How to be a "determined" "chapman and dealer" in prose without being either "vulgar" or merely "technical or professional"?'.[8] This is indeed a pertinent question, and it surely reveals the complexity of Hazlitt's distinctive sociolinguistic predicament. However, an exhaustive consideration of this topic requires more extensive contextualisation than Keach is able to provide in his short chapter. For instance, one aspect of this general issue (which Keach does not consider) is the fact that Hazlitt himself, along with many contemporaneous writers who explicitly expressed political allegiances that could be crudely classified as being in some sense 'radical' or 'republican', was frequently castigated by the Tory press for producing works of literature that contained allegedly 'vulgar' and (more specifically) 'ungrammatical' passages.[9] In an 1818 *Quarterly Review* assessment of *The Round Table*, for example,

John Russell wrote as follows, responding in part to an essay in which Hazlitt had soundly berated Edmund Burke for his political views:

> We were far from intending to write a single word in answer to this loathsome trash; but we confess that these passages chiefly excited us to take the trouble of noticing the work. The author might have described washerwomen for ever; complimented himself unceasingly on his own "chivalrous eloquence"; prosed interminably about Chaucer; written, if possible, in a more affected, silly, confused, ungrammatical style, and, believed, as he now believes, that he was surpassing Addison – we should not have meddled with him; but if the creature, in his endeavours to crawl into the light, must take his way over the tombs of illustrious men, disfiguring the records of their greatness with the slime and filth which marks his track, it is right to point him out that he may be flung back to the situation in which nature designed that he should grovel.[10]

This contemptuous and vitriolic harangue is representative of a particular kind of criticism that had become commonplace by the early nineteenth century, and which is characterised by its tendency to refer to linguistic and stylistic details when seeking, primarily for political reasons, to demonstrate both the intellectual and moral deficiency of the author being traduced. In this instance, Hazlitt had claimed of Burke that, as a result of his supremely eloquent opposition to the French Revolution, he 'has done more mischief than perhaps any other person in the world',[11] thus prompting Russell (a Tory, of course) to refute this assertion by revealing the full extent of Hazlitt's incompetence and insignificance – and Russell's procedure was as transparent as it was crude. Having stressed the general literary worthlessness of the *The Round Table*, he states bluntly that it would not have been mentioned at all if Hazlitt had not chosen to abuse Burke, and it is while cataloguing the various defects which disfigure the work that Russell describes Hazlitt's prose style as 'affected, silly, confused' and (most importantly for the present purpose) 'ungrammatical'.

Hazlitt's response to this type of socio-political linguistic analysis will be discussed later, but it is crucial here to emphasise the fact that he was not the only writer of the period to be condemned in this fashion. To consider just one obvious example, it is well-known that Shelley's early publications were elaborately dismissed by periodicals such as *The Anti-Jacobin Review and Magazine* and *The Quarterly Review*, and his (supposed) grammatical deviance was standardly mentioned in articles written by reviewers who were stringently opposed to his political views. An anonymous *Anti-Jacobin* contributor, for instance, ironically complimented Shelley for disdaining 'the common forms and modes of language' in *St. Irvyne: or The Rosicrucian*, adding with a sneer that one who aims at 'sublimity' should neither succumb to 'a slavish subjection to the vulgar restrictions of grammar' nor be guilty of 'a tame submission to the *Jus et Norms loquendi*'.[12] Less obliquely, while writing for *The Quarterly Review*, W.S. Walker suggested that *Prometheus Unbound* contained 'absurdities' that were 'in defiance of common sense, and even of grammar'.[13] Obviously, writers who were repeatedly subjected to this kind of attack were fully aware of the fact that the very linguistic structures they deployed were deemed by their political opponents to be problematical. Hazlitt, for example, readily acknowledged that 'I have been [...] loudly accused of revelling in vulgarisms and broken English',[14] and politically motivated linguistic criticism of this kind may have been one of the things that prompted him to advocate a 'familiar' prose style that existed somewhere between the shamefully vulgar and the tiresomely pedantic. In his authoritative discussion of the so-called 'Cockney School', Jeffrey Cox has argued that the stinging attacks upon Hunt, Hazlitt, Keats, Shelley, Byron, and others that were printed in journals such as *Blackwood's Magazine* 'constituted an enormously powerful act of cultural definition that still influences our understanding of what we call the second generation of romantic writers',[15] and he later elaborates this point in greater detail:

> The *Blackwood's* attacks were literally reactionary, a conservative response to the preexisting positive presentation of the group; each feature of the attack – its abuse of Hunt and his friends on social, sexual, stylistic, and ideological grounds – re-presents as a failing a key aspect of the circle's poetic project [...] These attacks were in fact a counterattack, an act of recognition by ideological enemies of the gathering of writers around Leigh Hunt.[16]

As this cogent overview implies, the linguistic disagreements that typified some of the exchanges between these authors and their critics were only part of a much larger cultural divide. Nonetheless, they were a central concern, and therefore they surely deserve careful treatment.

A number of interconnected issues have been identified so far – ambivalence concerning vulgar idioms, politically motivated critical accusations of ungrammaticality, the need to distinguish and validate a 'familiar' prose style – and, in this chapter, an attempt will be made to view Hazlitt's various pronouncements concerning these matters in the context of specific linguistic theories that prevailed in the late eighteenth and early nineteenth centuries.

4.3 The Grammars of English

It should be obvious by now that Hazlitt's essay 'On Familiar Style' will feature prominently in the ensuing discussion, and therefore it is worth quoting extensively from the opening lines:

> It is not easy to write a familiar style. Many people mistake a familiar for a vulgar style, and suppose that to write without affectation is to write at random. On the contrary, there is nothing that requires more precision, and, if I may so say, purity of expression, than the style I am speaking of. It utterly rejects not only all unmeaning pomp, but all low, cant phrases, and loose, unconnected, slipshod allusions. It is not to take the first word that offers, but the best word in common use; it is not to throw words together in any combinations we please, but to follow and avail ourselves of the true idiom of the language. To write a genuine familiar or truly English style, is to write as any one would speak in common conversation who had a thorough command and choice of words, or who could discourse with ease, force, and perspicuity, setting aside all pedantic and oratorical flourishes [...] Any one may mouth out a passage with a theatrical cadence, or get upon stilts to tell his thoughts; but to write or speak with propriety and simplicity is a more difficult task. Thus it is easy to affect a pompous style, to use a word twice as big as the thing you want to express: it is not so easy to pitch upon the very word that exactly fits it.[17]

Since Hazlitt is trying to distinguish consistently between a 'familiar' and a 'vulgar' style, he claims that while the latter permits the use of 'low, cant phrases, and loose unconnected, slipshod allusions', the former can only be achieved if 'precision', 'purity of expression', 'propriety and simplicity' characterise the discourse. Although seemingly innocuous, the vocabulary that Hazlitt uses largely reveals the extent to which contemporaneous linguistic theory influenced his attempts to identify and justify a 'familiar' prose style. Consequently, it is crucial to contextualise the vocabulary that he deploys. However, before this can be accomplished, it is necessary to assess the nature of Hazlitt's interest in English grammar in more detail, since it is in his writings about this topic that some of his intellectual associations are manifest most clearly.

As mentioned earlier, Hazlitt overtly associated his *Grammar* with the linguistic work of Horne Tooke. Specifically, he was keen to stress that his own *Grammar* was the first publication to present, in a practical school textbook format, certain aspects of the philological theory that Horne Tooke had propounded in his *Diversions*. In addition, he was also swift to argue that his *Grammar* was the first to propose an analytical framework for English that was not based on Graeco-Roman grammatical models, lamenting the fact that 'there has hitherto been no such thing as a real English Grammar'.[18] By contrast, he claimed that his publication presented the English language 'as it really is'.[19] In summary, then, by stressing the fact that his book was the first introductory volume to incorporate Horne Tooke's etymological insights, and by emphasising the fact that he rejected Latinate analyses of English, Hazlitt attempted to demonstrate that his *Grammar* was distinct from rival publications; and if there could be any doubt as to which particular books he considered to be his most immediate competitors, he clarifies this matter by referring directly to Lowth's *A Short Introduction* and Murray's *English Grammar*. Predictably, when Hazlitt cites these texts, he often does so in a negative manner, indicating how particular analyses proposed by Lowth and Murray are either inaccurate or else undesirable (or both). Indeed, when requested by Godwin to attack Murray's *Grammar* more forcibly, Hazlitt pointed out in a letter that 'I have hit at him several times, and whenever there is a question of a blunder, "his name is not far off"'.[20] To take just a few examples from the more pugilistic passages, when discussing substantives, Hazlitt comments that '[t]he definition given by Dr. Lowth, and generally adopted by others since his time, seems much too loose and general', and he continues by detailing the peculiar deficiencies of Lowth's formalism. Similarly, during his analysis of possessive pronouns, he notes that 'they are [...] very improperly set down as regular genitive cases of their respective pronouns by Murray, Lowth, and others', once again implying that the work of these influential grammarians was flawed.[21] However, although Hazlitt's *Grammar* is littered with such criticisms, he admits that his work is partly a compilation which makes extensive use of terminology and examples that are borrowed from Lowth and Murray. For example, his analysis of the tense system is adapted directly from Murray's: although he changes some of the names of the tenses (e.g., 'Past Tense' rather than 'Preterimperfect' and 'Present Perfect' for 'Preterperfect'), parts of Hazlitt's analysis has been imported, in only a slightly modified form, straight from Murray's text:

Murray (1795):

Irregular verbs are those which do not form their preterimperfect tense, and their perfect participle, by the addition of *ed* to the verb; as

Present	Preterimp.	Perfect Part.
I begin,	I began,	begun.
I know,	I knew,	known.[22]

Hazlitt (1809):

Irregular verbs are those which do not form their past or imperfect tense, and their perfect participle, by the addition of *ed* or *d* to the verb; as

Present	Imperfect or Past	Perfect Participle
I begin.	I began.	Begun.
I know.	I knew.	Known.[23]

These extracts only differ in minor details of wording and formatting. Therefore, Hazlitt's text obviously exists in an ambivalent relationship to certain earlier works, sometimes seeking to associate itself with them in order to benefit from the lustre of their authority, sometimes seeking to distance itself from them in order to reveal the apparent flaws and errors that litter the analyses they adopt.

Although Hazlitt's *Grammar* is intricately intertwined with those of Lowth and Murray, his interest in their work is revealed in other texts too. In the aforementioned extract from the *Spirit of the Age* essay devoted to Horne Tooke, for example, having summarised the most distinctive features of the latter's etymology-based grammatical theory, Hazlitt comments that

> Dr. Lowth described Mr. Harris's *Hermes* as 'the finest specimen of analysis since the days of Aristotle' – a work in which there is no analysis at all, for analysis consists in reducing things to their principles, and not in endless details and subdivisions. Mr. Harris multiplies distinctions, and confounds his readers. Mr. Tooke clears away the rubbish of school-boy technicalities, and strikes at the root of his subject.[24]

The severity of this assessment is considerable: not only is Harris condemned for producing an analytical system that cannot actually analyse anything, but Lowth is also castigated by association since he trumpets the supposed glories of Harris' *Hermes* in his own *Grammar*.[25] Similarly, in a recently attributed 1824 *Examiner* essay, Hazlitt describes John Wilson Croker as being one

[...] who affects literature, and fancies he writes like Tacitus, by leaving out the conjunction *and*; who helps himself to English out of Lindley Murray's *Grammar*, and maintains, with a pragmatical air, that no one writes it but himself [...][26]

Evidently the grammar-related rebuke here is directed towards the type of person who would use a grammar textbook in a mindless fashion in order mechanically to facilitate the writing of literature. Significantly, a number of similarly mocking references in contemporaneous works suggest that this approach to literary composition was becoming more prevalent. Perhaps the most revealing of these is the short piece of humorous doggerel that the young Percy Shelley concocted, seemingly with the assistance of his sister, and which was published in *Original Poetry, by Victor and Cazire* (1810). This light-hearted poem describes the sufferings of an author who struggles to write grammatically:

Here I sit with my paper, my pen and my ink,
First of this thing, and that thing, and t'other thing think;
Then my thoughts come so pell-mell all into my mind,
That the sense or the subject I never can find:
This word is wrong placed, – no regard to the sense,
The present and future, instead of past tense,
Then my grammar I want; O dear! what a bore,
I think I shall never attempt to write more [...][27]

The horror of this woeful predicament is eventually alleviated by the fortuitous arrival of Murray's *English Grammar* and John Entick's *New Spelling Dictionary* (1771):

But come, try again – you must never despair,
Our Murray's or Entick's are not all so rare,
Implore their assistance – they'll come to your aid,
Perform all your business without being paid,
They'll tell you the present tense, future and past,
Which should come first, and which should come last,
This Murray will do – then to Entick repair,
To find out the meaning of any word rare.[28]

In the first decades of the nineteenth century, then, grammarians and lexicographers such as Murray and Entick had attained the status of *quasi* linguistic deities who could be invoked by suppliant authors in order to facilitate the arduous process of literary composition: grammar textbooks could be used to regulate tenses, word order, and so on, while dictionaries could be used resolve problems involving vocabulary; and, as indicated previously, Hazlitt (like the young Shelley siblings) felt contempt for such mechanical and subservient compositional procedures. This no doubt partly explains his occasional irritation with books such as Murray's. However, since Hazlitt's attempts to demonstrate the respectability of a 'familiar' prose style were directly influenced by such textbook grammars (especially Murray's), it is essential to appreciate the sort of advice concerning grammaticality and, more importantly, literary style, that were contained in such publications. Consequently, the pathway back to Hazlitt leads directly through the work of Lowth and Murray.

4.4 Perspicuity: Purity, Propriety, and Precision

Since the word 'grammar' is often problematised by the philosophical, ideological, political, and polemical contexts in which it occurs, the definitions offered by Lowth and Murray are delightfully revealing. For Lowth,

> [t]he principal design of a Grammar of any Language is to teach us to express ourselves with propriety in that Language, and to be able to judge of every phrase and form of construction, whether it be right or not.[29]

The word 'propriety' is crucial since it specifies a stylistic quality that can be acquired and (presumably) appreciated as a result of studying 'Grammar'. It is also significant that Lowth refers to the general ability 'to express ourselves', and does not confine himself to one particular modality, be it speech or writing: grammaticality is associated with language in general, irrespective of the manner in which communication occurs. Having provided this overview of 'the design of Grammar', Lowth then defines 'Grammar' itself as follows: 'Grammar is the Art of rightly expressing our thoughts by words', and this all seems clear enough: presumably, those sentences that rightly express thoughts by means of words are classified as 'grammatical', while those that fail to do so are 'ungrammatical'.[30] In fact, even allowing for the implied subjectivism of 'rightly', a summary such as this is rather too clear, since Lowth was more subtle than his unwarranted posthumous reputation as an arch prescriptivist would suggest. In particular, he seems to have mistrusted overly simplistic dualities of this kind, and he was well aware that the grammatical status of linguistic structures sometimes depends on context and genre. For example, when discussing pronouns, although his general advice is that gender should be used consistently (e.g., *he* should be used to refer to a male antecedent), he acknowledges that

4.4 Perspicuity: Purity, Propriety, and Precision

structures which contravene this recommendation may be tolerated in poetry, and, having quoted these lines from *Henry VI, Part II* (Act 3, Scene 2),

> Oft have I seen a timely-parted ghost,
> Of ashy semblance, meagre, pale, and bloodless,
> Being all descended to the lab'ring heart;
> *Who*, in the conflict that *it* holds with death,
> Attracts the same for aidance 'gainst the enemy.

he comments as follows:

> If the Poet had said *he* instead of *it*, he would have avoided a confusion of Genders, and happily compleated the spirited and elegant Prosopopoeia, begun by the Personal Relative *who*. The Neuter Relative *which* would have made the sentence more strictly grammatical, but at the same time more prosaic.[31]

Lowth's response is appropriately complex: although this passage contains a 'confusion of Genders' which is usually undesirable, in this particular case it serves to augment the inherent poetry of the extract, and therefore this specific 'confusion' is both desirable and advantageous. Observations such as this, which are by no means rare in Lowth's *A Short Introduction*, imply a sophisticated awareness of different literary styles and genres, and other passages indicate that (from Lowth's perspective) certain grammatical conventions could be associated even with specific generic subtypes. For instance, during his analysis of prepositions, he notes that those associated with relative pronouns often appear at the ends of sentences and clauses rather than before their corresponding relatives, and he goes on to observe that

> [t]his is an Idiom which our language is strongly inclined to; it prevails in common conversation, and suits very well with the familiar style in writing; but the placing of the Preposition before the Relative is more graceful as well as more perspicuous; and agrees much better with the solemn and elevated Style.[32]

The stranded preposition at the end of the first clause here (i.e., the very structure that is appropriate 'common conversation' but not for 'the solemn and elevated Style') alerts us to the self-referential implications of this passage: since such structures are well suited to 'the familiar style', grammar textbooks are presented as being comparatively lowly commodities that need not be written in 'graceful' and 'perspicuous' prose. Although some of the distinctions that Lowth makes here are rather fine, his main point appears to be that structures such as clauses which terminate with prepositions can only be classified as being either 'grammatical' or 'ungrammatical' when they are considered in relation both to the genre and style of the passage in which they are situated. In this way, grammar and style are seen to be inextricably interconnected. As will be shown later, this prepares the ground for Hazlitt's reflections upon the 'familiar' style in the first decades of the nineteenth century.

Predictably, similar issues are addressed by Murray in his *English Grammar*, and, like Lowth before him, he too attempts to provide initial definitions of the most important terms, pinning down the word 'grammar' as: 'the art of speaking and writing the English language with propriety'.[33] Although this formulation appears to unite the two separate definitions proposed by Lowth, it also asserts its own independence. First, Murray states particularly that the word 'Grammar' can be associated with both 'speaking and writing', while Lowth had not referred so explicitly to the particular modality used for communication. Also, Murray seems to have substituted the phrase 'with propriety' in the place of Lowth's adverb 'rightly', and this is significant since it was partly Murray's use of the word 'propriety' that was to establish its centrality in grammatical discourse well into the nineteenth century. In general, Murray's approach to stylistic matters was more systematic than Lowth's, and, in order to appreciate the emphasis of the guidelines that he propounded, it is essential to understand the manner in which he drew upon contemporaneous discussions of literary 'style'.

With convenient frankness, Murray acknowledged that many of the ideas presented in his Appendix were 'chiefly extracted from the writings of Blair and Campbell', and the particular 'writings' referred to here are Hugh Blair's *Lectures on Rhetoric and Belles Lettres* and George Campbell's *The Philosophy of Rhetoric.*[34] Although these texts have already been described, it is important to show how Murray drew upon them while compositing his influential stylistic guidelines. For instance, Campbell stated that his intention in *The Philosophy of Rhetoric* was

[...] to ascertain, with greater precision, the radical principles of that art, whose object it is, by the use of language, to operate on the soul of the hearer, in the way of informing, convincing, pleasing, moving, or persuading.[35]

To this end, he devoted part of his discussion specifically to stylistic matters, and he emphasised in particular the importance of stylistic purity. Campbell defines purity, rather grandly, as 'grammatical truth',[36] although he elsewhere clarifies this notion:

Pure English, then, implies three things: *first*, that the words be English;

4.4 Perspicuity: Purity, Propriety, and Precision

second, that their construction, under which, in our tongue, arrangement also is comprehended, be in the English idiom; *thirdly*, that the words and phrases be employed to express the precise meaning which custom hath affixed to them.[37]

If these are the three requirements which induce stylistic purity, then it follows that there are various kinds of linguistic structures which should be avoided in order for these criteria to be observed. Accordingly, Campbell identifies particular kinds of 'barbarism' which prevent purity being achieved. For instance, he identifies 'obsolete', 'new', and 'new-modelled' words as being problematical – and his discussion of these provided Murray with specific instances which he could incorporate into his own analysis.[38] Campbell, for instance, presents the word 'delicatesse' as being a 'new' word, and he considers this to be an undesirable lexical item because the word 'delicacy' already exists.[39] Similarly, he offers 'incumberment' as an instance of a 'new-modelled' word since it is merely a reworked version of the existing word 'encumbrance'.[40] These examples are of particlar relevance here primarily because Murray borrowed them directly and incorporated them into his own discussion of literary style.[41]

If Campbell emphasised the importance of stylistic purity and provided Murray (and others) with persuasive instances of undesirable usage, Hugh Blair offered a more fully articulated analysis. In his *Lectures on Rhetoric and Belles Lettres*, for example, while confessing (rather disconcertingly) that '[i]t is not easy to give a precise idea of what is meant by Style', he introduced a tripartite framework for stylistic analysis which centred on the three alliterative terms '*Purity, Propriety, and Precision*'[42]. In essence, he argued that, if a discourse possesses these qualities, then it will inevitably possess the desirable quality of '*Perspicuity*':[43]

> Perspicuity in writing, is not to be considered as merely a sort of negative virtue, or freedom from defect. It has a higher merit: It is a degree of positive beauty. We are pleased with an author, we consider him as deserving praise, who frees us from all fatigue of searching for his meaning; who carries us through his subject without any embarrassment or confusion; whose style flows always like a limpid stream, where we see to the very bottom.[44]

The idea that perspicuity constitutes a 'positive beauty' when matters of style are considered was one that exerted a potent influence over Murray (and, eventually, Hazlitt). However, the three qualities which Blair associated with perspicuity are closely related to qualities that

Campbell had discussed in *The Philosophy of Rhetoric*. Blair defines purity as

> [...] the use of such words, and such constructions, as belong to the idiom of the Language which we speak; in opposition to words and phrases that are imported from other Languages or that are obsolete, or new-coined, or used without proper authority.[45]

and this clearly recalls Campbell's definition, given above. In addition, though, Blair defines propriety as

> [...] the selection of such words in the Language, as the best and most established usage has appropriated to those ideas which we intend to express by them.[46]

while he states that the word precision

> [...] imports retrenching all superfluities, and pruning the expression so, as to exhibit neither more nor less than an exact copy of his idea who uses it.[47]

These comments proved to be influential. Returning to Murray's Appendix, it is immediately apparent that he effectively incorporated Blair's analytical framework directly (and sometimes *verbatim*) into his own work. For example, he introduces the three alliterative stylistic qualities, purity, propriety, and precision, and the whole Appendix is devoted to the task of demonstrating that the desirable property of perspicuity can be analysed in terms of these subcomponents. When focusing on perspicuity in relation to words and phrases, for instance, Murray considers purity, propriety, and precision in turn, and he starts by defining purity as

> [...] the use of such words or constructions as belong to the idiom of the language which we speak, in opposition to words and phrases that are obsolete, or new-coined, or new-modelled, or ungrammatical, or not English.[48]

This is one of many instances in which Murray has clearly modelled his definition directly on Blair's (quoted above), yet he has made a number of intriguing changes which insinuate a subtly different approach to stylistic analysis. Whereas Blair had claimed that words and phrases which are used 'without proper authority' contravene the purity restriction, Murray instead refers to words and phrases that are 'ungrammatical'. It is not clear whether by 'authority' Blair intended to imply specifically grammatical correctness or not, but certainly Murray has placed the emphasis explicitly upon this aspect of stylistic regulation.

4.4 Perspicuity: Purity, Propriety, and Precision

As examples of the sorts of words and phrases that should be avoided, Murray cites such things as 'Quoth he' (obsolete), 'Delicatesse' (new-coined; 'delicacy' is preferable), and 'incumberment' (new-modelled; 'incumberance' is preferable), and, as mentioned above, both 'delicatesse' and 'incumberment' are words that Campbell had classified as being impure.[49] Having determined purity in this manner, Murray then deals with propriety (again with reference to words and phrases), and he defines this quality as being

> [...] the selection of such words as the best usage has appropriated to those ideas which we intend to express by them, in opposition to low expressions, and to words and phrases which would be less significant of the ideas that we mean to convey.[50]

This definition is essentially a collage of phrases that appear in Blair's description of this quality.[51] Indeed, a representative example of the way in which Murray adapted his sources is accorded when he adds that '[s]tyle may be pure, and yet deficient in propriety', indicating that the stylistic qualities that he advocates are not necessarily dependent upon one another. Murray's succinct statement can be directly compared with the corresponding passage in Blair's discussion:

> Style may be pure, that is, it may all be strictly English, without Scotticisms or Gallicisms, or ungrammatical irregular expressions of any kind, and may, nevertheless, be deficient in Propriety.[52]

By eliminating Blair's clarificatory asides, Murray presents a parsimonious statement of the relationship between two stylistic qualities which he deemed to be essential to perspicacious writing, and he often simplifies his sources in this manner, converting elaborate and finely wrought passages into pithy, pedagogical epigrams.

As examples of structures that do not possess the quality of propriety, Murray cites 'low expressions' (e.g., 'topsy turvey'), 'defective words' (e.g., the omission of articles and prepositions that are required), the use of the same relative pronoun with reference to different antecedents, 'technical terms' (e.g., 'larboard'), 'double meaning or ambiguity', 'unintelligible words or phrases', and 'an exuberance of metaphor'.[53] Finally, having propounded these strictures, he turns to the quality of precision, and declares that this involves '[r]etrenching superfluities, and pruning the expression, so as to exhibit neither more nor less than an exact copy of the person's idea who uses it'.[54] Obviously, this is taken unmodified from Blair's definition (quoted earlier), once again revealing the extent of Murray's reliance on his predecessors. Seeking to clarify, though,

Murray again reworks Blair's discussion in order to identify three ways in which words can fail to express thoughts:

1st, They may either not express that idea which the author intends, but some other which only resembles or is a-kin to it; or secondly, They may express that idea, but not fully and completely; or thirdly, They may express it, together with something more than is intended. Precision stands opposed to these faults, but chiefly to the last.[55]

In this case the inescapable subjectivity of this quality is conspicuous – who but the 'author' has access to the intended ideas in order to determine whether they have been expressed 'fully and completely' or not? – and this may account for the moralising tone of Murray's approach: linguistic responsibility is essential if precision is to be achieved.

It should be noted in passing that (like Blair) Murray does not restrict these qualities solely to prose. Indeed, in his Appendix he cites a number of passages from poetry, and argues particularly that the stylistic guidelines he is expounding can be applied to poetical as well as to prose compositions. While discussing the types of writing that contravene his rules concerning propriety, for example, he quotes the opening five lines from Dryden's 'A Song for St. Cecilia's Day, 1687', remarking that this extract contains 'scarcely a glimpse of meaning, though it was composed by an eminent poet'.[56] Murray's discussion raises a number of enmeshed issues involving considerations of genre and style, and, in general, his approach to such matters was less flexible than Lowth's. In short, then, the stylistic guidance that Murray offers in the Appendix to his *Grammar* is not restricted only to prose, and his advice can be paraphrased as follows: if an author creates a text that possesses the (independent) qualities of purity, propriety, and precision, then the text will also be perspicuous – and, in Murray's system (as in Blair's), this quality is desirable since it constitutes a 'positive beauty'.[57]

4.5 Familiarising the Perspicuous

Given Hazlitt's attested familiarity with the work of Campbell, Blair, Lowth, and Murray, it is no surprise that his own *Grammar* deploys a similar analytical vocabulary. However, what is most intriguing is the fact that, even as early as 1809, Hazlitt was seeking to argue that the 'familiar' style (as opposed to a formal, grammatically 'correct' style) was respectable – and not only when confined to select sub-genres. For example, when considering copula verbs, Hazlitt states that

4.5 Familiarising the Perspicuous 109

[...] the verb To be, with whatever word it is compounded, always requires the same case before and after it, when the same thing or person is meant, as "I am *he*".[58]

Having stated this 'rule', though, he immediately considers some examples of 'wrong construction' including the Shakespearian example '"Art thou proud yet", "Aye, that I am not thee"'. Unwilling, perhaps, to allow Shakespeare to be condemned so mechanically, Hazlitt adds:

It cannot be denied that custom has made this construction in many cases familiar and almost necessary. There is a stiffness and formality in saying [...] "That I am not thou", &c which takes away all the spirit of the language. It is perhaps best either to use these and such phrases in the common way, or to avoid using them at all.[59]

For Hazlitt, then, the language of the age (rather like the age itself) was characterised by a 'spirit'. In order to preserve this 'spirit', pedantic correctness should be avoided, and linguistic choices should be determined by consideration of 'the common way'. If this is not possible, then problematic structures should simply be rejected. Despite the fact that this seems to be general advice which is not confined to a specific genre or style, the Shakespearian origin of these subversive reflections should not be entirely disregarded, since it demonstrates that (like Lowth and Murray before him) Hazlitt recognised that judgements concerning grammaticality and the appropriateness of literary styles were intertwined with deliberations concerning genre and register. He agreed, for instance, with 'Dr. Lowth' that the English system of associating grammatical gender only with gendered entities 'has an advantage over most other languages in the poetical and rhetorical style, as the personification of inanimate things is rendered more remarkable when there is occasion for it', and he quoted from *Paradise Lost* (specifically, Book 6: 781-784) in order to substantiate this claim.[60]

The particularity of Hazlitt's stance concerning such matters can be appreciated when he overtly identifies grammatical rules that apply only to prose and not to poetry. When discussing the fact that English sentences should be ordered so that the subject precedes, and the direct object follows, the verb, he notes unambiguously that '[t]he rule above stated is confined to prose; for in poetry the inversion of the common order of the words is scarcely ever considered as an objection, and it is often accounted an elegance', and literary examples, this time from Pope, Denham, and Milton, are adduced as evidence.[61] Further, this passage confirms the suspicion that the word 'common', which has already started to insinuate itself into this discussion, was a vital term in Hazlitt's critical vocabulary. Indeed, as Keach has observed ' "[c]ommon" is a recurrent term for Hazlitt [...] and his use of it makes us see how much more readily it sheds its pejorative senses than does "vulgar" '.[62] In his own *Grammar*, then, Hazlitt was inclined to emphasise the importance of the 'common way' of speaking and writing, and, when forced to chose between grammatical niceties and actual practice, he generally sided with the latter, unless he felt that a given (sub-)genre (e.g., poetical discourse) benefited when 'common' conventions were disregarded. When considered in relation to the type of stylistic recommendations encountered in Campbell, Blair, Lowth, and Murray, Hazlitt's position confronts in a direct manner contemporaneous preoccupations concerning literary qualities such as perspicuity. In essence, a central difficulty that Hazlitt raises concerns the literary status of the 'familiar' style: is such a style inevitably outside the realm of perspicuity?

Although the discussion so far has considered a few examples of Hazlitt reflecting upon 'common' linguistic forms, none of the passages cited actually motivates his conviction that 'familiar' usage merits being classified as a valid medium for literary expression. However, a justification (of sorts) is contained in the following extract (quoted in part earlier and repeated here for convenience), which appears when the 'syntax' of adjectives is discussed in his *Grammar*:

Some writers object to such sentences as the following "the quarrel became *so universal* and national," "the *truest* happiness consists in the satisfaction of a good conscience," [...] We think, however, that these phrases are sanctioned not only by such high authority, but such constant use, that they have become parts of the language; and that to object to them is to introduce primness and formality under the pretence of propriety. The idioms of every language are in general the most valuable parts of it, because they express ideas which cannot be expressed so well in any other way. And the reason of this is, that they are either abbreviated methods of expressing things of constant recurrence, or have been invented to supply the defects of the general structure of language. To decide on the propriety of every phrase from a principle of *abstract* reasoning, besides unsettling the only acknowledged standard of propriety, would also be to cramp and mutilate the language, and render it unfit for the real purposes of life.[63]

This is an intricate passage. Once again, there is an impatience with the unremitting imposition of grammatical rules, and crucially, he states explicitly that the quality of 'propriety' cannot be induced by mere stylistic hypercorrectness, since unreflecting obedience to grammatical rules amounts to nothing except 'primness and formality'. This observation

4.5 Familiarising the Perspicuous

enables him to describe 'idioms' as 'the most valuable parts' of any given language. In section 3.5, it was argued that Hazlitt's views concerning the linguistic validity of idioms had been inspired by his general acceptance of Horne Tooke's pronouncements about such matters. Seemingly, then, he initially came to prize familiar idioms so highly both because he recognised their abbreviating role (in certain contexts), and because he believed that they could supply defects which would otherwise undermine the 'general structure of language' – and it is of considerable interest that he related both these things specifically to the notion of 'perspicuity'. For Hazlitt, then, the avoidance of 'idioms' for reasons of abstract principle could only 'cramp and mutilate the language', rendering it unfit for 'the real purposes of life', and these remarks manifest the underlying pragmatism that characterised his attitude towards language throughout his life: he consistently stressed the practical, social function of linguistic communication as opposed to more abstract, theoretical concerns. However, as noted previously, he also recognised that particular stylistic registers define themselves in opposition to familiar linguistic practice, and, in these cases (presumably) the recognised stylistic conventions of literary genres preserve the language from disfigurement. Nevertheless, Hazlitt's position here is precariously poised: if common usage determines acceptable practice, and if pedantic hypercorrectness and (say) poetical discourse both deviate away from this norm, then why is the former unacceptable while the latter is desirable?

Although Hazlitt's *Grammar* is not as well-known as his essay 'On Familiar Style', it should already be apparent that the latter is closely related to those sections of his early grammatical work that focus upon the relationship between grammar and style. The first lines of the essay were quoted previously, but they will be repeated here:

It is not easy to write a familiar style. Many people mistake a familiar for a vulgar style, and suppose that to write without affectation is to write at random. On the contrary, there is nothing that requires more precision, and, if I may so say, purity of expression, than the style I am speaking of. It utterly rejects not only all unmeaning pomp, but all low, cant phrases, and loose, unconnected, slipshod allusions. It is not to take the first word that offers, but the best word in common use; it is not to throw words together in any combinations we please, but to follow and avail ourselves of the true idiom of the language. To write a genuine familiar or truly English style, is to write as any one would speak in common conversation who had a thorough command and choice of words, or who could discourse with ease, force, and perspicuity, setting aside all pedantic and oratorical flourishes [...] Any one may mouth out a passage with a theatrical cadence, or get upon stilts to tell his thoughts; but to write or speak with propriety and simplicity is a more difficult task. Thus it is easy to affect a pompous style, to use a word twice as big as the thing you want to express: it is not so easy to pitch upon the very word that exactly fits it.[64]

Given the foregoing discussion, it should now be obvious that Hazlitt is here unambiguously attempting to associate the 'familiar' style with precisely those desirable stylistic qualities advocated both by rhetoricians such as Campbell and Blair, and by grammarians such as Lowth and Murray; and, in attempting to accomplish this, he is clearly seeking to justify and validate such a style with reference to the late eighteenth-century belletristic rhetorical and grammar textbook traditions. The now familiar alliterative triumvirate of purity, precision, and propriety are all conspicuous in these opening lines as Hazlitt endeavours to persuade his readers that 'familiar' prose is not devoid of perspicuity. Indeed, the basic structure of the argument that Hazlitt develops here suggests that his discussion is partly a reflection upon the Blair-Murray analysis of perspicuity since he refers in turn to each of the three desirable stylistic qualities which are required by perspicacious writing. Stylistic purity was associated with the avoidance of 'obsolete', 'new-coined', 'new-modelled', and 'ungrammatical' words, and Hazlitt is eager to demonstrate that since a 'familiar' style consistently avoids lexical and phrasal items of this sort it can therefore be associated with 'purity of expression'. Further, he mocks 'those who hoard up and make a cautious display of nothing but rich and rare phraseology – ancient medals, obscure coins, and Spanish pieces of eight', adding that, while '[a] sprinkling of archaisms is not amiss', 'a tissue of obsolete expressions is more fit for keep than wear'.[65] Writers who produce such sequences of arcane and obsolete words are outside the realm of the 'familiar', and therefore these sections of Hazlitt's essay can be viewed essentially as a reworking of Murray's rather more plodding guidelines concerning stylistic purity. In a similar manner, when Hazlitt condemns '[t]he florid style' for being 'a spangled veil' that conceals rather than reveals ideas, he is clearly seeking to indicate that the 'familiar' style is necessarily characterised by 'precision' since it avoids the various 'superfluities' that Murray had selected for condemnation.[66] Indeed, Hazlitt provocatively claims that 'nothing requires more precision' than the 'familiar' style since (by definition) when writing in this manner one has to seek to avoid all undesirable linguistic excrescences and 'unmeaning pomp'. As for the final component in Murray's stylistic triad, we are told that the 'familiar' style requires the writer to produce sentences that are characterised by

4.5 Familiarising the Perspicuous 113

'propriety and simplicity'. Once again, if Blair and Murray are indeed lurking beneath this injunction, then Hazlitt's list of undesirable words and phrases – 'low, cant phrases, and loose, unconnected, slipshod allusions' – certainly seems partially to overlap with the list that Murray provided in his Appendix and which included such things as 'low expressions', 'defective words', and 'unintelligible allusions'.[67] Accordingly, if the Blair-Murray perspective is adopted, the very fact that the 'familiar' style is inevitably characterised by purity, propriety, and precision, ensures that perspicuity follows of necessity. It is no surprise, then, when Hazlitt claims that such a style is distinguished by the use of structures which are prevalent in the type of 'common conversation' that occurs when a speaker holds forth with 'ease, force, and perspicuity'.[68] Significantly, even though Hazlitt's stylistic recommendations are similar to those presented by Blair and Murray, his manner of conveying them is markedly different. Rather than merely cataloguing particular desirable qualities and providing a list of examples to indicate problematical usage (as Murray had done), Hazlitt parodically debunks alternatives to the 'familiar' style by incorporating contrary approaches into the prose of his own essay. Accordingly, his description of the 'gaudy' florid style contains such needlessly ornate words and phrases as 'rhodomontade' and 'little fantoccini beings', thus exemplifying the absurd monstrosity of the style he is deriding, and this kind of imitative ridicule is a technique that Hazlitt uses extensively in his writing.[69]

It seems likely, then, that Hazlitt's argument in 'On Familiar Style' involves a reconfiguring of the influential belletristic stylistic guidelines presented by Campbell and Blair, and succinctly summarised by Murray in the Appendix of his *English Grammar*. Crucially, though, Hazlitt is here seeking to demonstrate that the 'familiar' style can achieve the status of linguistic respectability that is accorded by the desirable stylistic quality of perspicuity. However, his awareness of the grammar textbook tradition does not cease here, and there are a number of other linguistic structures embedded in his text which insinuate his playful and self-referential awareness of late eighteenth-century grammatical theory. The most conspicuous example is probably the prominent appearance of a stranded clause-final preposition at the end of the second sentence in the extract quoted above. When considering this structure, it should be recalled that Lowth had explicitly associated clause-final prepositions of this type with 'the familiar style', while associating the alternative structure with 'a solemn and elevated Style'.[70] Hazlitt could easily have written 'the style of which I am speaking', thereby ensuring that the preposition preceded its associated relative pronoun. This small detail suggests that he is teasing his audience in this instance (and throughout the essay in fact), toying with their knowledge of Lowth and Murray (at the very least), just as he characteristically toys with their knowledge of Shakespeare, Milton, and others in his essays, challenging his readers to recognise the echoes and references that are woven into his text, encouraging them to situate his words within a larger contextual and cultural framework.

Accordingly, in 'On Familiar Style', Hazlitt attempts to demarcate a domain of stylistic respectability in which the 'familiar' style can exist, and he seeks to do this both by reconsidering such belletristic stylistic qualities as purity, precision, and propriety and by showing that 'familiar' usages can be endowed with these properties. The difficulty of creating an intermediary linguistic space of this kind is revealed later in the same essay when he rebukes those critics who stubbornly maintain that language can be used in a manner that is either grammatical and perspicuous or else ungrammatical and vulgar:

> I have been (I know) loudly accused of revelling in vulgarisms and broken English. I cannot speak to that point; but so far I plead guilty to the determined use of acknowledged idioms and common elliptical expressions. I am not sure that the critics in question know the one from the other, that is can distinguish any medium between formal pedantry and the most barbarous solecism. As an author I endeavour to employ plain words and popular modes of construction, as, were I a chapman and dealer, I should common weights and measures.[71]

Some of the distinctions here are subtle. For Hazlitt there is certainly a clear difference between 'vulgarisms and broken English' on the one hand, and 'acknowledged idioms and common elliptical expressions' on the other, and he is frustrated by critics (especially those that condemn his own work) who acknowledge no intermediate ground between 'formal pedantry' and 'barbarous solecism '. Such a dichotomy excludes a 'familiar' style which inevitably situates itself between these extremes, and, as was shown earlier, Hazlitt articulated his opposition to such a simplistic perspective frequently from 1809 onwards. For example, he reveals his annoyance concerning such matters in his 1817 essay 'On Common-Place Critics', when he observes that such critics are likely to maintain (predictably) that 'no writer can be called elegant who uses the present for the subjunctive mood, who says, *If it is* for *If it be*', the point being that this kind of unbending prescriptivism is adopted only by mediocre readers.[72] However, even if it is (be?) possible to identify

4.5 Familiarising the Perspicuous

a space between pedantry and solecism, a difficulty presents itself when an attempt is made to distinguish 'common' elements from 'vulgar' elements. One of the most distinctive features of Hazlitt's own prose style is his use of idiomatic structures (both lexical and phrasal) that have been extracted directly out of the discourse of everyday life, and which therefore remove his writing from the domain of formal pedantry. To select an obvious example, his celebrated 1822 essay 'The Fight' contains vocabulary that is derived from the actual conversations that he had heard while witnessing the boxing match described in the piece, and words and phrases such as 'the FANCY', '*frowzy*', 'the *swells*', '*pluck*', 'it was a *cross*' (i.e., the fight was fixed) are sprinkled throughout the text.[73] Indeed, as Stewart Wilcox demonstrated in the 1940s, while writing 'The Fight', Hazlitt purposefully revised his manuscript so that initially anodyne expressions were replaced by words and phrases that possessed greater idiomatic potency. As Wilcox observed, since Hazlitt wrote 'The Fight' around the same time that he wrote 'On Familiar Style', it is , William! 'On Familiar Style'

[...] especially appropriate to give a list of the most important revisions in diction and sentence structure of "The Fight". These alterations, being more vivid, or racy, or specific than the first words that occurred to him, show his flair for choosing the right word.[74]

The particular 'revisions in diction and sentence structure' that Wilcox has in mind here include changes such as the following:

My friend the trainer [...] very wisely fell asleep when any <thing else> *other game* was started (Leaf 15, Line 19)

There was a <stupid> blockhead of a fellow I left in town [...] (Leaf 20, Line 3)[75]

In these examples the angled brackets mark those sections of the text that were deleted and subsequently revised by Hazlitt, and certainly expressions such as '*other game*' and 'a blockhead of a fellow' would have been considered 'slang' idiomatic terms in 1822. Significantly, Hazlitt himself writes some of them in italics in order to indicate different degrees of sociolinguistic status. Typographical markings such as these are always significant since they can be used to signal (and problematise) the literary and linguistic validity of particular words or phrases, and, as David Higgins has shown, preoccupations with gender and social status figure prominently in 'The Fight' and therefore perhaps necessarily manifest themselves linguistically.[76] To consider another example, speaking of the phrase 'to cut an acquaintance' in 'On Familiar Style', Hazlitt observes of the word *cut* that 'I should hardly [...] use the word in this sense without putting it in italics as a license of expression'.[77] Appropriately enough, this particular expression appears in Robert Cromie's 1811 *Dictionary of the Vulgar Tongue: a Dictionary of Buckish Slang, University Wit, and Pickpocket Eloquence*, a text that can help to illuminate some of the sociolinguistic registers of the late eighteenth and early nineteenth centuries.[78] For instance, Cromie defines the word *cut* as follows

TO CUT. (Cambridge.) To renounce acquaintance with any one is to CUT him. There are several species of the CUT. Such as the cut direct, the cut indirect, the cut sublime, the cut infernal, &c. The cut direct, is to start across the street, at the approach of the obnoxious person in order to avoid him. The cut indirect, is to look another way, and pass without appearing to observe him. The cut sublime, is to admire the top of King's College Chapel, or the beauty of the passing clouds, till he is out of sight. The cut infernal, is to analyze the arrangement of your shoe-strings, for the same purpose.[79]

Apparently, this particular idiomatic expression originated in Cambridge, and this may partly account for the pseudo-academic classification of the different subtypes which augment the general definition. Its inclusion in Cromie's text certainly suggests that it was deemed to be an inelegant phrase, and this substantiates Hazlitt's claim that he would never use the expression without distinguishing it orthographically by placing it in italics. While this may well be a reasonable convention, it is not possible for the use of italics to be relied upon consistently to demarcate the region that separates 'acknowledged idioms', which are acceptable, from mere 'vulgarisms', which are unacceptable. An authorial classification of a certain word or phrase as being italicisable slang often reveals something about the sociolinguistic structure of English society in the early nineteenth century, but it is an unavoidably relativistic judgement, and therefore one that effectively destabilises, rather than secures, the boundary that divides the familiar from the vulgar.

In case there is any lingering doubt concerning the centrality of such issues to Hazlitt's own literary endeavours, it is worth noting that matters of style – especially concerning vocabulary – were explored in some detail in his 1819 'A Letter to William Gifford, Esq.'. In this letter, while rebutting a number of opinions attributed to Gifford, Hazlitt particularly rejects the accusation that he is 'a very eminent creator of words and phrases'.[80] His refutation is expressed as follows:

I have nothing to do at present with the merits of the words and phrases,

4.5 Familiarising the Perspicuous

which you here attribute to me, and make the test of my general style, as if your readers truly if they persisted would find only a constant repetition of them in my writings. I say that they are not mine at all; that they are not characteristic of my style [...] I do not believe you can refer to an instance in any thing I have written in which there is a single new word or phrase. In fact, I am as tenacious on this score of never employing any new words to express my ideas, as you, Sir, are of never expressing any ideas that are not perfectly thread-bare and common-place. My style is as old as your matter. This is the fault you at other times find with it, mistaking the common idiom of the language for 'broken English'.[81]

There are obvious associations here between Hazlitt's statements concerning 'new words' and the Blair-Murray criterion of stylistic purity. The above passage neatly reveals the manner in which Hazlitt sought to justify the kind of idiomatic style that he adopted by arguing that it conformed to the type of stylistic guidelines that eighteenth-century grammarians such as Lowth and Murray had propounded. This enabled him to describe his own prose style as being 'old' – and his tenacious avoidance of newly minted words once again foregrounds his preoccupation with idiomatic lexical purity. While a close analysis of the specific lexical items, phrases, and sentences that Hazlitt deploys at different times and in different places in his prose is beyond the scope of this book, such a study would greatly illuminate the various stylistic transitions that Hazlitt frequently negotiates in his essays – transitions into and out of formal styles, into and out of familiar styles, into and out of vulgar styles (often within a single paragraph). Indeed, in his writing, the instances of stylistic transition are often more revealing than the periods of comparative stylistic stasis, and he himself advocated such fluctuations. For instance, consider the following extract from his *Table Talk* essay 'On the Aristocracy of Letters'. Concerning the so-called 'learned languages', Hazlitt observes that

[t]hey presently lift a man up among the celestial constellations, the signs of the zodiac (as it were) and third heaven of inspiration, from whence he looks down on those who are toiling on in this lower sphere, and earning their bread by the sweat of their brain, at leisure and in scorn. If the graduates in this way condescend to express their thoughts in English, it is understood to be *infra dignitatem*[82] – such light and unaccustomed essays do not fit the ponderous gravity of their pen – they only draw to advantage and with full justice to themselves in the bow of the ancients. Their native tongue is to them strange, inelegant, unapt, and crude. They 'cannot command it to any utterance of harmony. They have not the skill.' This is true enough; but you must not say so, under a heavy penalty – the displeasure of pedants and blockheads. It would be sacrilege against the privileged classes, the Aristocracy of Letters.

What! will you affirm that a profound Latin scholar, a perfect Grecian, cannot write a page of common sense or grammar? Is it not to be presumed, by all the charters of the Universities and the foundations of grammar-schools, that he who can speak a dead language must be *a fortiori*[83] conversant with his own? Surely the greater implies the less. He who knows every science and every art cannot be ignorant of the most familiar forms of speech. Or if this plea is found not to hold water, then our scholastic bungler is said to be above this vulgar trial of skill, 'something must be excused to want of practice – but did you not observe the elegance of the Latinity, how well that period would become a classical and studied dress?' Thus defects are 'monster'd' into excellences, and they screen their idol, and require you, at your peril, to pay prescriptive homage to false concords and inconsequential criticisms, because the writer of them has the character of the first or second Greek or Latin scholar in the kingdom. If you do not swear to the truth of these spurious credentials, you are ignorant and malicious, a quack and a scribbler – *flagranti delicto!*[84] Thus the man who can merely read and construe some old author is of a class superior to any living one, and, by parity of reasoning, to those old authors themselves: the poet or prose-writer of true and original genius, by the courtesy of custom, 'ducks to the learned fool'.[85]

The general tenor of this passage is unambiguous: Classicists cannot excuse their inability to write English skillfully by arguing that they are beyond such meagre pursuits. Consequently, an explicit tension is established between the Graeco-Roman scholarly worldview, and the contrasting perspective of common practice and common sense. Given this context, Hazlitt's use of Latin tag phrases is conspicuous. He offers no translations, and therefore he presumably expects his audience to be familiar with such expressions as '*infra dignitatem*' and '*a fortiori*'. However, in an essay which partly argues against the needless use of Graeco-Roman learning, the satirical import of these lines is signalled by this code switching: as so often, Hazlitt is exemplifying the kind of prose style that he detests while seeking to destabilise it. Further, though, it is no coincidence that the astringently ironic statement 'He who knows every science and every art cannot be ignorant of the most familiar forms of speech' should be followed by the structure 'Or if this plea is found not to hold water, then our scholastic bungler is said to be above this vulgar trial of skill'. The inelegant clause-initial correlative conjunction perhaps leads us to expect the provokingly idiomatic phrase 'found not to hold water'. These kinds of syntactic patterns were, of course, closely associated with precisely the 'familiar forms of speech' that are being discussed, as are earthy pejorative noun phrases such as 'a quack and a scribbler'. The purpose behind Hazlitt's reflections manifests primarily itself in these transitions from a self-consciously Latinate style to an

4.5 Familiarising the Perspicuous

equally self-conscious familiar style which flirts with vulgarity, and the result is a teasing and satirical sketch of a particular kind of pompous obtuseness. Similar techniques can be perceived in the following passage from 'On Vulgarity and Affectation', and the patterns found here are equally pertinent:

A thing is not vulgar merely because it is common. 'Tis common to breathe, to see, to feel, to live. Nothing is vulgar that is natural, spontaneous, unavoidable. Grossness is not vulgarity, ignorance is not vulgarity, awkwardness is not vulgarity; but all these become vulgar when they are affected and shown off on the authority of others, or to fall in with *the fashion* or the company we keep. Caliban is coarse enough, but surely he is not vulgar. We might as well spurn the clod under our feet and call it vulgar. Cobbett is coarse enough, but he is not vulgar. He does not belong to the herd. Nothing real, nothing original, can be vulgar; but I should think an imitator of Cobbett a vulgar man. Emery's Yorkshireman is vulgar, because he is a Yorkshireman. It is the cant and gibberish, the cunning and low life of a particular district; it has 'a stamp exclusive and provincial.' He might 'gabble most brutishly' and yet not fall under the letter of the definition; but 'his speech bewrayeth him,' his dialect (like the jargon of a Bond-Street lounger) is the damning circumstance. If he were a mere blockhead, it would not signify; but he thinks himself a *knowing hand*, according to the notions and practices of those with whom he was brought up, and which he thinks *the go* everywhere. In a word, this character is not the offspring of untutored nature but of bad habits; it is made up of ignorance and conceit. It has a mixture of *slang* in it. All slang phrases are for the same reason vulgar; but there is nothing vulgar in the common English idiom. Simplicity is not vulgarity; but the looking to affectation of any sort for distinction is.[86]

Once again, the form and the content of this extract are closely intertwined, as Hazlitt shifts between different linguistic registers in order to reveal his purpose. For instance, his use of distinctive rhetorical figures such as parison ('Caliban is coarse enough [...] Cobbett is coarse enough') declares his sophistication, yet these refinements are juxtaposed with idiomatic expressions, such as '*the fashion*', that are associated with the hypothesised vulgarity. Once again, the potency of this kind of vocabulary can be gauged, in part, by consulting the slang dictionaries that were published in the late eighteenth and early nineteenth centuries. Conveniently, the italicised idiomatic expression '*the go*' is catalogued in Cromie's *Dictionary of the Vulgar Tongue*:

GO, THE. The dash. The mode. He is quite the go, he is quite varment, he is prime, he is bang up, are synonimous expressions.[87]

The fact that this noun phrase was incorporated into a slang dictionary, while being excluded from more respectable lexicographical publications such as Johnson's, indicates its lowly status. Although the precise expression *'knowing hand'* is not in Cromie's dictionary, the noun in this phrase is defined as follows:

HAND. A sailor. We lost a hand; we lost a sailor. Bear a hand; make haste. Hand to fist; opposite: the same as tete-a-tete, or cheek by joul.[88]

The nautical connotations were probably already being lost by the early nineteenth century, but the origin of this vocabulary item indicates why it was deemed to be vulgar. However, the subtlety of these judgements is signalled partly by the fact that Hazlitt does not write 'blockhead' in italics – and, appropriately, this word does not appear in Cromie's lexicon. Seemingly, then, although 'blockhead' was an inelegant word, it was not considered to constitute a slang term in the first decades of the nineteenth century.

In addition to these swift stylistic transitions, it is worth reflecting upon the literary quotations that are embedded in the extract, since these too establish its status and help to position it in the linguistic and literary context of the period. The cluster of (sometimes modified) quotations that augment the discussion of regional speech provide several beguiling perspectives. For example, the phrase 'a stamp exclusive and provincial' is taken from Leigh Hunt's *The Story of Rimini*, and this is a complex choice since (as already noted) Hunt was one of the writers, along with Hazlitt himself, who was consistently attacked by the conservative Tory critics for using 'cockney' expressions in his writings. It is of particular interest that a phrase from Hunt is used to refer to a regional variety of English which is associated with Emery's vulgarity. Immediately after this, Hazlitt turns to *The Tempest*, and the words 'gabble most brutishly' are clearly derived from Miranda's evocation of a time when Caliban would 'gabble like / A thing most brutish' (I.ii.359-360), before he had mastered language. Consequently, Caliban once again enters into one of Hazlitt's reflections upon natural language, in this case exemplifying a kind of natural incapability that would strictly avoid being classified as vulgarity, if only the true nature of the performance were not revealed. Appropriately, the quotation which indicates the character of this revelation is taken from Matthew 26:73: 'And after a while came to him they that stood by, and said to Peter, Surely thou also art one of them; for thy speech betrayeth thee'. Peter's accent (or perhaps his dialect) suggested that he was associated with the Galileans who followed Jesus, yet he denied this, and, in a comparable manner, the actor John Emery's speech reveals that he is

4.5 Familiarising the Perspicuous

simply one of 'the herd', linguistically at least, despite the fact that his speech may indicate otherwise occasionally.[89] Hazlitt is apparently not making a clear distinction here between dialects and sociolects, since he likens Peter's and Emery's regional varieties to 'the jargon of a Bond-Street lounger', thereby suggesting that any individuals who speak after the manner of an identifiable group, whether that group be defined geographically or socially, risks being associated with linguistic vulgarity. Needless-to-say, the intricate transitions that occur in this extract itself, the disconcerting movement into and out of lower registers, the artful juxtaposition of allusions to different literary works, all combine to prevent Hazlitt's essay being classified as vulgar – at least in accordance to the very criteria that he is in the process of presenting.

This brief analysis has indicated the extent of the stylistic diversity that Hazlitt introduced into his mature essays, and, at this point it is probably worth recalling that he condemned Samuel Johnson's prose because 'there is no discrimination, no selection, no variety in it'.[90] In other words, it is the monotony of Johnson's style that irritated Hazlitt, and therefore he advocated stylistic variety – and variety is certainly one of the most distinctive features of his own works. In general, though, critics who are enamoured of Hazlitt's prose style tend to analyse it only in a subjective and predominantly metaphorical manner. For instance, in the Introduction to the collection of Hazlitt's essays that he edited with David Chandler, Tom Paulin tell us that Hazlitt's prose is sometimes characterised by 'a unique sensuousness that is subtle and arresting' and that, occasionally, it 'flexes wittily into life'.[91] While this kind of prettily descriptive analysis may help to characterise the impact of Hazlitt's writing on particular readers, there is considerable scope for more probing stylistic explorations than this, especially given his own interest in such matters. For instance, a study that explored the precise contexts in which he used those particular clausal and phrasal constructions (e.g., clause-final prepositions) which he himself associated with the 'familiar' style, would certainly provide considerable insights into the shifting structures and purposes of his prose. Such literary critical stylistic concerns are of considerable importance given the various issues that have been raised in this discussion, and therefore the linguistic focus of Hazlitt's literary criticism will be evaluated in detail in the next chapter.

5
The Languages of Literature

5.1 Grammar and Literature

The main purpose of this chapter is to explore some of the ways in which Hazlitt's understanding of linguistic theory influenced his literary criticism. As noted previously, this is an aspect of his work that has been strangely neglected in the past – 'strangely' because these are numerous explicit associations which have so far eluded serious discussion. However, before addressing these issues directly, it is necessary first to locate his thinking about such subjects in the context of eighteenth-century linguistic theory, and, to this end, it is helpful to return briefly to Lowth's and Murray's textbooks.

Lowth's wide-ranging interests and abilities ensured that his grammatical work was closely connected to his literary preoccupations. Crucially, though, he did not associate great literature merely with exemplary grammatical practice:

The English Language hath been much cultivated during the last two hundred years. It hath been considerably polished and refined; it hath been greatly enlarged in extent and compass; its force and energy, its variety, richness, and elegance, have been tried with good success, in verse and in prose, upon all subjects, and in every kind of stile: but whatever other improvements it may have received, it hath made no advances in Grammatical accuracy.[1]

Although, for Lowth, literary forms such as 'verse' and 'prose' are involved in the complex process of determining the 'force', 'energy', 'variety', 'richness', and 'elegance' of the English language, they do not necessarily guarantee an absence of solecisms and troublesome grammatical vagaries, therefore he rejected the simplistic notion that the literary masterpieces of the most admired authors necessarily constitute the finest examples of English usage. Indeed, he was fully persuaded

5.1 Grammar and Literature

that refined native speakers and respected writers alike were frequently guilty of grammatical errors. As a result, such literary texts 'cannot be recommended as models of an accurate style'.[2] Rather than focusing only on instances of grammatically impeccable writing, therefore, Lowth provided examples of both good and bad practice, and he acknowledged that, since many of the passages were extracted from literary works, his analyses inevitably imply that 'the best writers' are grammatically fallible.[3] This assumption places the humble grammarian in a position of considerable authority, charged with the onerous duty of identifying good literary style.

Despite this, Lowth's views concerning linguistic transgression were rather more complex than is standardly acknowledged. For instance, his characteristic approach to the identification of different stylistic registers partly reveals itself when he discusses pronouns, and the arguments that he presents are typical of his general methodology. Noting that certain writers have used *ye* as a second person plural object pronoun 'very improperly, and ungrammatically', Lowth provides the following selections from Shakespeare and Milton:

"The more shame for *ye*: holy men I thought *ye*." Shakespear, Henry VIII.
"His wrath, which one day will destroy *ye* both." Milton, P. L. ii, 734.[4]

These are presented as examples of faulty grammar, since *ye* functions as an object rather than as a subject pronoun in both cases, and he observes that this kind of usage

[...] may perhaps be allowed in the Comic and Burlesque style, which often imitates a vulgar and incorrect pronunciation : as, "By the Lord, I know *ye*", as well as he that made *ye*. Shakespear, 1 Henry IV. But in the serious and solemn style, no authority is sufficient to justify so manifest a Solecism.[5]

So, certain constructions involving pronominal case are appropriate when the 'Comic and Burlesque style' is adopted, since they constitute risible deviations from accepted grammatical conventions, but they should not be used in the 'serious and solemn style'. Crucially, it seems, particular structures can only be classified as erroneous when considered in relation to specified stylistic registers. This profoundly relativistic view of grammaticality necessarily prioritises the task of distinguishing accurately and consistently between different kinds of writing.

If certain grammatical constructions can be used to distinguish different registers, then it is reasonable to assume that they can also distinguish different literary forms and genres – and Lowth returns to this problem repeatedly. His basic claim is the rather uncontroversial assertion that poetry can flout grammatical rules which should be observed in other types of discourse, such as prose. For instance, he observes that it is generally 'improper' to form adverbs 'with the Comparative and Superlative Termination', and this appears to be an inviolable grammatical dictat.[6] The structures that he has in mind here are words such as 'hardliest', 'easilier', and 'highliest', and he declares that these ought to take the periphrastic forms 'most hardly', 'more easily', and 'most high' respectively, arguing that the alternative morphological variants are unwelcome because they have become obsolete, and not because they are inherently invalid. Intriguingly, though, Lowth makes a slight concession: 'these Comparative Adverbs, however improper in prose, are sometimes allowable in Poetry', and he provides an example from Milton in order to validate his point.

"Scepter and pow'r, thy giving I assume;
And gladlier shall resign." Milton, P. L. vi. 73.[7]

No explanation is given as to why and when adverbs of this kind should be permitted in poetry, but, while discussing other structures, Lowth does sometimes attempt to elucidate the motivation for grammatical rule-breaking in literary contexts. Having introduced the personal pronouns, for example, and having discussed the manner in which pronominal gender is deployed in English, Lowth considers the following Shakespearian quotation:

"Oft have I seen a timely-parted ghost,
Of ashy semblance, meagre, pale, and bloodless,
Being all descended to the lab'ring heart,
Who, in the conflict that *it* holds with death,
Attracts the same for aidance 'gainst the enemy."
Shakespear, 2 Henry VI.[8]

Concerning these lines, he comments as follows:

It ought to be,
"*Which*, in the conflict that *it* holds." –

Or, perhaps more poetically,
"*Who*, in the conflict that *he* holds with death."[9]

According to Lowth, these lines contain a mismatch between the relative pronoun *who* and the neuter pronoun *it*: the former should be used to refer to human antecedents, while the latter should never be used in such contexts. Consequently it would be preferable if one of these pronouns were changed, and there are various possibilities. If *which* is inserted instead of *who*, neither the relative nor the personal pronoun requires a human antecedent. However, if *it* were replaced by *he*, then both pronouns would be explicitly associated with a human antecedent, and (significantly) this resolution would enforce compatibility 'more poetically'. Seemingly, the greater poetical force of the latter substitution results from the descriptive personification that it introduces.

In a similar manner, Murray used literary examples extensively in his *English Grammar*. He stated that he wanted to use extracts that had 'a moral and religious tendency', and he chose to use unattributed passages, presumably to avoid explicit literary censure: only an educated reader would be able to identify the quotations that are criticised for containing ungrammatical elements. Murray's focus on the moral implications of grammar also prompted him to select passages from scriptural texts, and, as a result, passages from the King James Version (KJV) of the Bible appear frequently, occasionally with chapter and verse references. Characteristically, though, Murray was perturbed by the fact that some of the examples of 'faulty composition' that he presented were illustrated with passages taken from scripture, and he justified this by referring to Lowth's remarks concerning the general worthiness of the KJV.[10] This suggests that Murray was keen to associate himself with Lowth's grammatical heritage: he invokes Lowth's authority both as a divine and as a grammarian in order to validate his own analytical methodology.

Like Lowth before him (and Hazlitt after him), Murray was clearly intrigued by the grammatical characteristics of different stylistic registers and different literary form, and he frequently contrasted the 'familiar' and the 'solemn' styles. During his discussion of articles, for instance, he notes that

In many cases, articles are omitted in common conversation, or in familiar style, which seem to have a propriety in writing, or in grave style.[11]

Grammar textbooks are often playgrounds for linguistic self-reference, and it is surely no coincidence that Murray deploys anarthrous noun phrases (e.g., 'familiar style' and 'grave style') in this passage: definite phrases such as '*the* familiar style' or '*the* grave style' would have implied a seemingly undesirable uniqueness, while indefinite structures such as '*a* familiar style' or '*a* grave style' would have indicated a seemingly undesirable plurality. As it stands, Murray's wording avoids these difficulties. Oddly, the implication of Murray's discussion here is that anarthrous constructions seem to be permissible in a wide range of different styles, including both the 'familiar' and the 'grave'. Typically, he identifies many distinct and distinctive stylistic groupings – as when he criticises certain writers for needlessly separating prepositions and nouns:

This, whether in the familiar or solemn style, is always inelegant, and should never be admitted but in forms of law, and the like, where fulness and exactness of expression must take place of every other consideration.[12]

For Murray, then, the familiar and solemn styles are distinct, yet they both differ in some respects from the legal style, which, since it prioritises exactitude over elegance, is permitted to use grammatical forms that should remain absent in other types of discourse.

Murray used (unattributed) literary examples in order to explore the relationships between distinct stylistic registers, and he also used them to elucidate the grammatical differences which distinguish literary forms – especially prose and poetry. For instance, after stating that adjectives should precede nouns (or 'substantives'), he adds that

Sometimes, however, for the sake of sound, especially in poetry, the adjective comes after the substantive; as, "The torrent tumbling through rocks abrupt" [...] And likewise when a clause of the sentence depends upon the adjective; as, "He is a minister faithful to his trust".[13]

Since adjectives sometimes post-modify, rather than pre-modify, Murray acknowledged that poetry permits a wider range of word order permutations than prose, and, at various places, he attempted to identify the specific grammatical forms that were permissible predominantly, and sometimes exclusively, in poetry. Incidentally, this extract exemplifies Murray's use of unattributed quotations: the line 'The torrent tumbling through rocks abrupt' is taken from James Thomson's 'Winter: A Poem' (1726), but since Murray offers no specific citation information (not even the author's name), presumably only well-read readers are intended to recognise this fragment.

This brief overview of Lowth's and Murray's grammar textbooks has highlighted the extensive use of literary quotations (whether attributed or unattributed), the need to exemplify both good and bad grammatical practice in works of literature, and the desire to identify the linguistic characteristics that distinguish both literary forms and stylistic registers. As has been asserted throughout, these are all concerns which preoccupied Hazlitt in the first years of the nineteenth century, and, as usual, his *Grammar* provides insights into his understanding of these topics. Like his celebrated predecessors, Hazlitt also used extracts from

5.1 Grammar and Literature 127

literature throughout his *Grammar*, and while it is merely platitudinous to observe that literary quotations are distinctively prevalent in his mature prose, his use of such fragments is perhaps more intricate than is generally acknowledged. For instance, sometimes he includes full and accurate direct quotations; sometimes rough paraphrases, sometimes covert allusions, and these all serve markedly different ends. While a direct quotation may simply exemplify commendable practice, an implicit paraphrase can usefully contextualise an argument being developed and delimit the range of possible interpretative responses. Such intricacies are well-known to editors of Hazlitt, as Tom Paulin and David Chandler have recently testified:

> Hazlitt is not an easy writer to annotate. He quoted compulsively, often freely adapting the material he was quoting; even when he is not quoting his writing is often densely allusive. His essays are full of references to people and events that most readers today will know little about; moreover many of them contain topical and personal allusions – some obscure, and intended only for the inner circle of his readers. Finally, Hazlitt had regular recourse to Latin and French quotations, proverbs, and tags. The problem for the annotator is knowing when to stop.[14]

It is not only editors who have struggled with such things, though, and many of Hazlitt's readers (both contemporaneous and subsequent) have sought to describe and account for his distinctive approach. De Quincey, for instance, was irked by the quotations and echoes that are so abundantly sprinkled throughout Hazlitt's prose, condemning them as 'vitreous scintillations for a moment', while, more sympathetically, David Bromwich devoted a whole chapter to 'The Politics of Allusions' in his influential *The Mind of a Critic*.[15] Bromwich's discussion adroitly stresses the importance of quotations in various kinds of literary criticism, emphasising especially the unavoidable centrality of the implied power relationships:

> [a] critic when he quotes something is interrupting the text to which his chosen passage belongs, and exhibiting his power in relation to another author he cares for, at the same time that he acknowledges the author's mastery over him. His wish is to take possession of what he was possessed by. No interesting act of quotation therefore can imply a single gesture of homage; the reader cannot help being interested in more than the accuracy of the result.[16]

While this description may well summarise the function, purpose, and effect of quotations that are introduced into works of literary criticism in order to exemplify strikingly admirable linguistic structures, it certainly does not accurately capture the role of the literary extracts that are cited in grammar textbooks. Indeed, as the following discussion will demonstrate, 'act[s] of quotation' in grammar textbooks and literary criticism alike are disconcertingly complex events.

Ostensibly, the literary fragments that Hazlitt included in his *Grammar* are intended to serve a similar purpose to those encountered in eighteenth-century grammar textbooks such as Lowth's and Murray's – that is, they illustrate both correct and incorrect usage. As a result, the authors and texts to which he refers unavoidably define a literary canon of some kind. Since Hazlitt went on to write extensively in a professional capacity about English literature, it is worthwhile considering the manner in which this particular grammar-determined 'canon' can be associated with the 'idiosyncratic canon' of authors that Bromwich identified in Hazlitt's mature literary essays.[17] Significantly, like Lowth (but unlike Murray), Hazlitt usually provides citation information for the extracts that he considers in his *Grammar*; therefore it is reasonably simple to identify the authors quoted – and it is to be expected that certain writers figure more prominently than others. Predictably, Shakespeare, Spenser, Milton, Dryden, Pope, Swift, and Prior appear most often, and, in addition, there are several quotations from the KJV and eighteenth-century periodical essays.

Already, this unadorned and unquantified list manifests several characteristic patterns. For instance, it is intriguing that there are no extracts from Sidney in Hazlitt's *Grammar*, a fact which appears to corroborate his later claim that 'Sir Philip Sidney is a writer for whom I cannot acquire a taste'.[18] However, a simple listing of authors does not reveal very much about the distinctive stances that Hazlitt adopted in relation to them. Consequently, it is important to determine which extracts have been included because they exemplify particular merits and which have been incorporated because they contain conspicuous demerits. This distinction indicates that the literary 'canon' which Hazlitt outlines is articulated in an intricate manner: if extracts from the work of a given author are only ever included in order to illustrate grammatical errors, then the implicit insinuation is that the writer concerned is far from admirable. This issue is of some importance since Hazlitt himself acknowledged that words and phrases used by great authors were often used to legitimise linguistic choices in daily conversation. For instance, in his essay 'On the Disadvantages of Intellectual Superiority', he narrates the following anecdote:

A gentleman told me that a lady had objected to my use of the word *learneder*, as bad grammar. He said, he thought it a pity that I did not take more care, but that the lady was perhaps prejudiced, as her husband held a government office. I looked for the word, and found it in a motto from Butler. I was piqued, and desired him to tell the fair critic that the fault was not in me, but in one who had far more wit, more learning, and loyalty than I could pretend to.[19]

This wry reflection (which, incidentally, terminates with another of those alluring clause-final prepositions, always anathema for the pedants) suggests that Hazlitt was willing to justify, sometimes ironically, his own lexical and grammatical selections by invoking the authority of noted writers – in this case, Samuel Butler, the author of *Hudibras*. More importantly, it illustrates his acceptance of the fact that literary examples were believed to possess the power to validate unconventional practices, and the political subtext of the above extract is typical. The husband of the disapproving lady 'held a government office'; Butler was an ardent Royalist, and therefore Hazlitt satirically motivates his own use of 'learneder' by citing from the work of an exemplary, loyal subject: surely such a respectable source could not be doubted, even by ultra-crepidarian Tory quibblers? The point, presumably, is that it is invariably daft to justify a grammatical construction by referring to the social and political convictions of the person responsible either for creating, or for criticising, it, and Hazlitt dismisses this approach by adopting it himself. Although this playfulness is distinctive, Hazlitt clearly felt that these matters were of considerable importance, and in order to explore his views in greater detail, the next section will focus specifically on his grammatical and critical evaluations of Alexander Pope.

5.2 Verbal Criticism

Even before the eighteenth century had ended, Pope's reputation as a poet had begun to be reassessed. In his *Lectures on Rhetoric and Belles Lettres*, for instance, Hugh Blair discussed Pope's work on several occasions and his comments convey a curious mixture of admiration and disenchantment:

[...] Homer is the most simple in his Style of all the great Poets, and resembles most the Style of the poetical parts of the Old Testament. They can have no conception of his manner, who are acquainted with him in Mr. Pope's Translation only. An excellent poetical performance that Translation is, and faithful in the main to the Original. In some places, it may be thought to have even improved Homer. It has certainly softened some of his rudenesses, and added delicacy and grace to some of his sentiments. But withal, it is no other than Homer modernised. In the midst of the elegance and luxuriancy of Mr. Pope's language, we lose sight of the old Bard's simplicity.[20]

For Blair, then, Pope's translations of the *Iliad* and the *Odyssey* do not capture the spirit of the originals, and the references to the 'elegance and luxuriancy' of his language are surely pejorative, implying a certain over-indulgence, perhaps. Elsewhere Blair criticises Pope for using mixed metaphors and for introducing confusing personifications – and observations such as this certainly suggest that his poetry did not merit unalloyed admiration.[21]

If certain doubts concerning Pope's validity were being expressed in the 1780s, then, by the start of the nineteenth century, a number of publications had effectively enforced an extensive reassessment of his reputation as a poet. In particular, the Preface to the 1800 edition of *Lyrical Ballads* was widely perceived as a strident attack upon the principles of Augustan poetic diction, while William Lisle Bowles' 1806 edition of *The Works of Alexander Pope* undermined the latter's reputation by formulating stylistic guidelines for the avoidance of artificiality.[22] Coleridge's views, though, were ambivalent. In his *Biographia Literaria* (1817), having identified Pope as being typical of 'that school of French poetry' the practitioners of which wrote in a style that had been 'condensed and invigorated by English understanding',[23] he noted that

> I was not blind to the merits of this school, yet, as from inexperience of the world, and consequent want of sympathy with the general subjects of these poems, they gave me little pleasure, I doubtless undervalued the *kind*, and with the presumption of youth withheld from its masters the legitimate name of poets. I saw, that the excellence of this kind consisted in just and acute observations on men and manners in an artificial state of society, as its matter and substance: and in the logic of wit, conveyed in smooth and strong epigrammatic couplets, as its *form*: that even when the subject was addressed to the fancy, or the intellect, as in the Rape of the Lock, or the Essay on Man; nay, when it was a consecutive narration, as in that astonishing product of matchless talent and ingenuity, Pope's Translation of the Iliad; still a *point* was looked for at the end of each second line, and the whole was, as it were, a sorites, or, if I may exchange a logical for a grammatical metaphor, a *conjunction disjunctive*, of epigrams. Meantime the matter and diction seemed to me characterized not so much by poetic thoughts, as by thoughts *translated* into the language of poetry.[24]

Although Coleridge confesses that Pope's work accorded him 'little pleasure', he was nonetheless prepared to recognised the literary merits of the *Iliad*. However, later comments in the *Biographia Literaria* indicate that he harboured specific doubts about the quality of Pope's translations. While considering the distinction between poetry and prose, Coleridge observes that, in the general style of 'the present age', metre is either non-existent or else tediously mechanical, and he adds that

> [...] the language from "Pope's translation of Homer", to "Darwin's Temple of Nature", may, notwithstanding some illustrious exceptions, be too faithfully characterized, as claiming to be poetical for no better reason, than that it would be intolerable in conversation or in prose.[25]

This view of the perceived artificiality of Pope's style is re-enforced when Coleridge refers to Pope's translation of Homer as being 'the main source of our pseudo-poetic diction'.[26] So, he makes a clear distinction between Pope's translations and his original compositions, and, to put it simply, the latter are deemed to be superior to the former.

To return to Hazlitt, it is generally accepted that he was inclined to defend Pope from the more intemperate criticism produced during the early years of the nineteenth century. Nonetheless, like Coleridge, he identified strengths and weaknesses in Pope's work. For instance, in his 1818 essay 'On the Question Whether Pope was a Poet', he stated that, while not 'a poet of nature', Pope was

> [...] a wit, and a critic, a man of sense, of observation, of the world; with a keen relish for the elegancies of art, or of nature when embellished by art, a quiet *tact* for propriety of thought and manners, as established by the form and custom of society, a refined sympathy with the sentiments and habitudes of human life, as he felt them, within the little circle of his family and friends.[27]

Although this passage is predominantly complimentary, it insinuates doubt. Pope is presented as a poet who can only appreciate the natural world when it has been 'embellished by art', and it is hard not to hear a latent derogatory jibe in the reference to 'the little circle of his family and friends'. Such ambivalence is characteristic of Hazlitt's response, and John Barnard is just one critic who has felt inclined to group Hazlitt with Byron and De Quincey, claiming that 'their firm sense of his [i.e., Pope's] virtues is tempered by a realisation of his limitations'.[28] These remarks are, however, rather high-level, and it is more rewarding to consider the manner in which Hazlitt responded explicitly to Pope's poetic language. For instance, in his *Grammar*, Pope's writings receive frequent drubbings, and the quotations used provide detailed examples of passages in which basic grammatical rules have been contravened. To select just a few specific examples, Hazlitt castigates Pope for 'incorrectly' using *whose* as the genitive of *which* in inappropriate ways, for using finite verbs without a nominative subject, for using pronouns that do not agree with their antecedents, and for associating different moods and tenses with verbs that are related by means of a conjunction or a relative pronoun – and all of these criticisms are supported by specific quotations.[29] Detailed, language-focused criticism of this kind certainly suggests that Hazlitt was unimpressed, at least from a grammatical perspective, by some of the linguistic structures which Pope deployed, a stance that perhaps evinces a more general disenchantment with eighteenth-century literary conventions of which Pope is merely one of the primary representatives.

Hazlitt's discussion of grammatical case constitutes a useful exemplum, since it provides insights into the manner in which he juxtaposed linguistic and literary concerns. While recommending correct usage, for instance, he condemns Pope for using finite verbs which take subjects that are not associated with nominative case, and, in order to illustrate this particular deformity, he quotes the following lines which come from *An Essay on Criticism* and *The Odyssey of Homer* respectively:

Whose own Example strengthens all his Laws,
And *is himself* that great Sublime he draws.

Will *martial flames* for ever fire thy mind,
And never, never *be* to Heaven resign'd?[30]

The problem in the first case is that the verb 'strengthens' does not have a nominative subject since 'whose' is 'the genitive of *which*', and it therefore contravenes grammatical rule III which requires all finite verbs to take nominative subjects.[31] In the second example, the noun 'mind', which is the accusative direct object of the verb 'fire', functions as the implied subject of the following clause, thus contravening the same rule. In both examples, therefore, Pope has used constructions which violate one of the basic rules of grammar.

If the grammatical regulations that Hazlitt presents are accepted as valid, then examples such as the above seem to be straightforward and irrefutable instances of ungrammaticality. However, only a few pages later, he introduces another grammatical stricture – namely, that 'the nominative case is placed before the verb and the objective case after it' – and this rule legitimises structures such as *I like him* while prohibiting structures such as *Him likes I*.[32] Having introduced this idea, though, Hazlitt observes that:

The rule above stated is confined to prose, for in poetry the inversion of the common order of the words is scarcely ever considered as an objection, and is often accounted an elegance.[33]

The observation that word order inversions in poetry are (often) inherently elegant at least attempts to provide an explanation for this generic lenience, and Hazlitt further substantiates his point by including the following couplet (which is also taken from Pope's *An Essay on Criticism*):

These Equal Syllables alone require,
Tho' oft the Ear the open Vowels tire.[34]

In this case, subject-object-verb and object-subject-verb word orders are used rather than the standard subject-verb-object pattern, but this violation is not condemned as a fault. Seemingly, then, there are at least two different kinds of rule breaking, the forbidden and the permissable, and the crucial question is why Pope's rule-breaking in this case is considered to be an elegance, while, in the previous example, his alleged grammatical deviations were undesirable and castigated accordingly. As noted previously, in the former case, Hazlitt objects to the fact that Pope has neglected to provide nominative subjects for the finite verbs that appear in the main clauses of the extracted sentences, and therefore (presumably) he believes that Pope has contravened a grammatical rule which is deemed inviolable irrespective of the form or style adopted. By contrast, in the second example, the main verbs are correctly associated both with nominative subjects (i.e., 'These' and 'the open vowels') and accusative direct objects (i.e., 'Equal Syllables' and 'the Ear'). Obviously, since the subjects and the objects both precede the main verbs, these examples contravene rule IV, but, despite this, these structures still satisfy the grammatical case-agreement rule that Hazlitt prioritised. This suggests that, for Hazlitt (as for Lowth and Murray), there is a prioritative hierarchy of grammatical rules: some are unbreakable in all contexts, while others are optional depending on the form and style of the composition. In general, the inviolable rules are concerned with basic lexical agreement properties (e.g., case, gender, number), while the optional rules merely involve permutations of natural word orders. The emphasis on agreement properties no doubt results from the fact that a lack of grammatical agreement could easily result in nonsensical, obfuscating structures, while word order shiftings mainly generate stylistic nuances of emphasis. If this summary does indeed accurately capture Hazlitt's basic stance, then his grammar-focused criticism specifically of Pope simply reflects his larger convictions concerning linguistic structure: when Pope contravenes inviolable rules, then he is condemned uncompromisingly.

Hazlitt's hierarchical understanding of grammaticality partly reveals itself in the following observation taken from his essay 'On the Prose-Style of Poets':

> [...] in poetry, from the restraints in many respects, a greater number of inversions, or a latitude in the transposition of words is allowed, which is not conformable to the strict laws of prose. Consequently, the poet will be at a loss, and flounder about for the common or (as we understand it) *natural* order of words in prose-composition. Dr. Johnson endeavoured to give an air of dignity and novelty to his diction by affecting the order of words usual in poetry. Milton's prose has not only this draw-back, but it has also the disadvantage of being formed on a classic model.[35]

So, it is the 'latitude in the transposition of words' which is accorded to poetry that is one of its defining characteristics, and so marked is this feature that, according to Hazlitt, it can impede poets who attempt to write prose since they are unaccustomed to certain kinds of grammatical constraint. Intriguingly, the type of grammatical hierarchy that Hazlitt recognised is more appropriate for languages which make extensive use of a fully-developed case system: since the nominative and accusative cases of English nouns are not usually manifest morphologically (e.g., the proper noun *Tom* can function as both a subject and an object), it is misleading to claim that word order permutations do not interfere with the semantic interpretation of a given sentential structure. Obviously, the semantic import of the structure *Tom likes Sue* can alter considerably if the word order is changed to *Sue likes Tom*. While the consequences of this issue will not be explored at length here, it certainly seems to be contrary to Hazlitt's claims elsewhere in the *Grammar* that his textbook was the first to avoid presenting English as if it could be analysed in accordance with a Graeco-Roman grammatical framework.[36]

Such details suggest that Hazlitt's early estimation of the worth of Pope's poetry was partly determined by his grammatical concerns, and, in general, his initial critical views of Pope were not especially favourable – and the assessments of Pope which appeared in Hazlitt's later lectures and essays are of particular interest since they sometimes develop ideas that had initially been introduced in his *Grammar*. In his 1818 lecture 'On Dryden and Pope', for instance, after giving a list of couplets from Pope's *An Essay on Criticism*, all of which rhyme using the word 'sense', Hazlitt continues

> I have mentioned this the more for the sake of those critics who are bigoted

idolisers of our author, chiefly on the score of his correctness. These persons seem to be of opinion that 'there is but one perfect writer, even Pope'. This is, however, a mistake: his excellence is by no means faultless. If he had no great faults, he is full of little errors. His grammatical construction is often lame and imperfect. [...] In the translation of the Iliad, which has been considered as his masterpiece in style and execution, he continually changes the tenses in the same sentence for the purposes of the rhyme, which shews either a want of technical resources, or great inattention to punctilious exactness. But to have done with this.[37]

Clearly, nine years after completing his *Grammar*, Hazlitt was still irritated by the small grammatical infelicities that he identified in Pope's work, and he felt obliged to reveal the extent of the latter's linguistic frailties when rebutting critics who were inclined (rather uncritically in Hazlitt's view) to idolise Pope's verse without reservation. Presumably, when he refers to 'bigoted idolisers of our author' Hazlitt has critics such as John Gibson Lockhart in mind, since these conservative readers were particularly inclined to praise Pope's poetry in an elaborate manner which (to Hazlitt's mind) betrayed a lack both of acumen and restraint. To take just one example, in one of the 1818 'Cockney School' pieces which appeared in *Blackwood's*, Lockhart (hidden behind his pseudonym 'Z.') railed against Keats for expressing reservations about the merits of Pope's work. In particular, Lockhart was angry because Keats devalued

[...] a certain class of English Poets, whom, with Pope at their head, it is much the fashion with the ignorant unsettled pretenders of the present time to undervalue. Begging these gentlemen's pardon, although Pope was not a poet of the same high order with some who are now living, yet, to deny his genius, is just about as absurd as to dispute that of Wordsworth, or to believe in that of Hunt. Above all things, it is most pitiably ridiculous to hear men, of whom their country will always have reason to be proud, reviled by uneducated and flimsy striplings, who are not capable of understanding either their merits, or those of any other *men of power* – fanciful dreaming tea-drinkers, who, without logic enough to analyse a single idea, or imagination enough to form an original image, or learning enough to distinguish between the written language of the Englishmen and the spoken jargon of the Cockneys, presume to talk with contempt of some of the most exquisite spirits the world ever produced [...][38]

Obviously, this kind of diatribe is as much an attack upon a particular social group as it is a defence of the merits of Pope as an author, and it exemplifies the kind of critical stance that Hazlitt was keen to debunk. The aggrandising socio-political advocation of Pope as a writer of whom the country 'will always have reason to be proud' suggests that the issues at stake here transcend the boundaries of mere literature. Pope is no longer simply a poet, he has become a symbolic cultural entity who represents a world-view that is threatened with destabilisation by the rising Regency generation.

Hazlitt, of course, was pleased to be able to destabilise certain world-views; his description of Pope's 'grammatical construction' as being 'lame and imperfect' certainly recalls passages in his *Grammar* such as those discussed above, and, given the putative hierarchy of grammatical rules outlined earlier, it is of particular interest that Hazlitt should express especial dissatisfaction with the manner in which Pope deploys tenses in his translation of the *Iliad*. Indeed, this remark associates Hazlitt's critical discussion of Pope's verse directly with some of the observations that he makes in his *Grammar*. In this case, the relevant passage concerns his analysis of tense and sentence structure. Specifically, Hazlitt notes that '[w]here the sense is the same, the mood or tense of the verb governed either by a conjunction or a relative pronoun ought to be the same'.[39] Having stated this guideline, he states that the following lines (from 'Epistle to Allen Lord Bathurst') contain an 'impropriety':

Him portion'd maids, apprentic'd orphans *blest*
The young who *labour*, and the old who *rest*.[40]

The perceived problem here is that while *blest* is in the simple past tense, the verbs *labour* and *rest* are both in the simple present; this temporal shift seems to have occurred primarily so that a couplet can be created, and this is precisely the problem that Hazlitt identified in Pope's *Iliad* nine years later. Crucially, though, in using this particular example, Hazlitt was actually modifying Lowth's discussion of the same example, since the latter had used this very quotation in his *A Short Introduction* in order to make exactly the same point. Lowth makes the case as follows:

It is not easy to give particular rules for the management of the Modes and Times of Verbs with respect to one another, so that they may be proper and consistent: nor would it be of much use; for the best rule that can be given is this very general one, To observe what the sense necessarily requires. But it may be of use to consider a few examples, that seem faulty in these respects; and to examine where the fault lies [...]

"Him portion'd maids, apprentic'd orphans *blest*,
The young who *labor*, and the old who *rest*." Pope, Moral Ep. iii, 267

"Fierce as he *mov'd*, his silver shafts *resound*" Iliad, B.i.

The first Verb ought to be in the same Time with the following.[41]

Since Hazlitt knew Lowth's *A Short Introduction* well, connections of this kind certainly suggest that some of the language-based criticisms which Hazlitt formulated later in his career were influenced (to an extent) by his early encounters with the English grammar textbook tradition, and explicit inter-relations of this kind reveal the origins of his approach. Like case mismatches, unwarranted shifts in tenses can cause profound and needless interpretative difficulties, and therefore Hazlitt advocates temporal agreement: a sentence should not contain gratuitous tense fluctuations, especially if these are induced primarily by exigencies of rhyme. Hazlitt's impatient conclusion – 'But to have done with this' – implies that the criticism of Pope's grammar which he offers here does not constitute a profound new insight; rather, it is presented as being merely a weary restatement of an obvious truth the veracity of which he felt he had demonstrated satisfactorily long ago.

So, Hazlitt considered Pope to be grammatically fallible. Nonetheless, despite this, he admired his work and refused merely to condemn it as being incompetent and outmoded. This stance is possible since, unlike some of his peers, Hazlitt never reduced the art of literary criticism to an algorithmic process of grammatical evaluation. Indeed, he explicitly disparaged such an approach when he sought to belittle some of the most influential contemporaneous critics. Indeed, in his admirably pugnacious 'A Letter to William Gifford, Esq.', Hazlitt explicitly confronted this kind of linguistically-focused criticism when he argued that polemical reviewers such as Lockhart and Gifford were usually motivated primarily by specific socio-political allegiances rather than by honest linguistic concerns. Having identified Gifford as being 'an ultra-crepidarian critic', Hazlitt goads him directly

[w]hen you damn an author, one knows that he is not a favourite at Clarence House. When you say that an author cannot write common sense or English, you mean that he does not believe in the doctrine of *divine right*. Of course, the clergy and gentry will not read such an author. Your praise or blame has nothing to do with the merits of a work, but with the party to which the writer belongs, or is in the inverse *ratio* of its merits. The dingy cover that wraps the pages of the Quarterly Review does not contain a concentrated essence of taste and knowledge, but is a receptacle of the scum and sediment of all the prejudice, bigotry, ill-will, ignorance, and rancour afloat in the kingdom.[42]

This should, by now, be a familiar complaint. According to Hazlitt, reviewers such as Gifford are primarily concerned with the cultural context of a given publication, and their supposedly 'literary' convictions are in fact dictated exclusively by socio-political considerations concerning the establishment hierarchy. If the author is an acquaintance of the Prince of Wales (the inhabitant of Clarence House), then his work will be well reviewed. Similarly, if he acknowledges the divine right of kings, then, once again, praise will be lavished upon his literary productions. However, if the alternative holds in either of these cases, then the author's work will be brutally condemned; its (alleged) literary failings will be mercilessly revealed, and a negative review of this sort will ensure that the clergy and the gentry dismiss the text without even reading it. So, the political affiliations of the author concerned, rather than the language deployed, are the main target, and apparent assaults upon literary validity are actually covert attacks upon the author's view concerning institutions such as the monarchy and the Church. In a comparable passage, in his *Spirit of the Age* essay about Gifford, Hazlitt writes as follows:

Mr. Gifford has no pretensions to be thought a man of genius, of taste, or even of general knowledge. He merely understands the mechanical and instrumental part of learning. He is a critic of the last age, when the different editions of an author, or the dates of his several performances were all that occupied the inquiries of a profound scholar, and the spirit of the writer or the beauties of his style were left to shift for themselves, or exercise the fancy of the light and superficial reader. [...] In appreciating a modern one [i.e., writer], if it is an enemy, the first thing he thinks of is to charge him with bad grammar – he scans his sentences instead of weighing his sense; or if it is a friend, the highest compliment he conceives it possible to pay him is, that his thoughts and expressions are moulded on some hackneyed model. His standard of *ideal* perfection is what he himself now is, a person of *mediocre* literary attainments: his utmost contempt is shown by reducing any one to what he himself once was, a person without the ordinary advantages of education and learning. It is accordingly assumed, with much complacency in his critical pages, that Tory writers are classical and courtly as a matter of course, as it is a standing jest and evident truism, that Whigs and Reformers must be persons of low birth and breeding, imputations from one of which he himself has narrowly escaped, and both of which he holds in suitable abhorrence. He stands over a contemporary performance with all the self-conceit and self-importance of a country schoolmaster, tries it by technical rules, affects not to understand the meaning; examines the hand-writing, the spelling, shrugs up his shoulders and chuckles over a slip of the pen, and keeps a sharp look-out for a false concord and – a flogging.[43]

5.2 Verbal Criticism

Once again, Gifford is presented as being a 'mechanical' reader who simply parses the sentences of a text he wishes to debunk, neglecting the content, in order to expose examples of 'bad grammar' – in other words, he is an exponent of 'verbal criticism' – and, as noted earlier, linguistic probings of this kind are riddled with socio-political implications. While 'Tory writers' are assumed to be educated ('classical and courtly'), Whigs and Reformers (i.e., Hazlitt, Hunt, and their associates) must necessarily be 'persons of low birth and breeding', and therefore lacking in grammatical competence. Accordingly, Gifford (and other critics of the same type) resorted to the various 'rules' that they encountered in eighteenth-century grammar textbooks and treatises on belletristic rhetoric, using these regulations as weapons with which to attack their ideological opponents. Consequently, in Hazlitt's depiction, Gifford behaves like a pompous and socially-superior teacher in a rural school who assesses the work of his students only in accordance with 'technical rules' – and this kind of unengaged analysis is ridiculed as being petty and pointlessly stunted.

So, Hazlitt rejected verbal criticism partly because it involved the unthinking application of sometimes dubious grammatical rules, and his more general contempt for elaborate, but ultimately purposeless, formal systems is expressed most cogently in 'On the Ignorance of the Learned':

> How little has the human understanding been directed to find out the true and useful! How much ingenuity has been thrown away in defense of creeds and systems! How much time and talents have been wasted in theological controversy, in law, in politics, in verbal criticism, in judicial astrology and in finding out the art of making gold! What actual benefit do we reap form the writings of a Laud or Whitgift, or of Bishop Bull or Bishop Waterland, or Prideaux' Connections or Beausobre, or Calmet, or St Augustine, or Puffendorf, or Vattel, or from the more literal but equally learned and unprofitable labours of Scaliger, Cardan, and Scioppius? How many grains of sense are there in their thousand folio or quarto volumes? What would the world lose if they were committed to the flames to-morrow? Or are they not already "gone to the vault of all the Capulets"? Yet all these were oracles in their time, and would have scoffed at you or me, at common sense and human nature, for differing with them. It is our turn to laugh now.[44]

In this startling passage, verbal cricism is condemned, along with greatly admired grammatical treatises such as Joseph Scaliger's *De Causis Linguae Latinae* (1540) and Caspar Schoppe's (a.k.a. Scioppius) *Grammatica Philosophica* (1628). The accusation is that such approaches to linguistic analysis are as futile and useless as alchemy, astrology, and certain branches of theology since they are contrary to 'common sense and human nature'. Seemingly, Hazlitt believed that these disparate pursuits shared similar failings mainly because they are all examples of impractical and pointless systematisation.

As mentioned above, though, Hazlitt himself was unfailingly attentive to the linguistic structures that were deployed by the authors he himself assessed in his capacity as a critic. Given this, is it worth considering why he is not guilty of the same narrow pedantry that he identifies in Gifford's work. In general, Hazlitt's own grammar-based assessments (such as those of Pope) differ mainly because he always sought to distinguish linguistic structure from the perceived wider purpose and content of the texts he considered. Consequently, he was quite capable of admiring a particular writer's style even though he entirely rejected the political views expressed in the work concerned – and his comments about Edmund Burke in a 1817 *Edinburgh Review* essay provide a representative example. Hazlitt states at the outset that he feels great 'reluctance' when he is required to anatomise the 'the vices and infirmities of such a mind as Burke's'.[45] Despite this, though, he criticises the latter's political views, emphasising inconsistencies, noting how Burke deployed 'the chicanery of a sophist', and querying his sudden transformation from an advocate of reform to 'the apologist of all courtly abuses'.[46] Nonetheless, although Hazlitt rejected Burke's political manouevering after the French Revolution, he still acknowledged that he was 'an acute and accomplished man of letters' and 'an ingenious political essayist'.[47] Indeed, although the passage is quite well-known, it is worth quoting Hazlitt's analysis of Burke's prose style at some length, since it demonstrates both the extent of his admiration and the linguistic focus of his assessment:

Burke's literary talents were, after all, his chief excellence. His style has all the familiarity of conversation, and all the research of the most elaborate composition. He says what he wants to say, by any means, nearer to more remote, within his reach. He makes use of the most common or scientific terms, of the longest or shortest sentences, of the plainest and most downright, or of the most figurative modes of speech. He gives for the most part loose reins to his imagination, and follows it as far as the language will carry him. As long as the one or the other has any resources in store to make the reader feel and see the thing as he has conceived it – in its nicest shades of difference, in its utmost degree of force and splendour – he never disdains, and never fails to employ them. Yet, in the extremes of his mixed style there is not much affectation, and but little either of pedantry or of coarseness. He everywhere gives the image he wishes to give, in its true and appropriate colouring : and it is the very crowd and variety of these images that have given to his language its peculiar tone of animation, and even of passion. [...] He is, with the exception of Jeremy Taylor, the most poetical of our prose writers, and at the same time his prose never degenerates into the mere effeminacy of poetry ; for he always aims at overpowering rather than at pleasing; and consequently sacrifices beauty and delicacy to force and vividness.[48]

Burke's stylistic versatility is praised, as is his use of familiar, conversational idioms, the variety of his sentence lengths, the imagery he develops, the poetical qualities of his prose – and these words of admiration are lavished upon a man whom Hazlitt certainly considered to be a political rival. As this single example demonstrates, for Hazlitt, literary style and political convictions were seperable: he could criticise both if necessary, but a condemnation of one did not automatically imply a condemnation of the other. In this way, his critical assessments were more subtle than those of Gifford, and he never based his broader evaluations primarily on small grammatical quibbles. Consequently, there is a clear, if fine, distinction between Gifford's frigid pedantry and Hazlitt's caloric appraisals.

5.3 Common Language

The preceding discussion of Hazlitt's response to Pope has indicated that his literary criticism interacts with his linguistic preoccupations in a range of complex ways. This raises the question as to whether the same is true of Hazlitt's critical assessments of other eighteenth-century writers. Since Samuel Johnson was recognised in the early nineteenth century as an equally important figure in the history of literature, Hazlitt's response to his writings provide an appropriate comparison. Indeed, his evaluation of Johnson's work is sufficiently well-known to require minimal elaboration. In brief, he was consistently irritated by the perceived artificiality and monotony of Johnson's prose, and the following representative example is taken from his 1819 lecture on 'On The Periodical Essayists', an extract which, although quoted in part above, requires more extensive consideration here:

The fault of Dr. Johnson's style is, that it reduces all things to the same artificial and unmeaning level. It destroys all shades of difference, the association between words and things [...] The structure of his sentences, which was his own invention, and which has been generally imitated since his time, is a species of rhyming in prose, where one clause answers to another in measure and quantity, like the tagging of syllables at the end of a verse; the close of the period follows mechanically as the oscillation of a pendulum, the sense is balanced with the sound; each sentence, revolving round its centre of gravity, is contained with itself like a couplet, and each paragraph forms itself into a stanza.[49]

The word 'artificial' was identified above as a key term in Hazlitt's critical vocabulary when stylistic matters are considered, and therefore it is no surprise that it figures prominently in his condemnation of Johnson: the lack of stylistic variation eradicates interpretative hierarchies, with the result that all things considered are falsely presented as if they were equally important. Intriguingly, Hazlitt maintains that this kind of style 'destroys [...] the association between words and things'. Presumably, the point here is that the words used in a piece of prose should be chosen and arranged in a manner that corresponds to the significance of the topic, or 'thing', being addressed. In addition to these concerns, it is intriguing that Hazlitt should offer an analogical account of Johnson's prose which deploys analytical terminology derived directly from the natural sciences (e.g., 'oscillation of a pendulum', 'revolving round its centre of gravity'). Such descriptions stress the mechanistic, predictable, cause-and-effect character of Johnson's style, and these are, of course, intended to constitute negative associations. Hazlitt considers prose of this kind to be inferior since it contains no unexpected shifts, no surprising turns; everything is seemingly regulated by *quasi* physical laws which apply entirely predictably, and with numbing uniformity. This view was essentially re-expressed three years later when, in his essay 'On Familiar Style', he wrote as follows:

The reason why I object to Dr. Johnson's style is that there is no discrimination, no selection, no variety in it. He uses none but "tall, opaque words," taken from the "first row of the rubric" – words with the greatest number of syllables, or Latin phrases with merely English terminations. If a fine style depended on this sort of arbitrary pretension, it would be fair to judge of an author's elegance by the measurement of his words and the substitution of foreign circumlocutions (with no precise associations) for the mother-tongue. How simple is it to be dignified without ease, to be pompous without meaning! Surely, it is but a mechanical rule for avoiding what is low, to be always pedantic and affected. It is clear you cannot use a vulgar English word if you never use a common English word at all. A fine tact is shown in adhering to those which are perfectly common, and yet never falling into any expressions which are debased by disgusting circumstances, or which owe their signification and point to technical or professional allusions. A truly natural or familiar style can never be quaint or vulgar, for this reason, that it is of universal force and applicability, and that quaintness and vulgarity arise out of the immediate connection of certain words with coarse and disagreeable, or with confined ideas. The last form what we understand by cant or slang phrases.[50]

5.3 Common Language

This is now familiar territory. Once again there are references to scientific procedures (e.g., 'measurement', 'mechanical rule'); once again there are implications of self-conscious and superfluous elaboration (e.g., 'arbitrary pretension', 'pedantic and affected'), and the basic argument is that a good prose style cannot be automatically produced in a mechanistically procedural fashion since such a style requires nuanced delicacy and variety. In Hazlitt's presentation, if Johnson's writings were to be taken as being representative embodiments of 'fine style', then desirable qualities such as 'elegance' could be trivially determined via an objective quantitative procedure. These lexical considerations prompt Hazlitt to reflect upon the socio-political implications of the words that prose writers deploy. Johnson is rebuked for systematically 'avoiding what is low', and this prompts Hazlitt to delineate a rough hierarchy of linguistic vulgarity. More specifically, he distinguishes between words that are 'vulgar' and words that are 'common' – but, in addition, he also indicates that some words are more common than others and can therefore be classified as being 'perfectly common'.

So, Hazlitt was consistently critical of the syntactic structures and vocabulary items that Johnson standardly used in his published prose writings, and he claimed that his unvarying prose style, which favoured grandiloquent polysyllabic Latinate constructions over simple English sentences, lacked versatility and delicacy. Given this, it is of especial interest that, in his 1819 lecture, Hazlitt explicitly contrasted Johnson's prose compositions with the anecdotal accounts of his informal conversational style which James Boswell had garnered in his *The Life of Samuel Johnson* (1791). For Hazlitt, the 'life and dramatic play' of Johnson's conversation 'forms a contrast' with his published writings.[51] Specifically, it was Johnson's incisive colloquial speaking style that appealed most:

> It is to be observed that Johnson's colloquial style was as blunt, direct, and downright, as his style of studied composition was involved and circuitous. As when Topham Beauclerc and Langton knocked him up at his chambers, at three in the morning, and he came to the door with the poker in his hand, but seeing them, exclaimed, 'What, it is you, my lads? then I'll have a frisk with you!' and he afterwards reproaches Langton, who was a literary milksop, for leaving them to go to an engagement 'with some *un-idead* girls.' What words to come from the mouth of the great moralist and lexicographer![52]

Hazlitt's exclamation at the end of this passage is, of course, one of delight rather than horror, and although he characteristically misrecollects the exact words that Boswell attributes to Johnson in these examples, the important parts (specifically the idiomatic expression 'have a frisk' and the non-standard italicised adjective '*un-idead*') have been correctly recalled. Once again, Cromie's 1811 *Dictionary of the Vulgar Tongue* can be of some use here. Unsurprisingly, the slang expression 'to frisk' is not found in Johnson's own *Dictionary*, but Cromie defines it as both a noun and a verb as follows:

FRISK. To dance the Paddington frisk; to be hanged.

TO FRISK. Used by thieves to signify searching a person whom they have robbed. Blast his eyes! frisk him.[53]

Curiously, Johnson's usage doesn't seem to conform fully to either of these definitions. It is plausible that, in his joking response to Topham Beauclerc and Bennet Langton, he means 'I will hang you all', but it is also possible that he was referring to his initial suspicion that the supposed intruders were intending to rob him. However, the OED offers the following definition of *frisk* as a noun: 'A brisk sportive movement; a frolic; also, a freak, whim', though it provides only two eighteenth-century examples to support this usage, and one of them is the line from Boswell that is quoted above. Whatever the exact meaning of this expression, from Hazlitt's perspective, words and phrases such as these, which Johnson would systematically avoid in his published prose, but which were sprinkled liberally throughout his informal conversation, endow the spoken exchanges in Boswell's account with a captivating directness and vitality. It is appropriate, given both Hazlitt's delight in Johnson's conversational informality and his general advocacy of non-standard idiomatic expressions, that his own prose style should be modified in response to the topic currently being considered here. In particular, his use of such words as the adjective 'downright' and the noun 'milksop' clearly implies that the colloquial style can be effectively incorporated into formal prose compositions and need not only appear in written transcriptions of conversational fragments.

It should be clear by now that, when assessing the prose works of an iconic eighteenth-century figure such as Dr Johnson, Hazlitt was swift both to condemn the avoidance of the colloquial style in literary compositions, and to express his delight in the use of common idioms in conversational exchanges. Significantly, this championing of idiomatic language was a consistent position that Hazlitt adopted when evaluating literary forms from all periods, and it is important to recognise the consistency of his style-focused criticism. For instance, in his lectures on Elizabethan literature, he explicitly praised Heywood for exploring 'the

5.3 Common Language

commonest circumstances of every-day life' by means of dialogue 'such as might be uttered in ordinary conversation', and this certainly suggests that (as far as Hazlitt was concerned) the stylistic features of 'ordinary conversation' could be beneficially exploited by playwrights during the sixteenth century.[54] Indeed, while discussing Heywood's work, Hazlitt elaborates his view as follows:

It is not so much that he uses the common English idiom for everything (for that I think the most poetical and impassioned of our elder dramatists do equally), but the simplicity of the characters, and the equable flow of the sentiments do not require or suffer it to be warped from the tone of level speaking, by figurative expressions, or hyperbolical allusions.[55]

The emphasis here is evidently placed specifically upon the relationship between the kind of idiomatic linguistic structures which are associated with 'level speaking', and more elaborate and stylised rhetorical embellishments which involve 'figurative expressions, or hyperbolical allusions'. In essence, Hazlitt suggests that 'ordinary conversation' does not only require authors to use 'the common English idiom', but also to avoid the kind of artificial distortions that are caused by the inclusion of needlessly elaborate rhetorical devices. Intriguingly, Hazlitt's bold claim is that 'the most poetical and impassioned of our elder dramatists' expressed themselves using idiomatic English, and the implications is that the use of unadorned conversational expressions makes literary texts more, rather than less, poetical. If this is accepted, then it should be the case that the greatest dramatists should deploy idiomatic expressions frequently. Therefore, it is of interest that, in his well-known 1818 lecture 'On Shakespeare and Milton', Hazlitt writes about Shakespeare's style as follows:

His language is hieroglyphical. It translates thoughts into visible images. It abounds in sudden transitions and elliptical expressions. This is the source of his mixed metaphors, which are only abbreviated forms of speech. These, however, give no pain from long custom. They have, in fact, become idioms in the language. They are the building, and not the scaffolding to thought. We take the meaning and effect of a well-known passage entire, and no more stop to scan and spell out the particular words and phrases, than the syllables of which they are composed. In trying to recollect any other author, one sometimes stumbles, in case of failure, on a word as good. In Shakespeare, any other word but the true one, is sure to be wrong. If any body, for instance, could not recollect the words of the following description,

"—— Light thickens,

And the crow makes wing to the rooky wood,"

he would be greatly at a loss to substitute others for them equally expressive of the feeling.[56]

In the light of the foregoing discussion, there are various details embedded in the above extract which require further consideration. For instance, Hazlitt's claim that Shakespeare's 'mixed metaphors' should be classified as being 'abbreviated forms of speech', which 'give no pain from long custom' can be directly related to his awareness of the prominent role accorded to abbreviations in the work of certain eighteenth-century linguistic theorists. In particular, as mentioned previously, Hazlitt was profoundly influenced by the philological writings of Horne Tooke and, from the 1780s onwards, the latter had consistently stressed the importance of abbreviations and idiomatic structure in natural language. It is revealing, therefore, that, when determining which type of abbreviations these mixed metaphors could be, Hazlitt concludes that they should be categorised as 'idioms' – that is, indivisible structures (in Priestley's sense) that should be used in their entirety. At this stage it is worth returning to the passage from his *Grammar* that was quoted in section 3.5:

The idioms of every language are in general the most valuable parts of it, because they express ideas which cannot be expressed so well in any other way. And the reason of this is, that they are either abbreviated methods of expressing things of constant recurrence, or have been invented to supply the defects of the general structure of language. To decide on the propriety of every phrase from a principle of abstract reasoning, besides unsettling the only acknowledged standard of propriety, would also be to cramp and mutilate the language, and render it unfit for the real purposes of life.[57]

Even as early as 1809, then, 'idioms' were for Hazlitt 'the most valuable parts' of any given language because they reveal inherent linguistic structure and do not 'cramp or mutilate'. Cramping and mutilating are semantically related to warping – all three terms imply some kind of distortion from a natural state – and therefore the attitude towards grammatical hypercorrectness outlined here is similar to the recommended avoidance of elaborate rhetorical devices that he offered when discussing Heywood's style: the use of idiomatic expressions enables a writer to avoid artificiality, and, by so doing, to write in a style that is appropriate for 'the real purposes of life'. Clearly, Hazlitt believed that literature fell within the scope of this general recommendation since, as the above passage from 'On Shakespeare and Milton' indicates, he was happy to argue that an idiomatic style was highly desirable specifically in a literary context.

Idioms, then, are desirable. However, there is a distinction that must be made between different ways in which works of literature (in particular) can be associated with specific idioms. As noted above, certain writers (such as Heywood) incorporated existing idiomatic expressions directly into their literary works, and, by so doing, they ensured that their style avoided artificial distortions away from the language of ordinary conversation. By contrast, though, there are writers (such as Shakespeare) who not only deploy existing idioms, but who also create new idiomatic expressions which subsequently enter into the common stock of the language. In short, the fact that particular 'words and phrases' in Shakespeare have ultimately become idioms (in this sense) is presented by Hazlitt as a clear indication of the linguistic potency of Shakespearian drama. He especially appreciates the fact that numerous passages in Shakespeare can only be recollected in their entirety, as if they were irreducible linguistic units – a characteristic feature which (according to Hazlitt) arises from the fact that it is impossible to substitute one word in the place of another in the finest passages. Seemingly, then, Hazlitt's views concerning the role of idioms in literary works can be traced back directly to his early encounters with linguistic theory, and a focused consideration of interconnections of this kind prompts us to reassess certain aspects of Hazlitt's mature literary criticism.

6
Victorian Perspectives

6.1 Hazlitt's Influence?

The main chapters of this book have focused on Hazlitt's views concerning the relationship between language and literature, and his ideas have been discussed in the context both of his predecessors and of his contemporaries. But what of his successors? Did his advocacy of, say, the 'familiar' style and his rejection of the type of 'verbal' criticism practiced by John Gibson Lockhart, John Wilson, Francis Jeffrey, William Gifford, and others, exert a detectable influence over the next generation of writers and critics? As usual, the picture is complex. Certainly, the ideology adopted by Tory reviewers of the early nineteenth century enjoyed impressive longevity. Even as late as 1864, for instance, in a review of Browning's *Dramatis Personae* (1863), William Stigand was able to remark that

> [i]f the shades of Jeffrey and Gifford were to appear among us and to survey the poetic literature of the present generation, they would feel a stern satisfaction and a self-congratulatory delight at the remembrance of the hard-handed castigations which they had inflicted on the young poets of the commencement of the century.[1]

Seemingly, then, the great disciplinarian critics who hounded Hazlitt in the first decades of the nineteenth century bequeathed their tastes and value systems to a subsequent generation, and these heirs and successors took delight in condemning the linguistic structures that they encountered in the work of writers such as Dickens and Thackeray. In 1845, for instance, Thomas Cleghorn wrote a review of Dickens' *Martin Chuzzlewit* in which he noted particularly that Dickens

> [...] offends greviously against the rules of grammar, catching the infection from his own actors, he adopts their forms of expression, and offends the

shade of Lindley Murray with such barbarisms as 'It had not been painted or papered, hadn't Todgers', past the memory of man'. 'She was the most artless creature, was the youngest Miss Pecksniff'. 'Nature played them off against each other; *they* had no hand in it, the two Miss Pecksniffs' Indeed Mr Dickens seems often purposely to cast his language into the mould of the vulgar characters he represents, and as it were, to fondle their phrases, idioms, and ideas. He makes occasional use of the interjections 'bless you!', 'heaven knows', &c [...] Slang also seems to come naturally to his lips, for he founds a cumbrous joke in the first chapter on the words *my uncle*, and gives his readers credit for knowing this to be slang for pawnbroker.[2]

According to Cleghorn, then, Dickens trangresses linguistically because he uses pronouns which refer cataphorically to clause-final clarificatory noun phrases (e.g,. 'the youngest Miss Pecksniff', 'the two Miss Pecksniffs'), and these stylistic traits can be associated with his use of interjections and slang. Such things contravene 'the rules of grammar', and therefore Dickens offends 'the shade of Lindley Murray'. This is precisely the kind of 'verbal' criticism that Hazlitt had railed against several decades previously, and the fact that certain readers continued to focus on alleged linguistic flaws such as these suggests that Hazlitt and his fellow complainants had failed to convince the more traditional critics that literary works could beneficially deploy an idiomatic prose style which incorporated lexical and syntactic conventions that were primarily associated with spoken English.

Nonetheless, although particular critics may have ignored Hazlitt's advice, other writers were far more sympathetic. Robert Louis Stevenson, for instance, claimed that the *Plain Speaker* essay 'On the Spirit of Obligations', provided 'a turning-point in my life',[3] and he elsewhere recalled the educative methods that he had used while seeking to teach himself how to write memorable and effective sentences. His 'secret labours' involved imitating writers whose work he admired, and, as a result of these 'vain bouts',

[...] I got some practice in rhythm, in harmony, in construction and the co-ordination of parts. I have thus played the sedulous ape to Hazlitt, to Lamb, to Wordsworth, to Sir Thomas Browne, to Defoe, to Hawthorne, to Montaigne, to Baudelaire and to Obermann. I remember one of these monkey tricks, which was called *The Vanity of Morals*: it was to have had a second part, *The Vanity of Knowledge*; and as I had neither morality nor scholarship, the names were apt; but the second part was never attempted, and the first part was written (which is my reason for recalling it, ghostlike, from its ashes) no less than three times: first in the manner of Hazlitt, second in the manner of Ruskin, who had cast on me a passing spell, and third, in a laborious pasticcio of Sir Thomas Browne.[4]

Stevenson's literary interests were broad, and it is significant that Hazlitt's name should figure so prominently in this catalogue of authors. For Stevenson, the task of imitating Hazlitt's mannerisims while writing the first version of the *The Vanity of Morals* was seemingly an advantageous way of exploring the form and structure of the latter's prose, and he was convinced that exercises of this kind enabled him to develop his own style. In the mid nineteenth century, then, Hazlitt's prose could still be viewed as an exemplary model from which an aspiring writer could learn the skills of the craft.

Despite enthusiastic responses such as these, it is clear that Hazlitt's reputation began to wane during the second half of the century. This gradual diminishing was discussed in some detail in section 1.3, but it is worth considering an additional instance here. When Alexander Ireland sent a complimentary copy of his *List of the Writings of William Hazlitt and Leigh Hunt* to Dickens in 1868, he received the following reply:

> Many thanks for the book you have kindly sent me. My interest in its subject is scarcely less than your own, and the book has afforded me great pleasure. I hope it will prove a very useful tribute to Hazlitt and Hunt (in extending the general knowledge of their writings), as well as a deservedly hearty and loving one.[5]

Although this is essentially a functional letter which politely acknowledges the receipt of an unsolicited gift, Dickens' remarks suggest that, in the late 1860s, he still personally admired Hazlitt's (and Hunt's) work greatly, although, as his parenthetical observation concerning the desirability of extending 'the general knowledge of their writings' implies, neither author was widely read at the time.

6.2 Journalism and Urbanism

The various fragments juxtaposed above provide a few insights into the manner in which Hazlitt was viewed by several prominent Victorian authors who valued highly the kind of prose style that he had both advocated and deployed. However, Hazlitt's influence can also be considered in relation to the development of journalism in the nineteenth century. Since Hazlitt's repeated pleas for the use of a 'familiar' and 'common' style were often expressed in essays that had first appeared in magazines and periodicals, it is intriguing to determine the manner in which the prose style favoured by such publications developed as the century progressed. When confronting this daunting topic, it is worth recalling the remarkable proliferation in print media that occurred during the

6.2 Journalism and Urbanism

Victorian period, since, between the years 1830 and 1860 in particular, there was a tremendous increase in the range of publications that conveyed news in one form or another. This development was recorded in remarkable detail by Alexander Andrews in his *The History of British Journalism* (1859). Tracing the progression from simple newsheets – 'a miserable sheet of flimsy paper, blotted with coarse letter-press'[6] – to the full range of provincial and metropolitan newspapers that were available in the late 1850s, Andrews reveals both the extent and the rapidity of the development. Aware of the improving literacy standards of the general population, editors sought to appeal to new readership groups, and so specialist publications (such as magazines aimed specifically at women) began to appear.[7] As a result, the available print media became increasingly heterogenous, and this expansion was closely connected to changing demographic trends in nineteenth-century Britain. In particular, as Joanne Shattock and Michael Wolff have reminded us,

[w]e are familiar with Victorian Britain as the first urbanizing society. Journalism is the verbal equivalent of urbanism, and Victorian Britain was also the first "journalizing" society. The first generations of city-dwellers were also the first generations of newspaper readers. The mass media, however carefully some Victorians tried to insulate themselves, were the inescapable ideological and subliminal environment of the modern world. The press, in all its manifestations, became during the Victorian period the context within which people lived and worked and thought, and from which they derived their (in most cases quite new) sense of the outside world.[8]

This view of print media as constituting a type of 'verbal [...] urbanism' would perhaps lead one to expect that the linguistic forms associated with urban sociolects would dominate in such publications. However, in the event, contemporaneous readers frequently noted that this was not the case, and that the ubiquitous newspapers actually fostered curiously artificial linguistic conventions. Indeed, certain individuals were horrified by the damaging impact which they believed the language of the newspapers was having upon the speech habits of the populace. De Quincey's disquiet was considerable, and, writing in an 1840 essay concerning 'Style', he bewailed the decline of idiomatic English:

The pure racy idiom of colloquial or household English [...] may be looked for in the circles of well-educated women not too loosely connected with books. It is certain that books, in any language, will tend to encourage a diction too remote from the style of spoken idiom; whilst the greater solemnity, and the more ceremonial costume of regular literature must often demand such a non-idiomatic diction, upon mere principles of good taste. But why is it that in our own day literature has taken so determinate a swing towards this professional language of books, as to justify some fears that the other extreme of the free colloquial idiom will perish as a living dialect? The apparent cause lies in a phenomenon of modern life, which, on other accounts also, is entitled to anxious consideration. It is in newspapers that we must look for the main reading of this generation; and in newspapers, therefore, that we must seek for the causes operating upon the style of the age.[9]

Although Hazlitt is not mentioned in this passage, the concerns addressed are conspicuously Hazlittian. De Quincey is alarmed because, in his estimation, the 'pure racy idiom of colloquial or household English' has been usurped by an artificial discourse which he associates with 'the professional language of books'. As a result of this usurpation, the natural spoken idioms are being lost, and De Quincey considers this to be a profoundly undesirable development. In the above passage, he generally identifies the newspapers as the main culprits, but, in a later extract from the same essay, he specifies the precise nature of their guilt:

One single number of a London morning paper, which in half a century has expanded from the size of a dinner napkin to that of a breakfast tablecloth, from that to a carpet, and will soon be forced, by the expansion of public business, into something resembling the mainsail of a frigate, already is equal in printed matters to a very large octavo volume. Every old woman in the nation now reads daily a vast miscellany in one vol. royal octavo. The evil of this, as regards the quality of knowledge communicated, admits of no remedy. Public business, in its whole unwieldy compass, must always form the subject of these daily chronicles. Nor is there room to expect any change in the style. The evil effect of this upon the style of the age may be reduced to two forms. Formerly, the natural impulse of every man was, spontaneously to use the language of life; the language of books was a secondary attainment not made without effort. Now, on the contrary, the daily composers of newspapers have so long dealt in the professional idiom of books, as to have brought it home to every reader in the nation who does not violently resist it by some domestic advantages. The whole artificial dialect of books has come into play as the dialect of ordinary life. This is one form of the evil impressed upon our style by journalism; a dire monotony of bookish idiom has encrusted and stiffened all native freedom of expression, like some scaly leprosy or elephantiasis, barking and hide-binding the fine natural pulses of the elastic flesh. Another and almost a worse evil has established itself in the prevailing structure of sentences.[10]

De Quincey's amusing quantification of the growth of the newspapers – from the size of a dinner napkin to the size of a frigate sail in the space of about fifty years – evinces anxiety concerning the rapid proliferation and dominance of print media which make use of their own urban 'dialect'. This particular journalistic linguistic register is analogically associated with diseases of the skin which cause a crust to form over the pliant flesh beneath, and the effects of this 'barking' are considered to be unambiguously 'evil'. Significantly, he maintains that this linguistic disease has manifested itself in two distinct ways. Specifically, both the lexicon and syntax of English, as it is spoken in common conversation, have become more 'artificial', and this undesirable development has been caused by journalism. In order to illustrate the dreadful consequences that ensue when the dialect of the newspapers enters into everyday conversations, De Quincey recounts an incident in which he and his wife were forced to flee from a landlady because, when discussing the property for which she was responsible, she used such words as 'individuality', 'diplomatically', and 'anteriorly'.[11] Since she was fluent in this distinctive form of journalese, De Quincey considered her to be 'a student of the newspapers', and therefore 'a semibarbarian'.[12] Intriguingly, even the woman's marital status is impugned as a result of her familiarity with the popular press: De Quincey observes that '[s]he had no children: the newspapers were her children'.[13]

While the extremity of the condemnation offered in De Quincey's essay is partly the result of his own idiosyncratic predelictions, many of his near contemporaries expressed similar anxieties. For example, almost twenty years after De Quincey had voiced his fears concerning the loss of idiomatic English and the rise of the artificial diction associated with the newspapers, the theologian Henry Alford wrote about the 'Dialect of our journals' in his influential linguistic treatise *A Plea for the Queen's English*:

Our journals seem indeed determined to banish our common Saxon words altogether. You never read in them of a *man*, or a *woman*, or a *child*. A man is an "*individual*," or a "*person*," or a "*party*;" a woman is a "*female*," or if unmarried, a "*young person*," which expression, in the newspapers, is always of the feminine gender; a child is a "*juvenile*," and children *en masse* are expressed by that most odious term "*the rising generation*". [14]

By the 1860s, then, the language of the newspapers could still be described as a distinct 'dialect' which was characterised by the use of specific lexical items. Appropriately enough, just as De Quincey had been infuriated by the poor landlady's use of the word 'individuality', Alford rejects the use of the term 'individual', and correspondences of this sort in treatises condemning the use of linguistic structures associated with newspapers certainly suggest that it is indeed possible to identify some of the characteristic linguistic properties of nineteenth-century journalese. As the extracts cited above indicate, though, for contemporaneous critics such as De Quincey and Alford, this register was pernicious mainly because it has very little to do with common English or (to use Hazlitt's terminology) the 'familiar' style. It would be beneficial to explore in more detail the reasons why, contrary to Hazlitt's recommendation, the use of 'common' English declined in print media during the nineteenth century, and this fascinating topic awaits adequate consideration.

6.3 The Progress of Philology

So, although Hazlitt's essays were admired by certain celebrated Victorian authors, an artificial and non-idiomatic version of English came to be used widely in the magazines and newspapers of the Victorian period. In a similar way, it is useful to consider whether subsequent grammarians responded enthusiastically to his writings about language and linguistic analysis. It has already been mentioned that Godwin's various revisions of Hazlitt's *Grammar* effectively ensured that the original version of the text was destined to exert little, if any, influence over later generations of students, preventing it becoming a popular and dominant textbook. However, it is incorrect to conclude from this that Hazlitt's grammatical work was ignored entirely. While his *Grammar* never became a staple part of the linguistic education of British and North American school-children, it was certainly known to philologers from the mid to late nineteenth century, and this is of interest primarily because the development of the grammar textbook tradition during the Victorian period has been inexplicably neglected by linguists and historians alike. Indeed, Manfred Görlach has observed that 'there is no exhaustive analysis of the grammar book of English in the 19th century', adding that 'proper research into the 19th-century tradition of grammar books has barely started'.[15] The most significant attempt to address this difficult topic is still Ian Michael's *The Teaching of English: From the Sixteenth Century to 1870* (1987), and Michael is generally dismissive of the grammar textbooks that were published during the period 1830-1870:

Many nineteenth-century grammars were ordinary, routine productions. Their content and their methods scarcely distinguished one from another, and they are interesting only because they show the extent to which eighteenth-century practices could still be maintained even during a period when ideas about both language and teaching were being actively debated.[16]

However, not all the grammar textbooks that appeared during this period were as unremarkable as this broad overview suggests, and, in the

6.3 The Progress of Philology 155

context of Hazlitt's grammatical preoccupations, it is of particular interest that, as the century progressed, an increasing number of grammarians became dissatisfied with the kind of Graeco-Roman analytical framework that they had inherited from texts such as Murray's. Indeed, the gradual decline of interest in Murray's work occurred at the same time as more sophisticated research into comparative linguistics, and pedagogical reforms, began to advocate an approach to the analysis of English which was not hindered by the constraints of Classical models. Although this attitude starts to manifest itself early in the nineteenth century, it becomes more wide-spread as the decades pass. For instance, only nine years after Hazlitt's death, De Quincey surveyed the manner in which the English language had been analysed over the centuries, and he claimed that this 'capital subject' had been much neglected. Having referred to Johnson's *Dictionary* with tempered approval, criticising 'the slenderness of Dr Johnson's philological attainments', he continues as follows:

Of inferior attempts to illustrate the language, we have Ben Jonson's Grammar, early in the seventeenth century; Wallis, the mathematician's, Grammar (written in Latin, and patriotically designed as a polemic grammar against the errors of foreigners), towards the end of the same century; Bishop Lowth's little School-Grammar in the eighteenth century; Archdeacon Nares's Orthoepy; Dr Crombie's Etymology and Syntax; Noah Webster's various essays on the same subject, followed by his elaborate Dictionary, all written and first published in America. We have also, and we mention it on account of its great but most unmerited popularity, the grammar of Lindley Murray – an American, by the way, as, well as the eccentric Noah. This book, full of atrocious blunders (some of which, but with little systematic learning, were exposed in a work of the late Mr Hazlitt's), reigns despotically through the young ladies' schools, from the Orkneys to the Cornish Scillys. And of the other critical grammars, such as the huge 4to of Green, the smaller one of Dr Priestley, many little abstracts prefixed to portable dictionaries, &c., there may be gathered, since the year 1680, from 250 to 300; not one of which is absolutely without value – some raising new and curious questions, others showing their talent in solving old ones. Add to these the occasional notices of grammatical niceties in the critical editions of our old poets, and there we have the total amount of what has hitherto been contributed towards the investigation of our English language in its grammatical theory.[17]

This inevitably selective catalogue effectively charts the development of the teaching of English grammar from the sixteenth century (the period that Elia had recalled in 'The Old and the New Schoolmaster') to the early nineteenth, and De Quincey's list is characterised by typically rebarbative asides. Lowth's text is merely 'little', while Webster is both 'American' and 'eccentric'. However, the most elaborate condemnation is reserved for Murray. Although the *English Grammar* contains many 'atrocious blunders', it is nonetheless used as a teaching resource throughout the whole of the British Isles (in fact, as discussed earlier, its influence was much wider than this), and the sarcastic reference to 'young ladies' schools', which recalls the fact that it was written for The Mount School for girls in York, seeks to undermine Murray's authoritative status. In the context of the current discussion, though, it is De Quincey's parenthetical remarks concerning Hazlitt that are of the greatest interest. Hazlitt is somewhat grudgingly commended for revealing some of the errors that Murray had committed, though it is emphasised that this task had been accomplished with 'little systematic learning'. It is usually assumed – perhaps correctly – that De Quincey is referring here to Hazlitt's *Spirit of the Age* essay concerning Horne Tooke, since, as mentioned previously, that piece contains a number of passages which castigate Murray. Nonetheless, it is equally possible that De Quincey is in fact recalling Hazlitt's 1829 *Atlas* essay on 'English Grammar', or even his *Grammar* textbook. Whichever text he has mind, the point is that De Quincey's thinking about the teaching of English grammar (and Murray's work in particular) appears to have been influenced directly by Hazlitt's reflections upon this topic, which largely anticipated the shift away from Murray which occurred during the mid nineteenth century.

Hazlitt may have influenced the views of certain individuals concerning English grammar directly, but, in general, he seems merely to have anticipated later developments, while playing only a small part in the complex process of altering cultural and linguistic perceptions. For instance, it was mentioned in section 4.3 that his *Grammar* advocates an approach to the analysis of English which is not based upon a Graeco-Roman grammatical model, and certainly this kind of methodology became increasingly desirable as the nineteenth century progressed. For instance, already in 1854, only twenty-four years after Hazlitt's death, another literary-grammarian, William Barnes, felt obliged to comment as follows in the Preface to his *Philological Grammar*, quoting from Pablo Pedro de Astarloa y Aguirre's *Apología de la Lengua Bascongada* (1803)

What Señor Astarloa says in his Apologia de la Lengua Bascongada (Apology for the Basque Language) is true of English as well as Spanish: 'A blind slave to the Greek and Latin language, and a readiness to believe that every thing which imitates their idioms must be so far regular, has misdirected or fettered our whole literature'.[18]

6.3 The Progress of Philology

From the early nineteenth century onwards, then, in the field of Romance philology as well as the field of English-based linguistic research, there was a desire to move away from the unthinking imposition of Graeco-Roman case and tense systems, and to explore the inherent properties of these languages in their own terms – and this is exactly the philological position that Hazlitt had adopted as early as 1809. As noted previously, the kind of attitude that Barnes advocates in the above extract became more common as the nineteenth century approached its conclusion, and a number of grammar textbooks appeared which explicitly and extensively condemned the older Graeco-Roman framework. To select just one obvious example from many, in 1884 Henry Hutchinson published his elaborately entitled work

Thought-symbolism and Grammatic Illusions: being a Treatise on the Nature, Purpose and Material of Speech, and a Demonstration of the Unreality, the Useless Complexity, and the Evil Effects, of Orthodox Grammatic Rules in General

and in this impassioned study he sought to undermine the hegemony that the Classical regulation of English had enjoyed. In his Introduction, for instance, he refers to

the grammatic notions which classicism has imported into the English language, and to the forces which have, in fact, largely declassicized it, abolishing Greek and Latin modes, in spite of "learned" adherence, in name, to Greek and Latin formulae ; which, however well or ill they were fitted to represent the realities of the dead languages, succeed only in utterly misrepresenting those of the living one.[19]

Passages such as this introduce the terminology of Hutchinson's polemic: 'classicism' is the enemy, which has fostered the 'misrepresenting' of English. The cautionary quotation marks which adorn the word 'learned' insinuate Hutchinson's radical rejection of traditional approaches to grammatical analysis, and, indeed, he is often even more direct than this:

The Anglo-Saxon, modelled as it was largely upon the Latin, afforded some pretext for a grammatical doctrine of "cases," of accord of the verb with its subject, and for other classic survivals. Modern English has departed too far from the classic model to leave any pretext for their continuance, as such, in our speech ; they have, as it will be our task hereafter to show, absolutely no applicability, serve only to misrepresent it, and to produce inexplicable confusion in the minds of students who seek therein sound reasons for the English speech-mechanism.[20]

Intriguingly, Hutchinson's concerns arise from his understanding of the historical development of the English language – the very topic which, only fifty years earlier, De Quincey had claimed was much neglected. English may once have benefited from (for example) case-system analysis, but, given the inherent properties of modern English, such a model is now woefully stymied, and Hazlitt would no doubt have agreed wholeheartedly with this summary. Perhaps inevitably, like Hazlitt, Barnes, and others before him, Hutchinson finds that, by rejecting the grammatical tradition that he had inherited, he is required to reflect upon the implications of authority, especially linguistic authority. For instance, having observed that he himself paid due 'respect' unto the 'rules of grammar' until he was required to teach the subject to his own son, Hutchinson indicates that it was this pedagogical experience which caused him to see the 'radical inconsistency' of the conventional systems. He excuses this provocative conclusion with firmness:

With great respect for "authority" duly exercised and in its proper sphere, the present writer was not, however, disposed to yield to it the jurisdiction it laid claim to in the grammatical sphere – that, namely, of fettering and misrepresenting the language ; to concede to it the right to supersede reason and substitute its own rigid irrationality – the right to prescribe for the English or any other language rules having no foundation in its existing character, and having no recommendation but the fact that they love some resemblance to rules applicable to the dead languages of Greece and Rome. [21]

Once again, these remarks are in complete accordance with the kind of impatient frustration that Hazlitt had expressed when discussing the tradition of Lowth and Murray, (rather circumspectly), in the Preface to his *Grammar* and (more vitriolically) in some of his later essays. Hutchinson's metaphorical language is provocative and intentionally so – conventional case-system analysis imprisons the English language, places it in fetters, and imposes inflexible illogical regulations upon it. Indeed, just as, sixty years previously, Hazlitt had criticised the traditional analysis of case, so too Hutchinson addresses this particular problem, when having summarised the traditional view that there are three cases – 'nominative', 'objective', and 'genitive' – he continues:

On the threshold we are staggered with the manifest inconsistency between the definition of the thing called "case" and the fact of the things called "cases." [...] The doctrine of English case is certainly not an intelligible explanation of the facts, nor a true representation of them.[22]

The specific details of the alternative strategies that Hutchinson proposed – which emphasised the way in which semantic relations, rather than morphological forms, enable grammatical roles to be determined – need not be considered in detail, since his work is simply presented here

6.3 The Progress of Philology

as an example of the kinds of innovative and radical analytical schemes that were proposed in the later nineteenth century. As a result of such developments, there was a period of remarkable theoretical instability, which only began to settle into a more ordered form with the emergence of theoretical linguistics as an independent discipline in the first decades of the twentieth century. Presumably, though, the general shift away from Graeco-Roman formalisms was one that Hazlitt would have welcomed. Certainly, it is something for which he appealed repeatedly in his own work.

If the foregoing discussion has focused on the manner in which the grammar-textbook tradition in the nineteenth century gradually came to reject the formal analytical schemes that it had inherited from the most influential eighteenth-century treatises (as Hazlitt had recommended), then it is also worthwhile considering the manner in which nineteenth-century grammarians made use of Hazlitt's own writings when searching for examples with which to illustrate the various syntactic structures they wished to analyse. In other words, just as Hazlitt had gleaned numerous quotations from literary works in order to substantiate and exemplify his claims concerning both good and bad grammatical practice, so too did his nineteenth-century successors sift through his own essays and lectures for apposite examples. Obviously, this topic is too broad to be considered exhaustively within a mere subsection of a chapter. Indeed, the enquiry is dauntingly onerous partly because it addresses an aspect of Hazlitt's legacy that has never previously been studied. Despite this, though, the kind of connections that merit further attention can be indicated, and an obvious starting point is provided by Goold Brown's *The Grammar of English Grammars*. Brown was born in Providence, Rhode Island, in 1791, and he spent much of his adult life conducting a New York academy. As a result of his teaching experiences, he became convinced that the available English grammars were profoundly inadequate, and therefore he attempted to provide a better account of the structure and function of the language. Accordingly, he published his *Institutes of English Grammar* and his *First Lines of English Grammar* in 1823, while his *A Grammar of English Grammars* appeared twenty-eight years later. To some extent, he succeeded in his attempt: the clarity of his expositions was recognised, and his publications were extremely successful in North America. Of his various linguistic texts, it is the *Grammar of English Grammars* that is most significant, though. In this copious work, Brown attempted to provide a summary of the different analytical approaches that had been used in existing grammar textbooks, since he believed that this was the most effective way of identifying areas of agreement and disagreement. In the Preface, he notes that he had first conceived of this project 'about twenty-seven years ago' (that is, in 1824, just after he had published his first two textbooks) and he indicates that he had been aware of the self-reflective nature of the enterprise from the very beginning since, in writing his study, he had inevitably 'turned the eyes of Grammar, in an especial manner, upon the conduct of her own household'.[23] Therefore, like many of his contemporaries, Brown was motivated partly by a desire to resolve the many analytical conflicts and contradictions that undermined earlier textbooks and treatises. Accordingly, he provided a meticulously detailed survey of the parts-of-speech, etymology, syntax, and so on, indicating how different theorists had adopted different analytical interpretations of the same syntactic phenomena.

While the general structure and purpose of Brown's text are of some importance, what is of the greatest interest here is the use that he makes of literary quotations – especially quotations from Hazlitt. In many respects, Brown's use of passages from literature is conventional – that is, he generally cites a sentence, or a short extract, when considering the *pros* and *cons* of particular analyses or linguistic conventions. While discussing, for instance, the use of the possessive singular for words which end with an 's' (e.g., 'Moses" rather than 'Moses's') he notes that the use of the terminal 's' in such instances causes 'a concurrence of hissing sounds' which is undesirable, and this prompts him to recommend that this practice is not adopted.[24] However, despite this, he observes that

in prose the elision should be very sparingly indulged; it is in general less agreeable, as well as less proper, than the regular form. Where is the propriety of saying, *Hicks' Sermons*, *Barnes' Notes*, *Kames' Elements*, *Adams' Lectures*, *Josephus' Works*, while we so uniformly say, in *Charles's reign*, *St. James's Palace*, and the like? The following examples are right: "At Westminster and *Hicks's Hall*."– *Hudibras*. "Lord *Kames's* Elements of Criticism." – *Murray's Sequel*, p.331. "Of *Rubens's* allegorical pictures." – *Hazlitt*. "With respect to *Burns's* early education." – *Dugald Stewart*. "*Isocrates's* pomp;" – "*Demosthenes's* life." – *Blair's Rhet.*, p. 242. "The repose of *Epicurus's* gods." – *Wilson's Heb. Gram.*, p.93.[25]

This is representative of the kind of substantiating catalogues that Brown presents in order to motivate his various conclusions. In this case, his claim that, in prose, the use of the possessive singular form can sometimes be used, sparingly, is supported by a range of quotations from several texts. Samuel Butler, Lindley Murray, Dugald Stewart, Hugh

6.3 The Progress of Philology

Blair, and Charles Wilson appear alongside Hazlitt in order to legitimise this particular grammatical exception, and it is amusing that Butler should be included here since, as discussed earlier, Hazlitt had himself once quoted from the former's works in order ironically to validate his own use of the word 'learneder'. However, the combined authority of the writers Brown includes is considered to be sufficient to demonstrate that the use of the possessive suffix is, in this case, 'right'. This suggests that, for Brown at least, Hazlitt could be ranked alongside such linguistic experts as Murray, Blair, and Wilson, and that his willingness to use a particular form partly validates the construction concerned.

The situation is rather more complex than this brief account suggests, though, since Hazlitt is not always cited as an authority concerning grammatical structure, and Brown sometimes uses phrases and sentences from his works in order to illustrate erroneous constructions. The following is a typical passage of this kind:

Passive verbs should never be made to govern the objective case, because the receiving of an action supposes it to terminate on the subject or nominative. Errors: "Sometimes it *is made use of* to give a small degree of emphasis." – *L. Murray's Gram.*, 8vo, p.197. Say, "Sometimes it *is used*," &c. "His female characters *have been found fault with* as insipid." – *Hazlitt's Lect.*, p.111. Say, – "have been *censured*;" or, – "have been *blamed, decried, dispraised,* or *condemned*."[26]

In this case it is Hazlitt's use of a passive construction which attempts to assign the objective case to a nominative which causes offence, and Brown helpfully suggests alternative structures. In this example, Hazlitt is once again juxtaposed with Lindley Murray (who is also being condemned here), and the various lists of examples in which Hazlitt's name appears in Brown's discussion usually raise intriguing questions concerning the types of associations and implications that the latter attached to the authors and texts which he cited. To give one final example, when Brown considers a particular kind of subject-verb agreement, he comments that

Any phrase, sentence, mere word, or other sign, taken as one whole, and made the subject of an assertion, requires a verb in the third person singular; as, "To lie *is* base." – *Adam's Gram.*, p.154. "When, to read and write, *was* of itself an honorary distinction." – *Hazlitt's Lect.*, p.40. "To admit a God and then refuse to worship him, *is* a modern and inconsistent practice." – *Fuller, on the Gospel*, p.30. "*We is* a personal pronoun." – *L. Murray's Gram.*, p.227. "*Th has* two sounds." – *Ib.*, p.161. "The *'s is annexed* to each." – *Bucke's Gram.*, p.89. "*Ld. stands* for *lord*." – *Webster's American Dict.*, 8vo.[27]

In this example, Hazlitt is bundled together with a Scottish Classicist, a British Historian, a seventeenth-century Divine, and two American philologers. Apparently, grammatical niceties can posthumously acquaint a man with strange bed-fellows, and no doubt Hazlitt would have been greatly amused to find himself in such company. However, the persistent use of quotations from Hazlitt in grammar textbooks such as Brown's suggests that, despite the 'suppression' of his *Grammar*, his linguistic convictions, as manifest in his own prose, were still influential in North America in the middle of the nineteenth century, and this fact alone is of some interest since, as the century progressed, the British and American traditions of grammatical analysis began to diverge. It was observed earlier that, in his essay on 'The English Language', De Quincey had felt obliged to note the fact that Murray and Webster were 'Americans', and, from the 1830s onwards, English grammarians and amateur philologers alike, began increasingly to denounce the kind of structures that were starting to become associated with American varieties of English. For instance, in Percival Leigh's *The Comic English Grammar* (1840), he explicitly identifies 'American English' as being a distinct type of 'Comic English', and he catalogues a few examples of characteristic usage, include such elaborate structures as '*pretty particular considerable tarnation* degree'.[28] In a similar way, the aforementioned Henry Alford associated himself with this trend when he referred provocatively to 'the process of deterioration' which the American usage has inflicted upon British English. Not surprisingly, linguistic and socio-political concerns are inseparably intertwined as Alford exhorts us to

[l]ook at those phrases which so amuse us in their [i.e., the Americans'] speech and books ; at their reckless exaggeration, and contempt for congruity ; and then compare the character and history of the nation – its blunted sense of moral obligation and duty to man ; its open disregard of conventional right where aggrandisement is to be obtained ; and I may now say, its reckless and fruitless maintenance of the most cruel and unprincipled war in the history of the world.[29]

This type of harangue is not atypical, and it certainly suggests that social and ideological divides were explicitly associated with linguistic differences. Indeed, when required to concentrate exclusively on linguistic matters without referring to other concerns, Alford struggles to find convincing criteria with which to discredit the American forms. For instance, while ranting about the deficiencies of American orthography, he summarises the American practice of omitting the letter 'u' in words like 'honour/honor' and 'neighbour/neighor', and he argues in favour of the British forms by claiming that the American convention 'makes very ugly words, totally unlike anything in the English language before'.[30]

Acknowledging the divide which had started to separate British and American linguistics by the 1860s, it would be helpful to try to determine whether Hazlitt was indeed looked upon with greater linguistic favo(u)r by North American grammarians, and, if so, whether this was partly facilitated by his political allegiances. Initially, it would be revealing simply to establish whether his works were cited more often, and more approvingly, in North American grammar textbooks than they were in their contemporaneous British counterparts, and a detailed exploration of this kind could illuminate a wide range of linguistic and cultural preoccupations that remained prevalent throughout much of the nineteenth century. Indeed, such a study would provide invaluable insights into the reception history of Hazlitt's writings about linguistic theory – a topic that awaits serious critical discussion.

Notes

Chapter 1

1. Percival Presland Howe (ed.), *The Complete Works of William Hazlitt* (London: J.M. Dent, 1930-1934; from henceforth 'Howe'), Vol. XX, 212.
2. Howe, XX, 213.
3. Howe, XX, 212.
4. *The Tempest*, II.ii.
5. Richard Turley, *The Politics of Language in Romantic Literature* (London: Palgrave Macmillan, 2002), xvi.
6. Charles Lamb, *Elia. Essays which Have Appeared Under that Signature in the London Magazine* (London, 1823), 117.
7. Lamb 1823, 118.
8. Lamb 1823, 117.
9. Lamb 1823, 117. The phrase *cum multis aliis* means 'with many others'.
10. Leigh Hunt, *The Autobiography of Leigh Hunt; with reminiscences of his friends and contemporaries* (London, 1850), 78-79.
11. Hunt 1850, 78-79. The bilingual linguistic games that Hunt describes here were taken to a remarkable extreme by Luis van Rooten in his *Mots D'Heures: Gousses, Rames: The d'Antin Manuscript* (New York: Grossman, 1967).
12. A reconstruction of the sequence of events that preceded and ensued the publication of Hazlitt's *Grammar* is presented in Stanley Jones' 'The "Suppression" of Hazlitt's *New and Improved Grammar of the English Tongue*: A Reconstruction of Events', *The Library*, 6:9 (1987), 32-43.
13. William Carew Hazlitt, *Memoirs of William Hazlitt, with Portions of his Correspondence*, vol.1, (London: Richard Bentley, 1867), 168.
14. Quoted from Godwin's diary in Jones 1987, 34.
15. William Godwin, *New Guide to the English Tongue* (London: M.J. Godwin, 1809), 161.
16. Godwin 1809, 161.
17. Godwin 1809, 163. Godwin here seems to be re-working ideas that were presented in David Booth's *Introduction to an Analytical Dictionary of the English Language* (London, 1806), as discussed in section 2.5.
18. For instance, similar issues are raised by John Kersey in the 'Preface' to his *The New English Dictionary* (London: H. Bonwicke & R. Knaplock, 1702). Kersey states that 'to prevent the bulk of this Volume from

swelling beyond its due bounds, 'tis judg'd expedient only to leave out the common Terminations of the Verbs and Adverbs, that may be form'd from their Primitives with a very little application'. In this case, Kersey adopts an approach that enables him to reduce the number of separate lexical items that need to be listed in the dictionary, and he justifies this by claiming that derived forms can be easily generated from base-forms using well-defined rules.

19 *The Critical Review* 18:4 (1809), 444.
20 Edwin W. Marrs Jr. (ed.), *The Letters of Charles and Mary Anne Lamb*, vol.III, 1809-1817 (Ithaca and London: Cornell University Press, 1978), 37.
21 Herschel Sikes's, William Bonner's, and Gerald Lahey's, *The Letters of William Hazlitt* (London and Basingstoke: The Macmillan Press Ltd, 1979; from henceforth *Letters*), 110.
22 Hazlitt inscribed this presentation copy as follows: 'A Christmas Present from a Father to his Son. 1822'. This book is now in the Cambridge University Library (Keynes.k.7.28).
23 William Carew Hazlitt 1867, vol.1., 169.
24 Duncan Wu (ed.) *The Selected Writings of William Hazlitt* (London: Pickering & Chatto, 1998; from henceforth 'Wu'), vol. II, 261-262.
25 Wu, VI, 202.
26 Wu, VI, 202. The word '*Ultra-Crepidarian*' appears to have been coined by Hazlitt. It alludes to Pliny the Elder's account of Apelles' exchange with a shoemaker (*Naturalis Historia* Liber xxxv, 85). The latter criticised the way Apelles had painted a sandal in one of his pictures; Apelles accepted the criticism and corrected the image. Emboldened by this, the shoemaker then found fault with the manner in which Apelles had depicted the subject's leg. Rather than acquiescing, though, Apelles replied that a shoemaker should not judge beyond his sandals ('ne supra crepidam sutor judicaret'), and this phrase became well-known in a number of modified versions, including 'ne sutor ultra crepidam'. Hazlitt's point, obviously, is that certain critics are inclined to comment on matters about which they know nothing, and he suggests that linguistic matters are generally beyond the scope of their understanding. In particular, the fact that William Gifford, the editor of *The Quarterly Review*, had once worked as a cobbler, may have prompted this specific neologism. Significantly, in 1823, Hunt published his *Ultra-Crepidarius, a Satire on William Gifford,* thus perpetuating Hazlitt's coinage.
27 Wu, VIII, 36.
28 William Hazlitt Jnr., *Literary Remains of the Late William Hazlitt: with a notice of his life by his son.* (New York: Saunders & Otley, 1836), xxii.
29 William Carew Hazlitt 1867, vol.1, v.
30 Alexander Ireland, *William Hazlitt, Essayist and Critic: Selections from his Writings, with a Memoir, Biographical and Critical* (London and New York: F. Warne and Co., 1889), viii.
31 William Carew Hazlitt 1867, vol.2, 265. Hazlitt's essay, 'On the Disadvantages of Intellectual Superiority' can be found in Wu, VI, 250-258.
32 Caleb Thomas Winchester, *A Group of Essayists of the Early Nineteenth Century* (New York: The Macmillan Company, 1910), 52.
33 Winchester 1910, 53.

34 Jules Douady, *Vie de William Hazlitt L'essayiste* (Paris, 1907), v.
35 Douady 1907, 95-96.
36 Percival Presland Howe, *The Life of William Hazlitt* (London: M. Secker, 1922), 121.
37 Stewart C. Wilcox, *Hazlitt in the Workshop: The Manuscript of The Fight* (Balitore: The John's Hopkins Press, 1943), 67.
38 Wilcox 1943, 82.
39 Herschel Baker, *William Hazlitt* (Cambridge, Mass.: Harvard University Press, 1962), 171, 173.
40 Baker 1962, 173.
41 Roy Park, *Hazlitt and the Spirit of the Age: Abstraction and Critical Theory* (Oxford: Oxford University Press, 1971), 148.
42 David Bromwich, *Hazlitt: The Mind of a Critic* 2nd ed., (Oxford: Oxford University Press, 1999[1983]), 351.
43 Bromwich 1999[1983], 349.
44 Bromwich 1999[1983], 349.
45 Bromwich discusses Gifford mainly on pp.101-102, and Burke on pp.288-300.
46 Uttara Natarajan, *Hazlitt and the Reach of Sense: Criticism, Morals, and the Metaphysics of Power* (Oxford: Oxford University Press, 1998), 16.
47 Hans Aarsleff, *The Study of Language in England, 1780-1860* (Minneapolis: University of Minnesota Press, 2nd ed., 1983), 73.
48 Uttara Natarajan, Tom Paulin, and Duncan Wu, *Metaphysical Hazlitt: Bicentenary Essays* (London: Routledge, 2005), 134.
49 Turley 2002, 112.

Chapter 2

1 Howe, II, 126.
2 Thomas Hobbes, *Leviathan* (Cambridge: Cambridge University Press, 1996[1651]), 13.
3 Hobbes 1996[1651], 24.
4 Hobbes 1996[1651], 24.
5 Hobbes 1996[1651], 25. The Biblical account of the Tower of Babel is in Genesis 11:1-9.
6 Howe, XX, 69
7 John Locke, *An Essay Concerning Human Understanding*, Peter H. Nidditch ed. (Oxford: Oxford University Press, 1979[1689]), II, xii, 164.
8 *Essay*, III, i, 402.
9 *Essay*, III, ii, 405.
10 *Essay*, III, vii, 472.
11 *Essay*, III, ii, 472.
12 *Essay*, III, ix, 477.
13 *Essay*, III, ix, 479.
14 *Essay*, III, ix, 490.
15 *Essay*, III, x, 491.
16 *Essay*, III, xi, 512.
17 The particular texts are Adam Smith's *The Theory of Moral Sentiments* (Edinburgh and London: printed for A. Miller, A. Kincaid, and J. Bell, 1759), and Lord Monboddo's *Of the Origin and Progress of Language* (London: printed for A. Kincaid, W. Creech, and T. Cadell, 1773).

18 William Godwin, *Enquiry Concerning Political Justice* (London: 1793), Book I Chapter VI, 43.
19 Godwin 1793, Book I Chapter VI, 44.
20 Godwin 1793, Book I Chapter VI, 46.
21 It is well-known that Godwin later changed his mind about this issue when he became more familiar with literature from the Elizabethan period.
22 A few recent studies concerning this vast topic include Vivian Salmon, *The Works of Francis Lodwick: a Study of his Writings in the Intellectual Context of the Seventeenth Century* (London: Longman, 1972), M.M. Slaughter, *Universal Languages and Scientific Taxonomy in the Seventeenth Century* (Cambridge: Cambridge University Press, 1982), David Cram and Jaap Maat, *George Dalgarno on Universal Language* (Oxford: Oxford University Press, 2001), William Poole, 'Francis Lodwick's Creation: Theology and Natural Philosophy in the Early Royal Society', *Journal of the History of Ideas*, 66:2 (2005), 245-263.
23 Over the years a few people have attempted to account for this development. For instance, in *Sensible Words: Linguistic Practice in England, 1640-1785* (Baltimore and London: Johns Hopkins University Press, 1977), Murray Cohen argued that the development involved a shift from the 'grammar of things' to the 'grammar of the mind', but systematic analyses such as this are generally far too simplistic since they focus on selected trends only and so fail to confront the full complexity of the linguistic research that was produced during this period.
24 *Essay*, III, xi, 507.
25 William Smellie (ed.), *Encyclopedia Britannica* (London, 1771), 728.
26 By the time the second edition appeared, Harris had decided to alter the subtitle of his book, and, specifically, he omitted the words 'Language and'. It is not clear why he felt that this change was merited.
27 Detailed biographical information about Harris can be found in Clive Probyn's *The Sociable Humanist: The Life and Works of James Harris 1709-1780, Provincial and Metropolitan Culture in Eighteenth-century England* (Oxford: Clarendon Press, 1991), and Masataka Miyawaki's *James Harris's Theory of Universal Grammar* (Münster: Nodus Publikationen, 2002).
28 James Harris, *Hermes, or a Philosophical Inquiry concerning Universal Grammar* (London: printed by H. Woodfall, 1751), 2.
29 Harris 1751, 2.
30 Harris 1751, 11.
31 For more information about this aspect of Harris' work, see the discussion in Probyn 1991, 151-162.
32 Harris 1751, 10-11.
33 Harris 1751, 11.
34 Indeed, in one of the few such explicit references Harris criticises Locke (as Hazlitt would later) mainly for presenting his ideas as if they were original and were not derived from earlier authors, as discussed in Probyn 1991, 159.
35 These two quotations are from Probyn 1991, 152, and Patrice Bergheaud, 'Empiricism and Linguistics in Eighteenth-Century Great Britain' *Topoi* 4 (1985), 155, respectively.
36 Harris 1751, 27.

37 In this book, the phrase 'content word' will be used to refer to lexical items generally associated with traditional open-class categories such as noun, verb, and adjective, while the phrase 'function word' will indicate traditional closed-class categories such as preposition, pronoun, and conjunction.
38 Harris 1751, 241.
39 Harris 1751, 241-242.
40 Harris 1751, 242.
41 Harris 1751, 244.
42 Joseph Priestley, *A Course of Lectures on the Theory of Language and Universal Grammar* (Warrington: W. Eyres, 1762), 304.
43 Priestley 1762, 301.
44 The best biography of Horne Tooke is still Christina and David Bewley's *Gentleman Radical: A Life of John Horne Tooke* (London: I.B. Tauris, 1998).
45 This example is taken from John Horne, 'A Letter to John Dunning, Esq.' (London, 1778), 8.
46 Horne Tooke 1778, 8.
47 Wu, VII, 120.
48 Horne Tooke, *EPEA PTEROENTA, or The Diversions of Purley* (London: printed for J. Johnson, 1786), I, 4.
49 *Diversions*, I, 5.
50 *Diversions*, I, 24.
51 *Diversions*, I, 26.
52 *Diversions*, I, 51.
53 *Diversions*, I, 53.
54 Ian Michael, *The Teaching of English: From the Sixteenth Century to 1870* (Cambridge: Cambridge University Press, 1987), 6.
55 Standard summaries of the reasons for, and consequences of, standardisation can be found in Tony Bex and Richard J. Watts' (eds.), *Standard English: The Widening Debate* (London: Routledge, 1999), Laura Wright's (ed.), *The Development of Standard English, 1300-1800: Theories, Descriptions, Conflicts*, (Cambridge: Cambridge University Press, 2000), and Roger Lass' (ed.), *The Cambridge History of the English Language, III, 1476-1776* (Cambridge: Cambridge University Press, 1999).
56 For a detailed discussion of the parts-of-speech, see Ian Michael, *English Grammatical Categories and the Tradition to 1800* (Cambridge: Cambridge University Press, 1970).
57 For an insightful discussion of Lowth's *A Short Introduction*, see Geoffrey Pullum's article 'Lowth's Grammar: A Re-Evaluation', *Linguistics* 137 (1974), 63-78, and for a more recent reconsideration of its genesis, see Ingrid Tieken-Boon van Ostade's paper 'Robert Dodsley and the Genesis of Lowth's Short Introduction to English Grammar', *Historiographia Linguistica* 27:1 (2000), 21-36. The best biography of Robert Lowth is still Brian Hepworth's *Robert Lowth* (Boston: Twayne, 1978).
58 Jonathan Swift 'A Proposal for Correcting, Improving and Ascertaining the English Tongue: in a letter to the most honourable Robert Earl of Oxford and Mortimer, Lord High Treasurer of Great Britain' (London: printed for Benj. Tooke, 1712), 1.
59 Swift 1712, 1.

60 l'Académie français had been established in 1635 by Cardinal Richelieu.
61 Robert Lowth, *A Short Introduction to English Grammar* (London, 1762), ii. From time to time, the revised version of Lowth's text, which was published in 1795, will be cited. While being substantially the same as the 1762 edition, the later version contains augmented critical notes.
62 Lowth 1762, iii.
63 Lowth 1762, xiv.
64 Lowth 1762, xiv-xv.
65 Lowth 1762, 7.
66 Lowth 1762, 44.
67 Lowth 1762, 96.
68 Lowth 1762, 96.
69 Lowth 1762, 96.
70 Lowth 1762, 97.
71 Lowth 1762, 97.
72 A fine collection of articles which considers Murray's *English Grammar* from a range of perspectives can be found in Ingrid Tieken-Boon van Ostade's (ed.), *Two Hundred Years of Lindley Murray* (Münster: Nodus Publikationen, 1996). An account of his life is presented in Elizabeth Frank's *Memoirs of the Life and Writings of Lindley Murray*, David Reibel ed. (London: Routledge, 1996[1826]).
73 Murray 1795, iii.
74 Murray 1795, v.
75 Murray 1795, 91.
76 Murray 1795, 92.
77 As an example of the kind of influence referred to here, Murray's impact upon European attempts to devise a grammar for Maori is considered at length in Marcus Tomalin's ' '...to this rule there are many exceptions': Robert Maunsell and the Grammar of Maori', *Historiographia Linguistica*, 33:3 (2006), 303-334.
78 Kersey 1702, The Preface.
79 These examples are all taken from Kersey 1702, The Preface.
80 Kersey 1702, The Preface.
81 Kersey 1702, The Preface.
82 Kersey 1702, The Preface.
83 Kersey 1702, The Preface.
84 Kersey 1702.
85 Kersey 1702.
86 Recent reflections upon Johnson's *Dictionary* can be found in Robert DeMaria, *Johnson's Dictionary and the Language of Learning* (Chapel Hill: University of North Carolina Press, 1986), Allen Reddick, *The Making of Johnson's Dictionary, 1746-1773* (Cambridge: Cambridge University Press, revised ed., 1996), and Jack Lynch and Anne McDermott (eds.), *Anniversary Essays on Johnson's Dictionary* (Cambridge: Cambridge University Press, 2005).
87 Johnson, 'Preface' to *A Dictionary of the English Language* (London, 1755).
88 Johnson 1755, Preface.
89 These quotations are all taken from the 'Preface'.
90 Johnson 1755, Preface.
91 Johnson 1755, Preface.

92 Johnson 1755, Preface.
93 Johnson 1755, Preface.
94 Johnson 1755, Preface.
95 Johnson 1755, Preface.
96 David Booth, *Introduction to an Analytical Dictionary of the English Language* (London: Gale, Curtis, and Fenner, 1806), v.
97 Booth 1806, v.
98 Booth 1806, 11-12.
99 Booth 1806, 15.
100 Booth 1806, 15.
101 Booth 1806, 117.
102 Booth 1806, 24, 158.
103 Booth 1806, 158.
104 For a detailed discussion of this basic shift, see Samuel Howell, *Eighteenth-Century British Logic and Rhetoric* (Princeton: Princeton University Press, 1971).
105 The increased importance of print culture in the eighteenth century is discussed at length in David Kaufer's and Kathleen Carley's *Communication at a Distance: The Influence of Print on Sociocultural Organization and Change* (Hillsdale, New Jersey: Erlbaum, 1993).
106 Hugh Blair, *Lectures on Rhetoric and Belles Lettres*, Linda Ferreria-Buckley and Michael Halloran eds. (Illinois: Southern Illinois University, 2005[1785]), xxi.
107 For a detailed discussion of Campbell's philosophy of rhetoric in the context of the Scottish Enlightenment, see Arthur Walzer's *George Campbell: Rhetoric in the Age of Enlightenment* (Albany: State University of New York Press, 2003).
108 Campbell 1776, I, 13-14.
109 Campbell 1776, I, xi.
110 Campbell 1776, I, 25.
111 Campbell 1776, I, xiv.
112 Campbell 1776, II, iv.
113 The best biography of Blair is still Robert Schmitz's *Hugh Blair* (New York: King's Crown, 1948).
114 For more information about this, see Henry Meikle's, 'The Chair of Rhetoric and Belles Lettres in the University of Edinburgh', *University of Edinburgh Journal* 13 (1945), 89-103.
115 For more information, see Schmitz 1948, 94.
116 Some of the differences between the different versions of Blair's *Lectures* are discussed in Blair 2005[1785], xvi-xxiii.
117 Blair 2005[1785], 1.
118 Blair 2005[1785], 10.
119 Blair 2005[1785], 99.
120 Blair 2005[1785], 195.
121 Blair 2005[1785], 208.
122 Blair 2005[1785], 100.
123 Robert Harris, *Politics and the Nation: Britain in the Mid-Eighteenth Century* (Oxford: Oxford University Press, 2002), 44-45.
124 Jeffrey Cox, *Poetry and Politics in the Cockney School: Keats, Shelley, Hunt and their Circle* (Cambridge: Cambridge University Press, 1998), 31. Another useful text which explores some of these issues is Kevin

Gilmartin's *Writing Against Revolution: Literary Conservatism in Britain, 1790-1832* (Cambridge: Cambridge University Press, 2007).
125 Mark Philp, 'The Fragmented Ideology of Reform', in Mark Philp's (ed.) *The French Revolution and British Popular Culture* (Cambridge: Cambridge University Press, 1991), 56. In a similar manner, J. Ann Hone has commented that 'Radicalism eludes convenient or concise definition, but it may at least be said that it involves the attempt to change the world and to change it for the better' [J. Ann Hone, *For the Cause of Truth: Radicalism in London* (Oxford: The Clarendon Press, 1982), 1.], but descriptions of this kind are usually too general to be of much practical assistance.
126 Hone 1982, 4-5.

Chapter 3

1 As mentioned in the Introduction, the complexity of the genesis of Hazlitt's *Grammar* is considered in Jones 1987, 32-43.
2 A few details concerning this part of his education can be found in *Letters*, 60-66, and William Stephenson's *William Hazlitt and Hackney College* (London: The Lindley Press, 1930) provides a detailed discussion of New College. General overviews can be found in the usual biographical sources – for instance, Tom Paulin's *The Day-Star of Liberty: William Hazlitt's Radical Style* (London: Faber & Faber, 1998), 8-12, and A.C. Grayling, *The Quarrel of the Age: The Life and Times of William Hazlitt* (London: Phoenix Press, 2001), 31-48.
3 *Letters*, 65.
4 Wu, VI, 61-62.
5 Wu, VII, 120.
6 *Diversions*, I, 111.
7 Wu, VII, 121.
8 Howe, II, 270.
9 Natarajan 1998, 16.
10 *Diversions*, I, 51.
11 *Diversions*, I, 37.
12 The French sources of Horne Tooke's work are discussed at length in Aarsleff 1983, 46ff. For Horne Tooke's overview of these three different kinds of linguistic abbreviation, see *Diversions*, I, 26-28. The central aspects of Locke's philosophy of language are discussed in Vere Chappell (ed.), *The Cambridge Companion to Locke* (Cambridge: Cambridge University Press, 1994), especially chapter 5. However, for a recent attempt to demonstrate that Locke's linguistic work was unified and internally consistent, see Walter Ott's *Locke's Philosophy of Language*, (Cambridge: Cambridge University Press, 2004).
13 *Diversions*, I, 29-43.
14 *Essay*, III, v, 431-432.
15 For Horne Tooke's discussion of the words 'term' and 'idea', see *Diversions*, I, 37.
16 *Essay*, III, 471. Aristotle had distinguished between categorematic and syncategorematic terms in *De Interpretatione* (16b20 - 20a13), and the centrality of this distinction to Locke's work is discussed at length in

Gabriel Nuchelmans' 'The Historical Background to Locke's Account of Particles', *Logique et Analyse*, 29 (1986), 53-71.
17 *Essay*, III, 473.
18 *Diversions*, I, 41.
19 *Diversions*, I, 43.
20 *Essay*, III, 472, quoted in *Diversions*, I, 42.
21 *Diversions*, I, 29.
22 For instance, see Aarsleff 1983 and Olivia Smith , *The Politics of Language: 1791-1819* (Oxford: The Clarendon Press, 1984).
23 *Diversions*, I, 27.
24 *Diversions*, I, 84.
25 For this example, see *Diversions*, I, 86. James Harris classifies the word *that* both as a conjunction and as a pronoun in *Hermes*, 78-79, 242-249.
26 *Diversions*, I, 86.
27 *Diversions*, I, 135. Horne Tooke's attempts to demonstrate that all parts-of-speech can be reduced to two fundamental classes – namely nouns and verbs – is discussed at length in Patrice Bergheaud's 'Empiricism and Linguistics in Eighteenth-Century Great Britain', *Topoi* 4 (1985), 155-163.
28 Horne Tooke, *Diversions*, II, 19.
29 *Diversions*, II, 19.
30 *Diversions*, II, 404.
31 *Diversions*, II, 18.
32 John Cartwright sought 'Anglo-Saxon' antecedents in his *An Appeal, on the Subject of the English Constitution* (London, 1797). For a recent discussion of John Jebb's interest in the 'Anglo-Saxon Constitution', see Anthony Page's *John Jebb and the Enlightenment Origins of British Radicalism* (Westport Conn.: Greenwood Press, 2003), 176, 191, 228.
33 Gerald Newman, *The Rise of English Nationalism: A Cultural History, 1720-1830*, revised ed. (New York: Saint Martin's Press, 1997), 184.
34 Letter to Godwin, September 22, 1800, in Turnbull, A. (ed.), *Biographia Epistolaris* (London: G. Bell and Sons, Ltd., 1911), vol.1, letter 95.
35 James C. McKusick, *Coleridge's Philosophy of Language* (New Haven and London: Yale University Press, 1986), 43.
36 William Tooke offered Horne Tooke a remarkably low mortgage for the Wimbledon house and the associated land. For specifics, see Bewley and Bewley 1998, 116-117.
37 Bewley and Bewley 1998, 119.
38 Wu, VII, 115.
39 Wu, VIII, 36-37. The 'Fuseli' referred to here is, of course, the Swiss-born painter John Henry Fuseli.
40 Howe, II, 3.
41 Howe, II, 6.
42 Howe, II, 6.
43 Aarsleff 1983, 73-114. Booth is not mentioned at all, and while Salmon is cited once in a negative footnote on p.81, his *The First Principles of English Grammar* is not discussed.
44 For Hazlitt's criticism of Booth's analysis of verbs, see Howe, II, 9.
45 Howe, II, 65.
46 Stephen Land, *From Signs to Propositions: the Concept of Form in Eighteenth-century Semantic Theory* (London: Longman, 1974), 4.

47 Booth 1806, 11.
48 Booth 1806, 15.
49 Booth 1806, 21.
50 Booth 1806, 22.
51 Howe, II, 6-7.
52 Paul Hamilton, 'Hazlitt and the "Kings of Speech"', in Natarajan et al. 2005, 79; Natarajan 1998, 6.
53 Howe, II, 87.
54 Johnson 1755.
55 Priestley 1762, 231-232.
56 *Diversions*, I, 24.
57 *Diversions*, I, 3.
58 As mentioned in the Introduction, Godwin, who had commissioned Hazlitt to write his *Grammar*, maintained in *Political Justice* (esp. Book I, chapter 8) that natural language is perfectible.
59 Hazlitt's advocacy of the 'familiar' or 'common' style is discussed at length in chapter 4.
60 Wu, VII, 120.
61 For example, see the discussion in Paulin 1998, 249. Stephenson 1930 provides a detailed discussion of Hazlitt's education.
62 Obviously, the quotation here is from *Macbeth* 5.viii.
63 Wu, VII, 121.
64 *Diversions*, I, 111.
65 For a detailed discussion of early European analyses of Maori grammar, see Tomalin 2006.
66 Howe, II, 212.
67 Wu, VII, 121.
68 Natarajan 1998, 66.
69 Wu, VII, 122.
70 Horne Tooke discusses these issues in *Diversions*, I, 21-24.
71 *Essay*, II, xii, 164.
72 *Diversions*, I, 37.
73 *Diversions*, I, 37.
74 Park 1971, 98.
75 Howe, II, 270.
76 Howe, II, 271.
77 Howe, II, 277.
78 Howe, II, 272.
79 Howe, II, 271.
80 Howe, II, 280. When using this phrase, Hazlitt was recalling Anthony Willich's rather unreliable translation of Kant, *Essays and Treatises on Moral, Political and Various Philosophical Subjects* (London, 1798).
81 Howe, II, 280.
82 Park 1971, 20.
83 Tim Milnes, *Knowledge and Indifference in English Romantic Prose* (Cambridge: Cambridge University Press, 2003), 106.
84 Milnes 2003, 108.
85 *Diversions*, II, 404.
86 Howe, II, 278.
87 Howe, II, 280.

88 For a focused discussion of the problematical role of 'common sense' in Hazlitt's philosophy of mind, see Milnes 2003, 123-126.
89 Howe, II, 274.

Chapter 4

1 *Letters*, 43-45.
2 Grayling 2001, 27.
3 William Wordworth and Samuel Taylor Coleridge, *Lyrical Ballads, with a Few Other Poems* (London: printed for J. & A. Arch, 1798), i.
4 William Wordsworth and Samuel Taylor Coleridge, *Lyrical Ballads, with Other Poems*, 2nd ed. (London: Longman and Rees, 1800), vii.
5 Wordsworth and Coleridge 1800, xii.
6 William Keach, *Arbitrary Power: Romanticism, Language, Politics* (Princeton and Oxford: Princeton University Press, 2004), especially chapter 4.
7 Frederick Jones (ed.), *The Letters of Percy Bysshe Shelley*, vol.2 (Oxford: Oxford University Press, 1964), 108.
8 Wu, VI, 218-219.
9 Certain aspects of Hazlitt's involvement with contemporaneous periodicals are analysed in Gregory Dart's 'Romantic Cockneyism: Hazlitt and the Periodical Press', 2000, *Romanticism* 6.2, 143-162.
10 *The Quarterly Review*, 19, July 1818, 424-34. The essay 'On Washerwomen', to which Russell refers here and which he criticised most extensively in his review, was actually written by Leigh Hunt (as Russell well knew). For a brief summary of the details, see Grayling 2001, 212-213.
11 Wu, II, 105.
12 James E. Barcus (ed.), *Percy Bysshe Shelley: The Critical Heritage* (London and New York: Routledge, 1975), 51.
13 Barcus 1975, 257. This type of criticism persisted well into the nineteenth century, when Dickens was a frequent recipient of such politico-grammatical lashings. An insightful summary of such responses to Dickens can be found in Knud Sorensen's *Charles Dickens: Linguistic Innovator* (Arkona: Aarhus: 1985).
14 Wu, VI, 218.
15 Cox 1998, 21.
16 Cox 1998, 22.
17 Wu, VI, 217.
18 Howe, II, 5.
19 Howe, II, 5.
20 *Letters*, 110.
21 Howe, II, 26; Howe, II, 36.
22 Murray 1795, 67.
23 Howe, II, 54.
24 Wu, VII, 120.
25 Lowth praises Harris' *Hermes* in the Preface to his *Grammar*. For the specific reference, see Lowth 1762, xiv-xv.
26 This essay is reprinted in Tom Paulin's and David Chandler's collection *The Fight and Other Writings* (London: Penguin, 2000), 391-392.
27 Donald Reiman and Neil Fraistat (eds.), *The Complete Poetry of Percy*

Bysshe Shelley: Volume 1 (Baltimore and London: The Johns Hopkins University Press, 2000), 7.
28 Reiman and Fraistat 2000, 7.
29 Lowth 1762, x.
30 Lowth 1762, 1.
31 Lowth 1762, 35. The italics in the quotation from Shakespeare are Lowth's.
32 Lowth 1762, 127.
33 Murray 1795, iii.
34 Murray 1795, v.
35 Campbell 1776, I, vii.
36 Campbell 1776, II, 8.
37 Campbell 1776, I, 408.
38 Campbell 1776, I, 410-430.
39 Campbell 1776, I, 413.
40 Campbell 1776, I, 419-420.
41 These specific examples appear in Murray 1795, 179.
42 Blair 2005[1785], 99.
43 Blair 2005[1785], 99-100.
44 Blair 2005[1785], 100.
45 Blair 2005[1785], 100.
46 Blair 2005[1785], 101.
47 Blair 2005[1785], 101.
48 Murray 1795, 180.
49 Murray 1795, 179.
50 Murray 1795, 180.
51 Blair 2005[1785], 100-101.
52 Blair 2005[1785], 101.
53 These quotations are all found in Murray 1795, 180-184.
54 Murray 1795, 185.
55 Murray 1795, 185. This passage can be compared directly to Blair 2005[1785], 101. The most intriguing difference in this instance is that while Blair had referred to words which express an idea 'but not quite fully or completely', Murray chose to delete the mild intensifier.
56 Murray 1795, 182.
57 Murray 1795, 179.
58 Howe, II, 78.
59 These lines from Shakespeare are taken from *Timon of Athens* VI.iii; the Hazlitt quotation is from Howe, II, 78.
60 Howe, II, 28.
61 Howe, II, 81.
62 Keach 2004, 82.
63 Howe, II, 87.
64 Wu, VI, 217.
65 Wu, VI, 219.
66 Wu, VI, 220; compare Murray 1975, 185.
67 Murray 1975, 180.
68 Wu, VI, 220.
69 Wu, VI, 220-221.
70 Lowth 1762, 127.
71 Wu, VI, 218-219.

72 Wu, II, 138.
73 Wu, IX, 61, 66, 69, 71, 72.
74 Wilcox 1943, 83.
75 Wilcox 1943, 83.
76 David Higgins, 'Englishness, Effeminacy, and the New Monthly Magazine: Hazlitt's 'The Fight' in Context', *Romanticism* 10:2, 62-81.
77 Wu, VI, 218.
78 The 'Classical Dictionary of the Vulgar Tongue' was originally published by Francis Grose in 1785, and the edited version, compiled by Robert Cromie, was printed as the *Dictionary of the Vulgar Tongue: a Dictionary of Buckish Slang, University Wit, and Pickpocket Eloquence* (London, 1811).
79 Cromie 1811.
80 Wu, V, 350.
81 Wu, V, 350.
82 'beneath (their) dignity'.
83 'even more'.
84 'caught in the act'.
85 Wu, VI, 185-186. The phrase 'ducks to the learned fool' is adapted from *Timon of Athens*, IV.iii.
86 Wu, VI, 141-142.
87 Cromie 1811.
88 Cromie 1811.
89 John Emery had acted as the Yorkshireman Robert Tyke in Thomas Morton's *The School of Reform* on the 14th June 1816, and Hazlitt had reviewed his performance. His review was later reprinted in *A View of the English Stage*.
90 Wu, VI, 217.
91 Paulin and Chandler 2000, xv.

Chapter 5

1 Lowth 1762, iii.
2 Lowth 1762, vi.
3 Lowth 1762, vii.
4 Lowth 1795, 38.
5 Lowth 1795, 38.
6 Lowth 1795, 93.
7 Lowth 1795, 94.
8 Lowth 1795, 39.
9 Lowth 1795, 39.
10 Murray 1795, 103.
11 Murray 1795, 109.
12 Murray 1795, 123.
13 Murray 1795, 105.
14 Tom Paulin and David Chandler 2000, 553.
15 Thomas De Quincey, 'Charles Lamb' in *Works* (Author's Edition, Edinburgh, 1863), VIII, 128; Bromwich 1999[1983], chapter 8
16 Bromwich 1999[1983], 275.
17 Bromwich 1999[1983], 349.
18 Wu, V, 298.

19 Wu, VI, 255. The word appears in Butler's 'Satyr upon the Imperfection and Abuse of Human Learning', and Hazlitt used the lines as an epigraph to his essay 'On the Ignorance of the Learned'.
20 Blair 2005[1785], 494.
21 Blair 2005[1785], 164, 178-179.
22 An authoritative summary of Pope's reception in the Romantic era can be found in Robert J. Griffin's *Wordsworth's Pope: A Study in Literary Historiography* (Cambridge: Cambridge University Press, 1995), especially chapter 3. Obviously, the initial reception history of Pope's work can be followed in John Barnard's *Alexander Pope: The Critical Heritage* (London and New York: Routledge, 1995).
23 The edition of *Biographia Literaria* that will be used here is James Engell's and W. Jackson Bate's (eds.), *The Collected Works of Samuel Taylor Coleridge* (Princeton: Princeton University Press, 1983; from henceforth 'Coleridge 1983[1817]'), vols. 7 and 8. The quotation in the main text is from Coleridge 1983[1817], VII, 18.
24 Coleridge 1983[1817], VIII, 18-19.
25 Coleridge 1983[1817], VIII, 30.
26 Coleridge 1983[1817], VIII, 39.n.
27 Wu, 9, 27.
28 Barnard 1995, 32.
29 Howe, II, 36, 78, 82, 96.
30 Howe, II, 78. These lines are from *An Essay on Criticism* (Part II) and *The Odyssey of Homer* (Book XII) respectively. The italics are Hazlitt's.
31 Howe, II, 36, 78.
32 Howe, II, 80.
33 Howe, II, 81.
34 Howe, II, 81.
35 Wu, VIII, 6.
36 Howe, II, 5.
37 Wu, II, 234. The line 'there is but one perfect writer, even Pope' echoes Matthew 5:48.
38 *Blackwood's*, August 1818, iii, 520-521.
39 Howe, II, 96.
40 Howe, II, 96. As usual, the italics are Hazlitt's.
41 Lowth 1795, 118-121.
42 Wu, V, 344.
43 Wu, VII, 180-181.
44 Wu, VI, 65.
45 Howe, XVI, 130.
46 Howe, XVI, 131.
47 Howe, XVI, 132.
48 Howe, XVI, 133-134.
49 Wu, V, 93.
50 Wu, VIII, 217-218.
51 Wu, V, 94.
52 Wu, V, 94.
53 Cromie 1811.
54 Wu, V, 193.
55 Wu, V, 194.
56 Wu, II, 215.

57 Howe, II, 87.

Chapter 6

1 William Stigand, 'Review of *Poems* and *Dramatis Personae*', *Edinburgh Review*, LXX, 1884, 538-539.
2 Thomas Cleghorn, 'The Writings of Charles Dickens', in *North British Review* (May 1845), 65-87. The quoted extract can be found most easily in Philip Collins' (ed.) *Charles Dickens: The Critical Heritage* (London: Routledge, 1995), 188.
3 Robert Louis Stevenson, 'Books Which Have Influenced Me', British Weekly, May 13, 1887.
4 Robert Louis Stevenson, 'A College Magazine' in *Memories and Portraits*, (Glasgow: Richard Drew Publishing Ltd, 1990[1887]), 42-43.
5 Madeline House, Graham Storey, and Kathleen Mary Tillotson (eds.), *The Letters of Charles Dickens* (Oxford: Clarendon Press, 2002), vol.12, 123.
6 Alexander Andrews, *The History of British Journalism: from the foundation of the newspaper press in England, to the repeal of the Stamp act in 1855, with sketches of press celebrities*, 2 vols. (London: R. Bentley, 1859), vol.1, 1.
7 Approachable histories of these developments can be found in Kevin Gilmartin's *Print Politics: The Press and Radical Opposition in the Early Nineteenth Century* (Cambridge: Cambridge University Press, 1996), Hannah Barker's *Newspapers, Politics, and Public Opinion in Late Eighteenth Century England* (Oxford: The Clarendon Press, 1998), and Martin Conboy's *Journalism: A Critical History* (London: Sage Publications, 2004).
8 Joanne Shattock and Michael Wolff, (eds.), *The Victorian Periodical Press: Sampling and Sounding* (Leicester and Toronto: Leicester University Press and University of Toronto Press, 1982), xv.
9 De Quincey, *Works*, vol.12, 1863, 14.
10 De Quincey, *Works*, vol.12, 14-15.
11 De Quincey, *Works*, vol.12, 16.
12 De Quincey, *Works*, vol.12, 16.
13 De Quincey, *Works*, vol.12, 16.
14 Henry Alford, *A Plea for the Queen's English* (London: Strahan, 1864), 245-246.
15 Manfred Görlach, *English in Nineteenth Century England* (Cambridge: Cambridge University Press, 1999), 1, 16. No doubt (as Görlach notes) this neglect is partly due to the fact that considerable emphasis has been placed by researchers on the development of historical linguistics during the nineteenth century.
16 Michael 1987, 344.
17 De Quincey, *Works*, vol.2, 326-327.
18 William Barnes, *Philological Grammar* (London: J.R. Smith, 1854), vi.
19 Henry Hutchinson, *Thought-symbolism and Grammatic Illusions* (London: K. Paul Trench, 1884), vi-vii.
20 Hutchinson 1884, 10.
21 Hutchinson 1884, 11.
22 Hutchinson 1884, 58.

23 Goold Brown, *The Grammar of English Grammars* (New York: W. Wood & Co., 1851), iii, xvi.
24 Brown 1851, 490.
25 Brown 1851, 490.
26 Brown 1851, 500-501.
27 Brown 1851, 552.
28 Percival Leigh, *The Comic English Grammar: A New and Facetious Introduction to the English Tongue* (London: Richard Bentley, 1840), 15.
29 Alford 1864, 6.
30 Alford 1864, 10.

Bibliography

Whenever possible, the following editions of Hazlitt's works are used:

Howe, Percival Presland (ed.), *The Complete Works of William Hazlitt* 21 vols. (London: J.M. Dent, 1930-1934).
Wu, Duncan (ed.), *The Selected Writings of William Hazlitt* 9 vols. (London: Pickering & Chatto, 1998).

Primary Sources:

Alford, Henry, *A Plea for the Queen's English: Stray Notes on Speaking and Spelling* (London: W. Strahan, 1864).
Andrews, Alexander, *The History of British Journalism: from the foundation of the newspaper press in England, to the repeal of the Stamp act in 1855, with sketches of press celebrities*, 2 vols. (London: R. Bentley, 1859).
Astarloa y Aguirre, Pablo Pedro de, *Apología de la Lengua Bascongada* (Madrid: G. Ortega, 1803).
Barnes, William, *Philological Grammar: grounded upon English, and formed from a comparison of more than sixty languages. Being an introduction to the science of grammar and a help to grammars of all languages, especially English, Latin and Greek* (London: J.R. Smith, 1845).
Blair, Hugh, *Lectures on Rhetoric and Belles Lettres* (London: W. Strahan, T. Cadell, 1783).
——, *Lectures on Rhetoric and Belles Lettres*, Linda Ferreria-Buckley and Michael Halloran (eds.), (Illinois: Southern Illinois University, 2005[1785]).
Booth, David, *Introduction to an Analytical Dictionary of the English Language* (London: printed for Gale, Curtis, and Fenner, 1806).
Boswell, James, *The Life of Samuel Johnson* (London, 1791).
Bowles, Lisle, *The Works of Alexander Pope* (London: printed for J. Johnson et al., 1806).
Blount, Thomas, *Glossographia* (London, 1656).
Brown, Goold, *The Grammar of English Grammars* (New York: W. Wood & Co, 1851).
Campbell, George, *The Philosophy of Rhetoric* (London: W. Strahan, 1776).
Cartwright, John, *An Appeal, on the Subject of the English Constitution*, (Lon-

don, 1797).
Cawdrey, Robert, *A Table Alphabetical Of Hard Usual English Words* (London, 1604).
Cleghorn, Thomas, 'The Writings of Charles Dickens', *North British Review* (1845), 65-87.
Coleridge, Samuel Taylor, *Biographia Literaria*, printed in James Engell's and W. Jackson Bate's (eds.), *The Collected Works of Samuel Taylor Coleridge* (Princeton: Princeton University Press, 1983[1817]).
Cromie, Robert, *Dictionary of the Vulgar Tongue: a Dictionary of Buckish Slang, University Wit, and Pickpocket Eloquence* (London, 1811).
de Brosse, Charles, *Traité de la Formation Mèchanique des Langues et des Principes Physiques de l'Etymologie* (Paris, 1765).
Enfield, William, *Speaker, or Miscellaneous Pieces Selected from the Best English Writers* (London: printed for Joseph Johnson, 1774).
Entick, John, *New Spelling Dictionary* (London, 1771).
Grammaticus, Galfridus, *Promptorium Parvulorum* (London, 1499).
Godwin, William, *Enquiry Concerning Political Justice*, (London: printed for G.G.J. and J. Robinson, 1793).
——, *A New Guide to the English Tongue*, by 'Edward Baldwin, Esq.' (London: printed for M.J. Godwin, 1809).
——, *Outlines of English Grammar, Partly Abridged from Mr Hazlitt's New and Improved Grammar of the English Language* (London, 1810).
Harris, James, *Hermes, or a Philosophical Inquiry concerning Universal Grammar* (London: printed by H. Woodfall, 1751).
Hobbes, Thomas, *De Corpore Politico, or the Elements of Law, Moral & Politick* (London, 1649).
——, *Leviathan* (Cambridge: Cambridge University Press: Cambridge, 1996[1651]).
Horne Tooke, John, 'A Letter to John Dunning, Esq.' (London, 1778).
——, *EPEA PTEROENTA, or The Diversions of Purley*, Part I, (London: printed for J. Johnson, 1786).
——, *EPEA PTEROENTA, or The Diversions of Purley*, Parts 1 and 2, (London: printed for J. Johnson, 1798-1805).
Hume, David, *A Treatise of Human Nature* (London: printed for John Noon, 1739).
——, *Philosophical Essays Concerning Human Understanding* (London: printed for A. Millar, 1748).
Hunt, Leigh, *Ultra-Crepidarius; A Satire on William Gifford* (London, 1823).
——, *The Autobiography of Leigh Hunt; with reminiscences of his friends and contemporaries* (London, 1850).
Hutchinson, H., *Thought-symbolism and Grammatic Illusions* (London: K. Paul, Trench, 1884).
Johnson, Samuel, *A Dictionary of the English Language* (London: printed by W. Strachan, for J. and P. Knapton), 1755).
Kames, Lord (Henry Home), *Elements of Criticism* (Edinburgh, 1762).
Kersey, John, *The New English Dictionary* (H. Bonwicke & R. Knaplock, 1702).
Lamb, Charles, *Elia. Essays which Have Appeared Under that Signature in the London Magazine* (London, 1823).
Lancelot, Claude, Arnauld, Antoine, and Nicole, Pierre, *Grammaire Générale et Raisonnée* (Paris, 1660).

Leigh, Percival, *The Comic English Grammar: A New and Facetious Introduction to the English Tongue* (London: Richard Bentley, 1840).
Locke, John, *An Essay Concerning Human Understanding*, Peter H. Nidditch (ed.) (Oxford: Oxford University Press, 1979[1689]).
Lowth, Robert, *De Sacra Poesi Hebraeorum*, (Oxford, 1753).
——, *A Short Introduction to English Grammar* (London: printed by J. Hughes, 1762).
——, *A Short Introduction to English Grammar*, revised ed. (London: printed for J. Dodsley; and T. Cadell, Junior, and W. Davies, 1795).
Lye, Edward, *Dictionarium Saxonico et Gothico-Latinum* (London, 1772).
Monboddo, James Burnett, Lord, *Of the Origin and Progress of Language* (London: printed for A. Kincaid, W. Creech, and T. Cadell, 1773).
Murray, Lindley, *English Grammar, Adapted to the Different Classes of Learners* (York: printed by Wilson, Spence & Mawman, 1795).
Newton, Isaac, *Philosophiae Naturalis Principia Mathematica* (London, 1687).
Priestley, Joseph, *Course of Lectures on The Theory of Language, and Universal Grammar* (Warrington: printed by W. Eyres, 1762).
Sanctius, Franciscus, *Minerva, seu de Causis Linguae Latinae* (Salamanca, 1587).
Smellie, William (ed.), *Encyclopedia Britannica* (London, 1771).
Skinner, Stephen, *Etymologicon Linguae Anglicanae* (London, 1671).
Stevenson, Robert Louis, 'Books Which Have Influenced Me', *British Weekly*, May 13th (1887).
——, *Memories and Portraits*, reprint (Glasgow: Richard Drew Publishing Ltd, 1990[1887]).
Stigand, William, 'Review of *Poems* and *Dramatis Personae*', *Edinburgh Review*: LXX (1884), 538-539.
Swift, Jonathan, 'A Proposal for Correcting, Improving and Ascertaining the English Tongue: in a letter to the most honourable Robert Earl of Oxford and Mortimer, Lord High Treasurer of Great Britain' (London: printed for Benj. Tooke, 1712).
Thomson, James, 'Winter: A Poem' (London, 1726).
Wilkins, John, *An Essay towards a Real Character and a Philosophical Language* (London: printed for S. Gellibrand, Martyn, 1668).
Willich, Anthony Florian Madinger, *Essays and Treatises on Moral, Political and Various Philosophical Subjects* (London, 1798).
Wordsworth, William and Coleridge, Samuel Taylor, *Lyrical Ballads, with a Few Other Poems* (London: printed for J. & A. Arch, 1798).
Wordsworth, William and Coleridge, Samuel Taylor, *Lyrical Ballads, with Other Poems*, 2nd ed. (London: Longman and Rees, 1800).

Secondary Sources:

Aarsleff, Hans, *The Study of Language in England, 1780-1860* (Minneapolis: University of Minnesota Press, 1983).
Albrecht, William Price, *Hazlitt and the Creative Imagination* (Lawrence: University of Kansas Press, 1965).
Baker, Herschel Clay, *William Hazlitt* (Cambridge, Mass.: Harvard University Press, 1962).

Barcus, James E. (ed.), *Percy Bysshe Shelley: The Critical Heritage* (London: Routledge, 1975).

Barker, Hannah, *Newspapers, Politics, and Public Opinion in Late Eighteenth Century England* (Oxford: The Clarendon Press, 1998).

Barnard, John (ed.), *Alexander Pope: The Critical Heritage* (London and New York: Routledge, 1995).

Bergheaud, Patrice, 'Empiricism and Linguistics in Eighteenth-Century Great Britain', *Topoi* 4 (1985), 155-163.

Berkeley, George, *A Treatise Concerning the Principles of Human Knowledge* (London, 1710).

Bewley, Christina and Bewley, David K., *Gentleman Radical: A Life of John Horne Tooke, 1736-1812* (London: Tauris Academic Studies, 1998).

Bex, Tony and Watts, Richard J. (eds.), *Standard English: The Widening Debate* (London: Routledge, 1999).

Bromwich, David, *Hazlitt: The Mind of a Critic* (London: Yale University Press, 1999[1983]).

Chandler, Zilpha Emma, *An Analysis of the Stylistic Technique of Addison, Johnson, Hazlitt, and Pater* (Iowa City, Ia.: The University, 1928)

Chappell, Vere (ed.), *The Cambridge Companion to Locke* (Cambridge: Cambridge University Press, 1994).

Cohen, Murray, *Sensible Words: Linguistic Practice in England, 1640-1785* (Baltimore and London: Johns Hopkins University Press, 1977).

Collins, Philip, (ed.), *Charles Dickens: The Critical Heritage* (London: Routledge, 1995).

Conboy, Martin, *Journalism: A Critical History* (London: Sage Publications, 2004).

Cox, Jeffrey N., *Poetry and Politics in the Cockney School: Keats, Shelley, Hunt and their Circle* (Cambridge: Cambridge University Press, 1998).

Cram, David and Maat, Jaap, *George Dalgarno on Universal Language* (Oxford: Oxford University Press, 2001).

Dart, Gregory, 'Romantic Cockneyism: Hazlitt and the Periodical Press', *Romanticism* 6.2 (2000), 143-162.

Dechamps, Jules Albert, *Hazlitt et Napolèon* (Paris, 1939).

DeMaria, Robert, *Johnson's Dictionary and the Language of Learning* (Chapel Hill: University of North Carolina Press, 1986).

De Quincey, Thomas, *Works*, 15 vols. (Edinburgh, 1862-1878).

Douady, Jules, *Vie de William Hazlitt L'essayiste* (Paris, 1907).

Dyer, Gary, *British Satire and the Politics of Style, 1789-1832* (Cambridge: Cambridge University Press, 1997).

Frank, Elizabeth, *Memoirs of the Life and Writings of Lindley Murray*, David Reibel (ed.) (Routledge: London, 1996[1826]).

Gilmartin, Kevin, *Print Politics: The Press and Radical Opposition in the Early Nineteenth Century* (Cambridge: Cambridge University Press, 1996).

——, *Writing Against Revolution: Literary Conservatism in Britain, 1790-1832* (Cambridge: Cambridge University Press, 2007).

Grayling, A.C., *The Quarrel of the Age: the Life and Times of William Hazlitt* (London: Phoenix, 2001).

Griffin, Robert John, *Wordsworth's Pope: A Study in Literary Historiography* (Cambridge: Cambridge University Press, 1995).

Hamilton, Paul, 'Hazlitt and the "Kings of Speech" ', in Natarajan *et al.* 2005, 68-80.
Harris, Robert, *Politics and the Nation: Britain in the Mid-Eighteenth Century* (Oxford: Oxford University Press, 2002).
Hazlitt, William Jnr., *Literary Remains of the Late William Hazlitt: with a Notice of his Life by his Son.* (New York: Saunders & Otley, 1836).
Hazlitt, William Carew, *Memoirs of William Hazlitt, with Portions of his Correspondence*, 2 vols. (London: Richard Bentley, 1867).
Higgins, David, 'Englishness, Effeminacy, and the New Monthly Magazine: Hazlitt's 'The Fight' in Context', *Romanticism* 10:2 (2004), 62-81.
Hone, J. Ann, *For the cause of Truth: Radicalism in London* (Oxford: The Clarendon Press, 1982).
House, Madeline, Storey, Graham, and Tillotson, Kathleen Mary (eds.), *The Letters of Charles Dickens*, 12 vols. (Oxford: Clarendon Press, 2002).
Howe, Percival Presland, *The Life of William Hazlitt* (London: M. Secker, 1922).
Howell, Wilbur Samuel, *Eighteenth-Century British Logic and Rhetoric* (Princeton: Princeton University Press, 1971).
Ireland, Alexander, *List of the Writings of William Hazlitt and Leigh Hunt* (London, 1868).
——, *William Hazlitt, Essayist and Critic: Selections from his Writings, with a Memoir, Biographical and Critical* (London and New York: F. Warne & Co., 1889).
Jones, Frederick L. (ed.), *The Letters of Percy Bysshe Shelley*, 2 vols. (Oxford: Oxford University Press, 1964).
Jones, Stanley, 'The "Suppression" of Hazlitt's *New and Improved Grammar of the English Tongue*: A Reconstruction of Events', *The Library* 6:9 (1987), 32-43.
——, *Hazlitt, a Life: from Winterslow to Frith Street* (Oxford: The Clarendon Press, 1989).
Kaufer, David S. and Carley, Kathleen M., *Communication at a Distance: The Influence of Print on Sociocultural Organization and Change* (Hillsdale, New Jersey: Lawrence Erlbaum Associates, 1993).
Keach, William, *Arbitrary Power: Romanticism, Language, Politics* (Princeton N.J. and Oxford: Princeton University Press, 2004).
Land, Stephen K., *From Signs to Propositions: the Concept of Form in Eighteenth-century Semantic Theory* (London: Longman, 1974).
Lass, Roger, (ed.), *The Cambridge History of the English Language, Vol.III, 1476-1776* (Cambridge: Cambridge University Press, 1999).
Lynch, Jack and McDermott, Anne (eds.), *Anniversary Essays on Johnson's Dictionary* (Cambridge: Cambridge University Press, 2005).
McKusick, James C., *Coleridge's Philosophy of Language* (New Haven: Yale University Press, 1986).
Marrs, Edwin W. (ed.), *The Letters of Charles and Mary Anne Lamb, Vol.III, 1809-1817* (Ithica and London: Cornell University Press, 1978).
Meikle, Henry, 'The Chair of Rhetoric and Belles Lettres in the University of Edinburgh', *University of Edinburgh Journal* 13 (1945), 89-103.
Michael, Ian, *English Grammatical Categories and the Tradition to 1800* (Cambridge: Cambridge University Press, 1970).
——, *The Teaching of English: From the Sixteenth Century to 1870*, Cambridge: Cambridge University Press, 1987).

Milnes, Tim, *Knowledge and Indifference in English Romantic Prose* (Cambridge: Cambridge University Press, 2003).
Miyawaki, Masataka, *James Harris's Theory of Universal Grammar* (Münster: Nodus Publikationen, 2002).
Natarajan. Uttara, *Hazlitt and the Reach of Sense: Criticism, Morals, and the Metaphysics of Power* (Oxford: Clarendon Press, 1998).
Natarajan, Uttara, Paulin, Tom, and Wu, Duncan, *Metaphysical Hazlitt: Bicentenary Essays* (London: Routledge, 2005).
Nattrass, Leonora, *William Cobbett: The Politics of Style* (Cambridge: Cambridge University Press, 1995).
Newman, Gerald, *The Rise of English Nationalism: A Cultural History, 1720-1830*, revised ed. (New York: Saint Martin's Press, 1997).
Nuchelmans, Gabriel, 'The Historical Background to Locke's Account of Particles', *Logique et Analyse*, 29 (1986), 53-71.
Ott, Walter R., *Locke's Philosophy of Language* (Cambridge: Cambridge University Press, 2004).
Page, Anthony, *John Jebb and the Enlightenment Origins of British Radicalism* (Westport Conn.: Greenwood Press, 2003).
Park, Roy, *Hazlitt and the Spirit of the Age: Abstraction and Critical Theory* (Oxford: Clarendon Press, 1971).
Paulin, Tom, *The Day-Star of Liberty: William Hazlitt's Radical Style* (London: Faber & Faber, 1998).
Paulin, Tom and Chandler, David (eds.), *The Fight and Other Essays* (London: Penguin, 2000)
Pearson, Hesketh, *The Fool of Love (a Life of William Hazlitt)* (London: H. Hamilton, 1934).
Philp, Mark, 'The Fragmented Ideology of Reform' in Philp 1991, 50-77.
—— (ed.), *The French Revolution and British Popular Culture* (Cambridge: Cambridge University Press, 1991).
Poole, William, 'Francis Lodwick's Creation: Theology and Natural Philosophy in the Early Royal Society', *Journal of the History of Ideas*, 66:2 (2005), 245-263.
Priestley, John Boynton, *William Hazlitt* (London: Longman, 1960)
Probyn, Clive T., *The Sociable Humanist: The Life and Works of James Harris 1709-1780, Provincial and Metropolitan Culture in Eighteenth-century England* (Oxford: Clarendon Press, 1991).
Pullum, Geoffrey K., 'Lowth's Grammar: A Re-Evaluation', *Linguistics* 137 (1974), 63-78.
Reddick, Allen, *The Making of Johnson's Dictionary, 1746-1773*, revised ed. (Cambridge: Cambridge University Press, 1996).
Reiman, Donald H. and Fraistat, Neil (eds.), *The Complete Poetry of Percy Bysshe Shelley*, 2 vols. (Baltimore and London: The Johns Hopkins University Press, 2000).
Salmon, Nicholas, *The First Principles of English Grammar* (London, 1798).
Salmon, Vivian, *The Works of Francis Lodwick: a Study of his Writings in the Intellectual Context of the Seventeenth Century* (London: Longman, 1972).
Schmitz, Robert Morell, *Hugh Blair* (New York: King's Crown, 1948).
Schneider, Elizabeth, *The Aesthetics of William Hazlitt: a Study of the Philosophical Basis of his Criticism* (Philadelphia, Pa., London: University of Pennsylvania Press, Humphrey Milford, 1933).

Shattock, Joanne, and Wolff, Michael, (eds.), *The Victorian Periodical Press: Sampling and Sounding* (Leicester and Toronto: Leicester University Press and University of Toronto Press, 1982).
Sikes, Herschel Moreland, Bonner, William Hallam, and Lahey, Gerald, (eds.), *The Letters of William Hazlitt* (London and Basingstoke: The Macmillan Press Ltd, 1979).
Slaughter, Mary, *Universal Languages and Scientific Taxonomy in the Seventeenth Century* (Cambridge: Cambridge University Press, 1982).
Smith, Adam, *The Theory of Moral Sentiments* (Edinburgh and London: printed for A. Miller, A. Kincaid, and J. Bell, 1759).
Smith, Olivia, *The Politics of Language: 1791-1819* (Oxford: Clarendon Press, 1984).
Sorensen, Knud, *Charles Dickens: Linguistic Innovator* (Arkona: Aarhus: 1985).
Stephenson, William, *William Hazlitt and Hackney College* (London: The Lindley Press, 1930).
Tomalin, Marcus, ' "...to this rule there are many exceptions": Robert Maunsell and the Grammar of Maori', *Historiographia Linguistica*, 33:3 (2006), 303-334.
——, ' "Vulgarisms and Broken English": The Familiar Perspicuity of William Hazlitt', *Romanticism* 13:1 (2007), 28-52.
——, ' "The new-invented patent-lamp of etymology": Hazlitt, Horne Tooke, and the Philosophy of Language', *Eighteenth-Century Studies* 42:1 (2008), 61-90.
Turley, Richard Marggraf, *The Politics of Language in Romantic Literature* (Basingstoke: Palgrave Macmillan, 2002).
Turnbull, Andrew, *Biographia Epistolaris: being the biographical supplement of Coleridge's Biographia Literaria; with additional letters, etc.*, 2 vols. (London: G. Bell and Sons, Ltd, 1911).
van Ostade, Ingrid Tieken-Boon (ed.), *Two Hundred Years of Lindley Murray* (Münster: Nodus Publikationen, 1996).
——, 'Robert Dodsley and the Genesis of Lowth's Short Introduction to English Grammar', *Historiographia Linguistica* 27:1 (2000), 21-36.
van Rooten, Luis, *Mots D'Heures: Gousses, Rames* (New York: Grossman, 1967).
Wilcox, Stewart Conger, *Hazlitt in the Workshop: The Manuscript of The Fight* (Baltimore: The John's Hopkins Press, 1943).
Winchester, Caleb Thomas, *A Group of Essayists of the Early nineteenth Century* (New York: The Macmillan Company, 1910).
Waller, Alfred Rayney, and Glover, Arnold (eds.), *The Collected Works of William Hazlitt* (London: J.M. Dent, 1902).
Walzer, Arthur E., *George Campbell: Rhetoric in the Age of Enlightenment* (Albany: State University of New York Press, 2003).
Wardle, Ralph Martin, *Hazlitt* (Lincoln: University of Nebraska Press, 1971).
Wright, Laura, (ed.) *The Development of Standard English, 1300-1800: Theories, Descriptions, Conflicts* (Cambridge: Cambridge University Press, 2000).

Index

Aarsleff, Hans, 64, 84, 167, 172, 173
abbreviation, 37, 38, 66–68, 79–81, 83, 84, 110, 111, 145, 146, 172
Aberdeen, 53
ablatives, 83
abnegatives, 83
abstract nouns, 69, 81, 88, 89, 92
abstract reasoning, 110
abstraction, 18, 76, 79, 81, 111, 146, 167
accusative case, 134
active voice, 41
actors, 120, 148
Addison, Thomas, 17, 54, 96
adjectives, 34, 41, 50, 69, 74, 79, 110, 126, 144, 169
adjunctives, 83
adverbs, 41, 50, 67, 69, 104, 124, 166
adversatives, 83
aesthetics, 18, 89
affectation, 98, 111, 119, 140
affixation, 9, 80, 105
agriculture, 49
Albrecht, William Prince, 18
Alford, Henry, 153, 154, 162, 179
algebra, 61
algorithms, 137
allegory, 160
alliteration, 105, 106, 112
allusions, 2, 3, 17, 82, 98, 111, 113, 121, 127, 142, 145
alphabets, 43
amateurs, 162
ambiguity, 28, 30, 31, 34
ambivalence, 74, 97, 100, 130, 131
America, 42, 44, 155, 159, 161–163
American English, 162, 163
Ammonius, 33
analogy, 2, 19, 27, 32, 47, 77, 82, 142, 152
anecdotes, 15, 73, 128, 143

Anglican Church, The, 39
Anglo Saxon, 38, 70, 153, 157, 173
anomalies, 47, 83
antecedents, 25, 33, 107, 124, 125, 132, 173
anthologies, 44
anti-empiricism, 89
Anti-Jacobin Review and Magazine, The, 57, 96
anti-Jacobinism, 58
antiquarianism, 70
Apelles, 166
Arbuthnot, John, 11
Arcadia, 4
archaisms, 112
aristocracy, 51, 117
Aristotle, 30, 33, 52, 63, 67, 100, 172
arithmetic, 62
art, 33, 91, 102, 104, 118, 131
articles, 34, 41, 107, 125
Articles of Religion, The, 5
artificial languages, 30, 31, 35
artificial memory, 6
artificial rules, 9
artificiality, 11, 13, 130, 131, 141, 145–147, 151–154
artisans, 72
artists, 33, 72
artlessness, 149
arts, 52, 53, 94
Asia, 56
Astarloa, Pablo Pedro de, 156
Augustan period, The, 130
Australia, 83
authority
    intellectual, 1
    linguistic, 1, 28, 38, 42, 44, 100, 106, 110, 119, 123, 125, 156, 158, 161
    literary, 54, 129, 161
    pedagogic, 3

Index

Babel, 167
bad grammar, 138
Bagehot, Walter, 15
Baker, Herschel, 18, 167
Banchory, 53
bankers, 72
Banks, Joseph, 51
barbarisms, 149
Barcus, James E., 175
Barnard, John, 131, 178
Barnes, William, 156–158, 179
base-forms, 166
Basileus, 4
Basque, 156
Bate, W. Jackson, 178
Baudelaire, Charles, 149
Beadon, Richard, 37
Beauclerc, Topham, 143, 144
beauty, 105, 116, 141
Beck, Cave, 30
belles lettres, 23, 55, 171
belletristic rhetoric, 19, 22, 23, 28, 52, 57, 112–114, 139
Belsham, Thomas, 21, 61
Bentham, Jeremy, 21, 60
Bergheaud, Patrice, 168, 173
Berkeley, George, 10, 60, 66, 86
Bewley, Christina, 72, 169
Bewley, David, 72, 169
Bex, Tony, 169
Bible, The, 39, 61, 120, 125, 167
bigotry, 135, 137
bilingualism, 44, 165
biography, 17–20, 72, 169, 171
Bishopsgate, 4
Blackwood's Magazine, 97
Blair, Hugh, 23, 52, 54–58, 104–108, 110, 112, 113, 117, 129, 130, 161, 171, 176
blockheads, 117
Blount, Thomas, 45
Bonhours, Dominique, 52
Bonner, William, 166
Booth, David, 49–51, 74–77, 79, 88, 165, 171, 173
Boswell, James, 143, 144
botany, 5, 51
Bowles, William Lisle, 130
boxing, 115
Britain, 44, 51, 56, 151, 154, 162
British Constitution, The, 5
British Isles, The, 156
Bromwich, David, 19, 60, 127, 128, 167, 177
Brown, Goold, 159–162, 180
Browne, Sir Thomas, 149
Browning, Robert, 148

Burdett, Sir Francis, 37
Burke, Edmund, 19, 96, 140, 167
burlesque, 1, 123
Butler, Samuel, 129, 160, 161, 178
Byron, Lord George Gordon, 57, 95, 97, 131

Cadell, Thomas, 55
Caesar, Julius, 34
Caliban, 2, 119, 120
Calvinism, 53
Cambridge, 35, 116
Cambridge University, 166
Campbell, George, 23, 52–54, 58, 104–108, 110, 112, 113, 171
Canterbury, 39
Cardinal Richelieu, 170
Carley, Kathleen, 51, 171
Cartwright, John, 70, 173
case-systems, 50, 132–134, 137, 158
categorematic words, 67, 172
categories, 27, 30, 31, 34, 35, 41, 43, 50, 64, 75, 85, 88, 169
Cawdrey, Robert, 45
censure, 48
centenary, 16
centos, 13
Central America, 56
Chandler, David, 121, 127, 175, 177
Chandler, Emma, 17
Chappell, Vere, 172
Chaucer, Geoffrey, 96
chemisty, 5
childhood, 4
children, 1, 10, 29, 42, 62, 153
Christ, 39
Christ's Hospital, 6
Christmas, 62, 166
chronicles, 152
Church, The, 46, 58, 138
Cicero, 6, 7, 33
ciphering, 6
Clarence House, 137, 138
classical authors, 6, 33, 52, 54
classical education, 7, 62
classical heritage, 33
classical languages, 4–6, 118
classical metre, 13
classicism, 157
classicists, 72, 118, 162
classification, 69, 116
classrooms, 30, 44, 63
clauses, 4, 34, 36, 67, 76, 103, 104, 132, 133, 141
Cleghorn, Thomas, 148, 149, 179
clergy, 138
closed-class categories, 169

coarseness, 140
Cobbett, William, 119
Cockney School, The, 97, 120
Cockneyisms, 135
Cohen, Murray, 168
Coleridge, Samuel Taylor, 3, 71, 73, 95, 130, 131, 178
Colet, John, 4
Collins, Philip, 179
colloquialisms, 13, 143, 144, 151, 152
colonialisation, 83
comedy, 123
common sense, 90, 91, 97, 118, 137, 175
common usage, 9, 28, 41, 46, 48, 98, 109, 111, 114, 117–119, 134, 140, 142, 143, 145, 153, 154
common words, 11
communication, 28, 29
comparatives, 124
complex ideas, 27, 85
compounds, 77
concepts, 64, 87
conditionals, 83
conjugations, 4
conjunctions, 27, 34–37, 41, 43, 64, 67–69, 75–78, 81–83, 88, 101, 118, 132, 136, 169, 173
conjunctives, 83
connectives, 34
constellations, 86, 117
constitutional history, 70
continuatives, 35, 83
contradictions, 64, 65, 69, 84, 90, 160
conversation, 11, 13, 28, 29, 37, 72, 73, 98, 103, 111, 113, 115, 125, 128, 131, 140, 141, 143–145, 147, 153
copula verbs, 108
copulatives, 43, 73, 82, 83
Corrie, John, 61
corruption, 57, 70, 83
counter-examples, 43
Cox, Jeffrey, 58, 97
Cram, David, 168
Creation, The, 168
criticism, 122, 127, 128, 131–137
  linguistic, 97
  literary, 18, 23, 52, 144, 147
  political, 96
  pro-Tory, 12, 138
  the French tradition, 16
critics
  and quotation, 127
  common-place, 114
  disciplinarians, 148
  Hazlittians, 7, 77, 121
  in the nineteenth century, 148, 154
  literary, 7

  subcategories of, 12
Tories, 12, 52, 97, 114, 120, 134, 135, 137–140, 149
ultra-crepidarians, 166
Croker, John Wilson, 100
Crombie, Alexander, 155
Cromie, Robert, 116, 119, 120, 144, 177
culture, 30, 51, 70, 82, 94, 97, 114, 136, 138, 156, 163, 171
customs, 17

Dalgarno, George, 30, 168
Danish, 38
Darwin, Erasmus, 21, 131
de Brosse, Charles, 66
De Quincey, Thomas, 3, 15, 127, 131, 151–156, 158, 162, 177, 179
de Salignac, François, 52
debates, 3, 58, 66, 73, 94
Dechamps, Jules, 16
declaratives, 83
declensions, 4, 5
defects, 32, 79, 81, 110, 111, 118, 146
definitions, 14, 20, 32, 38, 41, 46, 53, 54, 62, 80, 97, 99, 102, 104, 106, 107, 116, 119, 144, 158
Defoe, Daniel, 149
deformity, 132
deities, 69, 101
DeMaria, Robert, 170
democracy, 70
Demosthenes, 6
Denham, John, 109
destiny, 69
dialects, 45, 79, 119, 121, 152, 153
dialogue, 37, 145
diaries, 165
diatribes, 135
dichotomies, 114
Dickens, Charles, 175
  Martin Chuzzlewit, 148, 149
  and ungrammaticality, 149
  and William Hazlitt, 15, 150
  and William Makepeace Thackeray, 148
diction, 17, 115, 130, 131, 134, 151, 153
dictionaries, 22, 44–46, 49, 101, 119, 120, 155, 165, 166, 170, 177
diffusion, 49
direct objects, 109, 132–134
discipline, 1, 29, 159
discourse, 28, 51, 54, 78, 98, 104, 105, 111, 115, 124, 126, 152
discoveries, 8, 73, 81
disjunctives, 67, 82, 83
Divine Right of Kings, The, 137, 138
divinity, 53, 162

doctrines, 137, 157, 158
Dodsley, Robert, 169
doggerel, 101
dogmatism, 85
Douady, Jules, 16, 167
drama, 143, 147
dramatists, 145
Dryden, John, 17, 41, 42, 54, 80, 108, 128
Dunning, John, 36, 169
Dutch, 38

eccentricity, 155
Edinburgh, 54, 55
education, 4–7, 38, 42, 43, 45, 52, 62, 72, 95, 138, 154, 172
effeminacy, 141
egalitarian, 70
elegance, 41, 49, 72, 76, 103, 114, 118, 122, 126, 130, 131, 133, 142
elision, 160
Elizabethan period, The, 168
ellipsis, 114, 145
eloquence, 13, 15, 53, 54, 96, 116
Emery, John, 119–121, 177
empiricism, 18, 20–22, 26, 33, 34, 37, 50, 60, 64–66, 71, 76, 78, 79, 85, 89–91
energy, 19, 89, 122
Enfield, William, 93
Engell, James, 178
England, 42, 52, 70, 168
English grammar, 1, 3, 7, 9, 40, 41, 61, 91, 98, 99, 137, 156
English language, The
    abuses of, 3, 12, 40, 47, 84, 122
    American varieties, 163
    and classical languages, 6, 27, 34, 83, 99, 117, 118, 155–158
    and German, 48
    and literature, 48, 52, 54, 104, 124, 155
    and pedagogy, 8, 10, 38, 42, 56, 101
    and politics, 137, 162
    and style, 105, 107, 117, 153, 154
    British varieties, 163
    its historical development, 157
    pedagogy, 155
    the structure of, 8, 10, 23, 39, 40, 44, 83, 98, 99, 158
English literature, 10, 48, 49, 52
Enlightenment, The, 53, 171
Entick, John, 101
epigrams, 107, 130
epigraph, 1, 178
epistemology, 64, 89, 90
errors, 83, 100, 123, 128, 135, 155, 156, 161

ethics, 53
ethnography, 2, 70
Eton, 35
etymology, 2, 21, 36, 37, 43, 48, 50, 51, 65, 68–71, 74, 75, 77, 79, 81, 82, 85–89, 91, 92, 99, 100, 155, 160
Europe, 16, 44, 51, 56, 170, 174
evangelisation, 42
evil, 152
explorers, 51

false morality, 69
familiar style, 17, 23, 56, 94, 95, 98, 103, 110–114, 116–119, 121, 125, 126, 140–142, 150, 174
fancy, 91, 130, 138
fashions, 17, 72
fate, 69, 87
Ferreria-Buckley, Linda, 52, 171
Fifeshire, 49
figurative language, 140, 145
forests, 51
Forfarshire, 49
forgery, 36
Fraistat, Neil, 175
France, 16
Frank, Elizabeth, 170
French, 16, 34, 48, 52, 56, 127
French poetry, 130
French Revolution, The, 96, 140
function words, 67
Fuseli, John Henry, 73, 173

Galileans, 120
Gallicisms, 107
games, 37, 63
gardens, 4, 46, 47, 51
gender, 38, 102, 103, 109, 115, 124, 133, 153
genealogy, 39
general knowledge, 4
Genesis, 167
genitive case, 99, 131, 132, 158
genius, 48, 62, 90, 118, 135, 138
genres, 30, 38, 39, 93, 102–104, 108, 109, 111, 123
gentry, 138
geography, 62
geometry, 61
German, 38, 48, 56
gesture, 72
ghosts, 76
gibberish, 119
Gifford, William, 12, 19, 57, 116, 137–141, 148, 166, 167
gifts, 72, 150
glossing, 82

Glover, Arnold, 16
God, 161
Godwin, William, 8–10, 14, 29, 46, 71, 99, 154, 165, 168, 173, 174
government, 36, 40, 57, 58, 129
grace, 130
grammar textbooks, 39
  and belletristic rhetoric, 19, 22, 112, 139
  and classical languages, 157
  and grammatical categories, 75
  and Lindley Murray, 23, 43, 44, 94, 102, 113, 122, 125, 126, 156
  and literature, 48, 128
  and pedagogy, 2, 8, 23, 44, 45, 74, 84, 93, 98, 101, 137, 156
  and philosophical grammars, 30, 35, 57, 93
  and Robert Lowth, 39, 40, 42, 64, 94, 103, 122, 126
  characteristics of the genre, 38, 39
  in North America, 163
  in the nineteenth century, 23, 159, 160, 162
  William Hazlitt's *Grammar*, 1, 10, 73, 80, 134
grammar-schools, 4, 6, 32, 118
grammarians, 14, 35, 38, 39, 42, 63, 68, 82–84, 94, 99, 101, 112, 117, 123, 125, 154, 155, 159, 162, 163
grammatical accuracy, 122
grammatical agreement, 133
grammatical analysis, 1, 4, 6, 9, 17, 42, 60–64, 75, 78, 84, 88, 157, 162
grammatical categories, 64
grammatical construction, 129
grammatical errors, 123, 128
grammatical exercises, 44
grammatical number, 133
grammatical principles, 43, 81
grammatical roles, 37, 66, 67, 158
grammatical rules, 4, 9, 43, 58, 109, 110, 123, 124, 131–133, 136, 148
grammatical structure, 5, 8, 11, 18, 43, 161
grammatical systems, 2, 75
grammatical theory, 38, 75, 100, 113, 155
grammaticality, 12, 43, 101–104, 106, 108, 109, 114, 123, 134, 135, 137, 141
grave style, 125
Grayling, A.C., 19, 93, 172, 175
Greece, 43, 158
Greek, 4, 6, 7, 10, 34, 50, 52, 61, 62, 69, 83, 98, 118, 134, 155–159
Griffin, Robert J., 178

Grose, Francis, 177

Hackney New College, 61, 82, 93, 172
Halloran, Michael, 52, 171
Hamilton, Paul, 78, 174
Hampshire, 39
hard words, 46
Hardy, Thomas, 36
Harley, Robert, 40
Harris, James, 22, 32–35, 38, 40, 41, 61, 63, 64, 68, 71, 75, 82–84, 91, 100, 168, 173, 175
Harris, Robert, 57, 171
Hawthorne, Nathaniel, 149
Hazlitt, William
  Characters of Shakespear's Plays, 10
  Essay on the Principles of Human Action, 8, 18, 20, 65
  Grammar, 1, 8–10, 14, 17, 18, 20, 23, 73, 80, 99, 100, 111, 127, 128, 134, 146, 154
  Lectures on English Philosophy, 10, 17, 20, 25, 65, 87, 92
  Lectures on the English Comic Writers, 10
  Lectures on the English Poets, 10
  Lectures on the Literature of the Age of Elizabeth, 10
  Spirit of the Age, 82, 85, 100, 156
  Table Talk, 12
  The Eloquence of the British Senate, 8, 13
  The Plain Speaker, 13
  The Round Table, 12
  'A Letter to William Gifford, Esq.', 12, 116, 137
  'English Grammar', 1, 3, 84, 156
  'On Common-Place Critics', 12, 114
  'On Criticism', 12
  'On Dryden and Pope', 134
  'On Familiar Style', 12, 17, 18, 95, 98, 111, 113, 114, 142
  'On Genius and Common Sense', 90
  'On Milton's Sonnets', 12
  'On Pedantry', 12
  'On Shakespeare and Milton', 145
  'On the Aristocracy of Letters', 117
  'On the Conversation of Authors', 13, 73
  'On the Difference between Writing and Speaking', 13
  'On the Disadvantages of Intellectual Superiority', 128, 166
  'On the Ignorance of the Learned', 62, 139, 178
  'On The Periodical Essayists', 141
  'On the Prose-Style of Poets', 13, 134

'On the Question Whether Pope was a Poet', 131
'On Vulgarity and Affectation', 12, 95, 119
'The Fight', 17, 115, 116, 177
'The Late Mr Horne Tooke', 63
and abstract ideas, 86, 89
and Alexander Pope, 131–137, 141
and allusions, 127
and belletristic rhetoric, 52, 54, 56, 110, 112
and Charles Dickens, 150
and Charles Lamb, 5, 10
and classical languages, 118
and common sense, 90, 91, 175
and conjunctions, 75
and conversation, 145
and David Booth, 75, 88, 173
and Edmund Burke, 96, 140
and education, 3
and empiricism, 18, 20, 78, 85, 89
and epistemology, 89
and etymology, 74, 75, 79, 81, 88
and gender, 82
and Goold Brown, 160–162
and grammar textbooks, 93, 99, 101, 102, 108, 133, 156, 158, 159
and grammatical rules, 109, 132–134, 137
and Hackney New College, 62, 172
and Hugh Blair, 56
and idealism, 60, 65
and idioms, 23, 79–81, 111, 117, 145–147
and Immanuel Kant, 89, 174
and indeclinable words, 78, 79
and James Harris, 35, 41, 75, 168
and John Arbuthnot, 11
and John Emery, 177
and John Horne Tooke, 10, 16, 21, 22, 37, 43, 60, 63–65, 71–74, 76, 82–89, 91, 92, 98
and John Locke, 25, 26
and John Thelwall, 72
and John Wilson Croker, 100
and journalism, 150
and Laurence Sterne, 13
and Leigh Hunt, 120
and lexicography, 49
and Lindley Murray, 99, 100, 102, 108–110, 114, 117, 128, 133
and linguistic authority, 128, 129
and linguistic reform, 1
and linguistic registers, 119, 121
and linguistic theory, 7, 11, 15, 17, 19–23, 25, 57, 59, 60, 63, 64, 74,
77, 78, 84, 92, 97, 120, 122, 148, 158, 159
and literary criticism, 7, 12, 19, 23, 121, 128, 137, 140–142, 147
and literary registers, 134
and literature, 2, 7, 126
and metaphor, 92
and metaphysics, 85–87, 92
and Michel de Montaigne, 19
and objectivism, 90
and pedagogy, 1, 3, 61
and philology, 21, 60, 157
and philosophical grammar, 23, 32, 61, 63, 93
and philosophy, 18, 20, 22, 86, 89, 90
and primitivism, 82
and radicalism, 52
and relativism, 90
and Robert Louis Stevenson, 149, 150
and Robert Lowth, 63, 93, 99, 100, 102, 108–110, 113, 117, 128, 133, 136
and Samuel Butler, 161, 178
and Samuel Johnson, 141–144
and semantic theory, 77
and stylistic registers, 18, 52, 125, 126, 140
and the Cockney School, 57, 97
and the familiar style, 17, 23, 94, 98, 102, 104, 108–110, 112, 113, 116, 117, 121, 150, 154, 176
and Thomas De Quincey, 127, 152, 155, 156
and Thomas Heywood, 145
and Thomas Hobbes, 26
and Tory critics, 12, 43, 96, 135, 139, 149, 175
and ultra-crepidarian critics, 166
and verbal critics, 12, 149
and vulgarity, 95, 97, 110, 114, 116, 143
and William Enfield, 93
and William Gifford, 19, 138, 139, 141
and William Godwin, 29, 174
and William Shakespeare, 120, 146, 147
his biography, 7, 61, 63, 93, 174
his death, 16, 23, 155, 156
his eloquence, 15
his influence, 148, 149, 154, 158, 159, 163
his prose style, 17–19, 96, 115, 117, 118, 120, 121, 127, 141, 150
language and politics, 95
on speech and writing, 13
reception history, 13–16, 18, 20, 150, 154–156, 163

Hazlitt, William Carew, 8, 10, 14–16, 165, 166
Hazlitt, William Jnr, 14
Heaven, 69, 117, 132
Hebrew, 39, 61
Hell, 69
Hepworth, Brian, 169
heresy, 2
heritage, 125
hexameters, 13
Heywood, Thomas, 144–146
hierarchy, 34, 39
hieroglyphics, 73, 145
Higgins, David, 115, 177
history, 56, 70, 162, 163
Hobbes, Thomas, 10, 25, 26, 60, 167
holiness, 123
holy orders, 35
Homer, 6, 7, 129–132, 178
homophony, 7
honours, 62
Horace, 6, 52
Horne Tooke, John
   Diversions, 2, 16, 22, 36, 37, 63, 80, 86
   'A Letter to John Dunning, Esq.', 36, 169
   and abbreviation, 37, 38, 66, 67, 79, 172
   and abstraction, 69, 89
   and antiquarianism, 70
   and common sense, 90, 91
   and David Booth, 50, 77
   and deduction, 91
   and empiricism, 21, 64, 66, 71, 76, 90
   and etymology, 21, 37, 38, 43, 65, 68, 70, 71, 74, 77, 88, 89, 91, 92, 99
   and idioms, 79, 80, 111, 146
   and imperfection, 81
   and indeclinable words, 79
   and James Harris, 38, 64, 71, 100
   and John Dunning, 169
   and John Locke, 66–68, 86
   and John Thelwall, 72
   and John Wilkes, 65
   and linguistic theory, 3, 14, 16, 37, 63, 66–68, 70, 72, 73, 75–77, 81, 82, 84, 87, 172, 173
   and metaphysics, 10, 85–88, 90, 92
   and morality, 69
   and pedagogy, 2
   and philology, 73, 86, 91, 98
   and philosophical grammar, 60, 61
   and philosophy, 71, 74, 87
   and primitivism, 82, 83
   and relativism, 90
   and Samuel Taylor Coleridge, 71
   and subaudition, 69
   and the sciences, 76, 84
   and William Hazlitt, 60, 63–65, 72–75, 81, 82, 84–86, 90, 98, 100, 156
   and William Tooke, 36
   his biography, 35, 36, 72, 169, 173
   his conversation, 73
   his education, 35
   his influence, 17, 18, 20–22, 63, 77
   his radicalism, 2
House, Madeline, 179
Howe, Percival Presland, 16, 17, 20, 165, 167
Howell, Samuel, 171
humanism, 168
Hume, David, 29, 60, 66
humour, 54
Hunt, Leigh, 3, 6, 7, 14, 43, 52, 57, 95, 97, 120, 135, 139, 150, 165, 166, 175
hunting, 46
husbandry, 46
Hutchinson, Henry, 157, 158, 179
hyperbole, 145
hypercorrectness, 110, 111, 146

idealism, 20, 21, 29, 60, 65, 71, 78, 89
ideas
   abstract, 85–87, 89
   and empiricism, 50
   and idioms, 80, 110, 146, 149
   and logic, 135
   and meaning, 11, 28, 50, 77, 78
   and things, 27, 78
   and words, 9, 27, 32, 50, 56, 79, 80, 85, 86, 106–108, 112, 117, 176
   complex, 27, 28, 50, 67
   particular, 86
   simple, 27
ideational ontology, 27
ideologies, 57, 66, 97, 102
ideology, 139, 151, 162
idiomatic style, 13
idioms
   and colloquialisms, 13, 151, 152
   and literature, 23, 48, 145, 147, 149
   and slang, 115, 116
   and ungrammaticality, 79
   and vulgarity, 95, 97
   bookish, 152
   common, 17, 79, 98, 111, 117, 144, 145, 147
   definition of, 80
   Edmund Burke's use of, 141
   John Arbuthnot's use of, 11
   John Horne Tooke's advocacy of, 80, 111

Laurence Sterne's use of, 13
new, 147
Thomas De Quincey's advocacy of, 152
William Hazlitt's advocacy of, 79–81, 84, 110, 111, 114, 116, 117, 146, 147
William Hazlitt's use of, 23
idiosyncracies, 44, 153
ignorance, 3, 5, 45, 47, 81, 118, 119, 135, 137
Iliad, The, 130, 135, 136
illogicality, 158
illusions, 81
images, 50, 135, 145, 166
imagination, 3, 53, 82, 135, 140
imperatives, 69
imperfect tense, 100
imperfection, 28, 40, 47, 81, 135, 136, 178
impropriety, 47, 136
inconsistency, 85, 158
indeclinable words, 21, 22, 65, 75, 78, 79, 82, 84, 85, 88, 92
independence, 104
individuals, 151
infancy, 4, 80
infinitives, 87
inflections, 14
informal style, 7
informality, 143, 144
inspiration, 117
intellect, 1, 4, 130
intellectualism, 73
intellectuals, 35, 51, 57, 71
intelligibility, 158
interjections, 41
interrogatives, 83
inversions, 109, 132–134
Ireland, Alexander, 14, 150, 166
irony, 55, 82, 97, 118, 129, 161
irrationality, 158
irregular verbs, 99, 100
irregularities, 44, 47, 107
Islip, 42
Isocrates, 52
Italian, 56
italics, 115, 116, 119, 120, 144, 178
Italy, 16

Japan, 44
jargon, 62, 69, 119, 121, 135
Jebb, John, 70, 173
Jeffrey, Francis, 148
Jesus, 120
Johnson, Samuel, 17, 46–49, 51, 79, 80, 120, 121, 134, 141–144, 155, 170

jokes, 6, 149
Jones, Frederick, 175
Jones, Stanley, 8, 19, 165, 172
Jonson, Ben, 155
journalese, 153
journalism, 24, 72, 150–153
journals, 97, 153
judgement, 36, 109, 116, 120, 142
justice, 117
Justice of the Peace, 32

Kames, Lord, 52, 160
Kant, Immanuel, 89, 174
Kaufer, David, 51, 171
Keach, William, 22, 95, 110, 175
Keats, John, 95, 97, 135
Kennetles, 49
Kersey, John, 45, 46, 48, 165, 166, 170
King James Version, The, 125, 128
kings, 4
knowledge, 5, 35, 40, 46, 49, 63, 93, 137, 138

l'Académie française, 40
Lahey, Gerald, 166
Lamb, Charles, 3, 4, 6, 10, 15, 149, 155, 165, 177
Land, Stephen, 76, 173
Langton, Bennet, 143
language planning, 31, 34, 35
language teaching , 5
languages, 9, 61, 62
Lass, Roger, 169
Latin, 4–6, 27, 34, 52, 61, 69, 83, 98, 99, 118, 127, 134, 142, 143, 155–159
latinists, 4
Lavoisier, Antoine, 76
law, 32, 35, 36, 53, 87, 126
laws, 31, 32, 71, 134, 142
lawyers, 42
learned style, 11
legal style, 126
Leigh, Percival, 162
letters, 37, 43, 71, 93, 95, 99, 116, 118, 150
lexicography, 9, 29, 44–49, 51, 57, 92, 101, 119, 143
lexicon, 45, 120, 153
liberty, 34
Lily, William, 4
Linacre, Thomas, 4
Lindley Murray, 133
linguistic analysis, 2, 7, 10, 27, 30, 33, 35, 37, 41, 47, 56, 61, 64, 69, 75, 78, 81, 88, 96, 100, 154, 168
linguistic categories, 31, 50
linguistic conventions, 151, 160

linguistic forms, 151
linguistic games, 165
linguistic imperfection, 28–32, 40, 47, 81
linguistic laws, 32
linguistic phenomena, 64
linguistic registers, 12, 94, 119, 152
linguistic structure, 3, 8, 10, 29, 30, 34, 37, 41, 79, 85, 97, 102, 105, 113, 127, 132, 134, 140, 145, 146, 148, 153
linguistic systems, 70
linguistic theory
  and belletristic rhetoric, 51
  and complexity, 83
  and diversity, 4, 26
  and empiricism, 21, 71
  and etymology, 68
  and James Harris, 34, 35
  and John Horne Tooke, 10, 20, 36, 37, 63, 74, 82, 92
  and John Locke, 29
  and lexicography, 92
  and Lindley Murray, 42
  and literary criticism, 23
  and literature, 94, 122
  and philosophy, 8, 22, 26, 30, 33, 38, 60, 66, 71, 85, 89
  and politics, 65
  and rhetoric, 52
  and Romanticism, 3, 21, 22, 25, 28, 39, 57, 168
  and science, 33
  and William Hazlitt, 7, 12, 15, 18–20, 22, 23, 25, 49, 60, 63, 92, 97, 98, 147, 163
  in the eighteenth century, 48, 57, 122
linguistic universals, 30–32, 34, 35
linguistics, 84, 155, 159, 161, 163, 168
linguists, 31, 51, 146
Linnaeus, Carolus, 76
literacy, 51
literalism, 26, 81, 82
literary canon, 128
literary conventions, 11
literary criticism, 7, 18, 23, 43, 121, 122, 127, 128, 137, 141, 147
literary forms, 58, 122, 123, 125, 126, 144
literary fragments, 128
literary judgements, 12
literary registers, 12
literary style, 13, 15, 19, 23, 52, 93, 102–105, 109, 123, 141
literature
  and Alexander Pope, 135
  and belletristic rhetoric, 52

  and grammar textbooks, 48, 101, 123, 126, 160
  and Lindley Murray, 43, 125
  and linguistic theory, 94, 148
  and Robert Louis Stevenson, 150
  and Robert Lowth, 39, 41, 122
  and Samuel Johnson, 48
  and style, 56, 94, 100, 115, 138, 144, 145, 147, 149, 151
  and vulgarity, 95
  and William Hazlitt, 80, 82, 96, 116, 128, 141, 146, 147, 159
  Elizabethan, 144, 168
  French, 48
  in the nineteenth century, 148
Locke, John, 10, 25–29, 31–35, 37, 38, 47, 50, 60, 66–68, 75, 76, 81, 85, 86, 90, 91, 167, 168, 172, 173
Lockhart, John Gibson, 57, 135, 137, 148
Lodwick, Francis, 30, 168
logic, 53, 54, 71, 90, 91, 130, 135
logocentrism, 26
London, 39, 49, 72, 152
Long Island, 42
Longinus, 52
Lowth, Robert
  A Short Introduction, 41, 102, 122
  and grammaticality, 123
  and James Harris, 41, 63, 84, 100, 175
  and Jonathan Swift, 39, 40
  and Lindley Murray, 104, 108
  and literary forms, 122–124
  and pedagogy, 40
  and Samuel Johnson, 47
  and stylistic registers, 23, 102, 103, 110, 112, 114, 117, 176
  and the grammar textbook tradition, 39, 158, 169
  and William Godwin, 8
  and William Hazlitt, 14, 23, 61, 63, 64, 99, 100, 102, 108, 109, 113, 133, 136
  his biography, 39, 169
  his definition of 'grammar', 102
  his influence, 42, 43, 58, 93, 94, 99, 104, 125, 128, 155
  his use of literature, 41, 42, 122–126, 128
loyalty, 58, 129
Lynch, Jack, 170

Maat, Jaap, 168
Macbeth, 82
magazines, 154
mankind, 33, 69
manners, 34, 72, 73, 95, 130, 131

Maori, 170, 174
Marischal College, 53
mass media, 151
materialism, 71, 85
Maunsell, Robert, 170
McDermott, Anne, 170
McKusick, James, 71, 173
Meikle, Henry, 171
metaphors, 56, 92, 121, 130, 145, 146, 158
metaphysics, 10, 20, 22, 53, 54, 71, 85, 87–90, 92, 167
Michael, Ian, 169
Mill, James, 21
Milnes, Tim, 21, 64, 89, 90, 174, 175
Milton, John, 12, 109, 114, 123, 124, 128, 134, 145, 147
Miyawaki, Masataka, 168
monarchy, 4, 5, 58, 65, 138
Monboddo, Lord, 3, 29, 167
monotony, 141
Montaigne, Michel de, 19, 149
moods, 132
morality, 42, 54, 71, 87, 93, 96, 108, 143, 149, 162
morphology, 9, 48, 49, 75, 124, 134, 158
Morton, Thomas, 177
mother-tongue, 45, 142
Mount School, The, 42, 156
Murray, Lindley
  English Grammar, 42, 43, 122
  and belletristic rhetoric, 23, 104–108, 113, 117, 176
  and literary forms, 126
  and morality, 108, 125
  and pedagogy, 43, 44, 101, 156
  and Robert Lowth, 125
  and stylistic registers, 23, 125, 126
  and the grammar textbook tradition, 8, 39, 44, 158
  and William Hazlitt, 8, 14, 23, 61, 99, 100, 102, 108, 109
  criticism of, 156, 162
  his biography, 42
  his definition of 'grammar', 102, 104
  his influence, 42, 44, 58, 93, 94, 99, 101, 102, 112, 149, 155, 160, 161, 170
  his stylistic guidelines, 104–108, 110, 112–114, 117, 176
  his use of literature, 43, 125, 126, 128
Murray, William, 65

Napoleon, 16
Nares, Robert, 155
narratives, 70, 130

Natarajan, Uttara, 20, 21, 60, 64, 65, 78, 167, 174
nationalism, 65, 70, 135
natural language, 2, 3, 20, 22, 23, 25, 26, 29–33, 37, 59, 67, 68, 70, 92, 120, 146
natural philosophy, 53
nature, 50, 131
negligence, 47
neo-Aristotelians, 33
neo-classicism, 77
neuters, 38, 41, 103, 124
New Brentford,, 36
New College, Oxford,, 39
New York, 42, 159
New Zealand, 83
Newburgh, 49
Newman, Gerald, 70, 173
newspapers, 151–154
Newton, 31, 33
Nidditch, Peter, 167
nominalism, 86
nominals, 69
nominative case, 132, 158, 161
nonsense, 71, 84, 133
North America, 83, 154
noun phrases, 34, 118
nouns, 5, 34, 43, 44, 50, 67, 69, 74–77, 79, 81, 85, 87–89, 92, 119, 120, 125, 126, 132, 134, 144, 149, 169, 173
novels, 15, 63
Nuchelmans, Gabriel, 173

object pronouns, 123
objective case, 132, 158, 161
objectivism, 90
objects, 42, 67, 89
Odyssey, The, 132, 178
Old English, 69, 70
Old Testament, The, 129
ontology, 27, 69
open-class categories, 169
oratory, 8, 13, 73, 98, 111
Orkney Islands, The, 155
ornaments, 11
orthography, 39, 43, 45, 47, 116, 162
Ott, Walter, 172
Oxford, 12, 32, 39, 40
Oxford English Dictionary, The, 144

Page, Anthony, 173
painting, 12, 18, 173
Pamela, 4
paradise, 70
paranomasia, 10
Paris, 16
Park, Roy, 18, 19, 60, 86, 89, 167

parliament, 32, 57, 61, 65
parody, 1, 113
participles, 46, 69, 85, 87, 99, 100
particles, 11, 27, 35, 38, 67, 68, 75, 76, 173
parts-of-speech, 14, 19, 37, 39, 41, 62, 66, 74–76, 78, 81, 85
passive voice, 41
pastoral, 56
patent-lamp, 92
Pater, Walter, 17
patriotism, 65, 155
Paulin, Tom, 20, 82, 121, 127, 167, 172, 174, 175, 177
Pearson, Hesketh, 18
Pecksniff, Miss, 149
pedagogy, 1–4, 6–9, 38, 39, 44, 46, 93, 107, 155, 158
pedantry, 12, 81, 84, 97, 98, 109, 111, 114, 115, 117, 140–142
Pennsylvania, 42
periodicals, 96, 128, 150, 175
periphrasis, 124
personification, 109, 125, 130
perspicuity, 41, 98, 103, 105, 106, 108, 110–114
persuasion, 53
Philoclea, 4
philology, 3, 5, 7, 8, 10, 13, 15–17, 21, 22, 25, 26, 30, 31, 35–38, 44, 60, 65, 72, 73, 75, 86, 91, 92, 98, 146, 154, 155, 157, 162
philosophers, 30, 33, 35, 43, 57, 76, 79, 83
philosophical grammar, 22, 23, 30–32, 35, 38, 40, 57, 59, 60, 63, 64, 68, 83, 91, 93
philosophical idealism, 65
Philosophical Society, The, 53
philosophy, 3, 7, 8, 17, 18, 20, 22, 25–30, 32, 33, 37, 38, 53, 60, 63, 65, 66, 71, 72, 74, 75, 78, 81, 84–91, 102, 168, 171, 172, 175
Pitt 'The Younger', William, 36, 57
plagiarism, 26
Plato, 33, 37, 43
playwrights, 145
Pliny, 166
pneumatics, 5
pneumatology, 53
poetry, 39, 56, 58, 69, 95, 97, 101, 103, 108–111, 118, 124–126, 129–136, 141, 145, 148
poets, 135, 148, 155
polemic, 102
political activism, 36
political ideology, 66

politicians, 56, 72
politics, 11, 19, 20, 29, 43, 48, 57, 58, 65, 70, 72, 80, 95–97, 102, 129, 138, 140, 141, 163, 175
Poole, William, 168
Pope, Alexander, 23, 54, 109, 128–137, 140, 141, 178
Port-Royal, 66
positives, 83
power, 20, 89, 167
pragmatics, 78, 101
pragmatism, 111
precision, 8, 28, 40, 45, 56, 98, 104, 106–108, 111–114
prefixes, 48, 50
prejudice, 3, 76, 81, 129, 137
prepositions, 27, 34, 41, 67, 69, 75–78, 88, 103, 104, 107, 113, 114, 121, 126, 129, 169
presbyterians, 54
prescriptivism, 44, 102, 114, 118
Priestley, John Boynton, 18
Priestley, Joseph, 22, 35, 38, 61, 80, 146, 155, 169
priests, 125
primitive language, 83
primitivism, 82
Prince of Wales, The, 138
Prior, Matthew, 80, 128
Probyn, Clive, 168
pronouns, 19, 36, 41–44, 68, 81, 99, 102, 103, 107, 114, 123–125, 132, 136, 169, 173
pronunciation, 123
propositions, 61
propriety, 11, 28, 56, 79, 98, 102, 104, 106–108, 110, 112–114, 125, 131, 146, 160
prose, 14, 15, 54, 95–97, 103, 108, 109, 112, 113, 117, 118, 121, 122, 124, 126, 127, 131, 132, 134, 141–144, 150, 160, 162
prose style, 11, 15, 17, 19, 49, 54, 97, 98, 102, 115, 117, 118, 121, 140, 143, 144, 149, 150
prosody, 4
prosopopoeia, 103
pseudonyms, 135
psychology, 89
Ptolemaic epicycles, 33
Pullum, Geoffrey, 169
puns, 7
purity, 47–49, 54, 56, 83, 98, 104–108, 111–114, 117, 151
Purley Lodge, 36, 37

Index

Quarterly Review, The, 12, 57, 96, 97, 137, 166, 175
Quintilian, 52, 53
quotations, 127

radicalism
   and John Horne Tooke, 36, 72, 169
   and the Cockney School, 52
   heterogeneity of, 59
   linguistic, 2, 3, 69, 83, 157, 159
   philosophical, 21
   political, 2, 43, 58, 65, 70
rationality, 90
reason, 49, 91, 158
Reddick, Allen, 170
reductivism, 64, 66, 68, 79
refinement, 95
reform
   and the Whigs, 58
   educational, 6
   electoral, 58
   heterogeneity of, 59
   linguistic, 2, 3, 9, 40, 47, 58, 155
   political, 36, 58, 65, 70, 138–140
   social and literary, 11
Regency period, The, 14, 15, 136
Reibel, David, 170
Reiman, Donald, 175
relative pronouns, 103, 107, 114, 124, 125, 132, 136
relativism, 90, 116, 123
religion, 5, 42, 43, 125
Renaissance, The, 4, 51
revolution, 36, 42, 57, 89, 96, 140
rhetoric, 8, 22, 23, 51–55, 109, 112, 119, 139, 145, 146, 171
rhetoricians, 28, 52, 57, 112
Rhode Island, 159
rhyme, 134, 135, 137, 141
rhythm, 4, 149
Rollin, Charles, 52
Romanticism
   Alexander Pope's reputation, 178
   and linguistic theory, 3, 7, 57
   and literature, 19
   and philology, 3
   and radicalism, 58
   and socio-politics, 94
   and the imagination, 3
   as a cultural movement, 3, 24
   language and politics, 22, 57
   second generation, 97
Rome, 34, 158
Royalists, 129
rule-breaking, 124

rules, 9, 28, 43, 44, 47, 58, 62, 86, 90, 91, 108–110, 124, 131–134, 136, 138, 139, 142, 149, 158, 166, 170
Rushworth pond, 72
Ruskin, John, 149
Russell Institution, The, 10
Russell, John, 96, 175
Russian, 38, 56

sacrilege, 117
sailors, 120
Salisbury, 32
Salmon, Nicholas, 74, 173
Salmon, Vivian, 168
Sanctius, 33
Scaliger, Joseph, 33, 139
scepticism, 31, 63, 82, 84, 85
Schmitz, Robert, 171
Schneider, Elizabeth, 18
scholars, 9, 39, 45, 72
scholarship, 18, 19, 21, 70, 118, 138, 149
scholasticism, 67, 73, 118
school-children, 1, 9, 62, 63, 73, 94, 100, 154
schoolmasters, 2–5, 7, 8, 49, 138
schools, 1, 4, 6, 9, 155
Schoppe, Caspar, 139
science, 5, 33, 50, 84, 92, 118, 140, 142, 143, 168
scientific methodology, 31
scientific theories, 5
scientists, 72, 76
Scotland, 51, 52, 162
Scotticisms, 107
Scottish Enlightenment, The, 53, 171
sects, 12
secularism, 2
semantic ambiguity, 28
semantic theory, 77
semantics, 27, 36, 67, 75, 77, 79, 80, 134, 146, 158
sensations, 66
sense, 101, 138
sensory perception, 26, 89
sentences, 12, 19, 34, 36, 41, 43, 68, 76, 77, 80, 83, 102, 103, 109, 110, 112, 113, 115, 117, 126, 133–143, 149, 160, 161
sentiment, 4, 95, 130, 131, 145
sentiments, 53
sermons, 54, 160
Shacklewell, 4
Shakespeare, William, 82, 109, 114, 123, 124, 128, 145–147, 176
Shattock, Joanne, 151, 179
Shelley, Percy Bysshe

Original Poetry, by Victor and Cazire, 101
Prometheus Unbound, 97
St. Irvyne: or The Rosicrucian, 97
'Julian and Maddalo', 95
and grammar textbooks, 101
and linguistic vulgarity, 95
and philology, 3
and the Cockney School, 43, 57, 97
and the familiar style, 95
and Tory critics, 96
and ungrammaticality, 97
Sidney, Sir Philip, 48, 128
signification, 11, 28, 29, 67, 68, 77, 107
signs, 68, 71, 117
Sikes, Herschel, 166
simplicity, 50, 83, 84, 98, 112, 113, 119, 130, 145
sin, 26
Skinner, Stephen, 70
slang, 116, 119, 120, 142, 144, 149
Smith, Adam, 29, 52, 167
Smith, Olivia, 21, 173
social structure, 3
society, 11, 28, 34, 42, 70, 116, 130, 131, 151
socio-politics, 3, 5, 7, 8, 11, 12, 18, 29, 46, 70, 94–96, 135, 137–139, 143, 162
sociolects, 121, 151
sociolinguistics, 3, 49, 95, 115, 116
solecisms, 114, 115, 122, 123
solemn style, 126
Sorensen, Knud, 175
sorites, 130
South America, 56
Spanish, 56, 156
speech, 28, 91
spelling, 43, 45, 138
spelling-books, 62, 63
Spenser, Edmund, 128
spoken English, 149
standardisation, 26, 39, 169
Stephenson, William, 172, 174
Sterne, Laurence, 13
Stevenson, John, 54
Stevenson, Robert Louis, 15, 149, 150, 179
Stewart, Dugald, 160
Stigand, William, 148, 179
Storey, Graham, 179
Strahan, William, 55
Stuart, John, 65
students, 5, 12, 35, 39, 54, 55, 62, 139, 153, 154, 157
style, 7, 8, 13, 49, 54, 56, 94–98, 102–105, 107–119, 121–123, 125, 126, 129–131, 133, 135, 138, 140–152, 154
stylistic analysis, 105, 106
stylistic conventions, 111
stylistic guidelines, 13, 94
stylistic registers, 11–13, 18, 23, 56, 57, 93, 94, 109, 111, 123, 125, 126, 142
stylistics, 17, 28, 48
subcontinuatives, 83
subdisjunctives, 83
subject pronouns, 123
subject-verb agreement, 161
subjectivity, 102, 108
subjects, 41, 42, 101, 109, 132–134, 157, 161
subjunctives, 114
Sublime, The, 56, 132
sublimity, 97
substantives, 9, 41, 76, 99, 126
subversion, 2, 7, 109
suffixes, 48, 50, 161
superiority, 83
superlatives, 124
suppositives, 83
Swedish, 38
Swift, Jonathan, 39, 40, 128
syllables, 43, 133, 141, 142, 145
syllabus, 6, 61
syncategorematic words, 67, 79, 172
synonyms, 119
syntactic categories, 27, 43
syntactic rules, 39
syntax, 4, 6, 14, 16, 43, 58, 80, 83, 118, 143, 149, 153, 155, 159, 160

Tacitus, 100
taxonomy, 30, 31, 34, 168
Taylor, Jeremy, 141
teaching, 8–10, 35, 38, 42, 54, 156, 159, 169
tenses, 14, 99–101, 132, 135–137, 157
terminations, 142, 166
Ternan, 53
textbooks, 154
Thackeray, William Makepeace, 15, 148
theatricality, 98
Thelwall, John, 36, 72
theology, 30, 153, 168
theories, 97
theorists, 160
Thetis, 6
Thomson, James, 126
thought, 27
Tillotson, Kathleen Mary, 179
Tomalin, Marcus, 170, 174
Tooke, William, 36, 37, 173
Tories, 58

Tory critics, 52, 57, 95, 96, 120, 129, 175
Tory reviewers, 148
Tory writers, 138
Tower of London, The, 36
tradesmen, 45
tradition, 1, 11, 19, 21, 23, 37, 39, 40, 44, 46, 52, 60, 63–67, 71, 89, 93, 113, 137, 158, 159
transitivity, 83
translation, 13, 39, 44, 89, 118, 129–131, 135, 136, 174
treason, 36
Treason Trials, The, 36
treatises, 139, 153, 159, 160
truth, 63, 69, 81, 82, 87, 89, 90, 118, 137
Turley, Richard, 3, 7, 22, 165
Tyke, Robert, 177
typography, 115

ultra-crepidarian critics, 12, 129, 166
uncertainty, 28, 34, 76
understanding, 26, 28, 29, 31, 81–83, 88, 90, 166
ungrammaticality, 40, 79, 96, 97, 102, 104, 106, 107, 114, 123, 125, 132
universal grammar, 22, 31–35, 61, 168, 169
universal languages, 30, 168
universality, 142
universals, 31, 34, 35, 86
universities, 118
urbanisation, 151
urbanism, 151

van Ostade, Ingrid Tieken-Boon, 169, 170
van Rooten, Luis, 165
vanity, 31, 149, 150
verb phrases, 34
verbal criticism, 54, 139, 148, 149
verbal critics, 12
verbs, 5, 14, 41, 43, 44, 46, 48, 62, 67–69, 74–77, 79, 85, 87, 88, 99, 100, 108, 109, 132, 133, 136, 144, 157, 161, 166, 169, 173
Victorian period, The, 23, 151, 154
Victorians, 14, 15, 150, 151, 154
violations, 133
Virgil, 7
virtue, 42
vocabulary, 9, 46, 49, 58, 98, 101, 108, 110, 115, 116, 119, 120, 142, 143
vowels, 133
vulgarity, 95, 97, 98, 111, 114, 116–121, 123, 142, 143, 149, 177

Wadham College, 32

Waller, Alfred Rayney, 16
Wallis, John, 155
Walzer, Arthur, 171
War of Independence, The, 42
Wardle, Ralph, 18
Warrington Academy, The, 35
washerwomen, 96
Watts, Richard, 169
Webster, Noah, 155, 161, 162
Wem, 61, 82, 93
Westminster, 35, 160
Wilcox, Stewart, 17, 115, 167
wilderness, 51
Wilkes, John, 65
Wilkins, John, 30, 31, 35, 76
William, Tooke, 37
Willich, Anthony, 89, 174
Wilson, Charles, 161
Wilson, John, 148
Wimbledon, 173
Wimbledon Common, 72
Winchester, 39
Winchester College, 39
Winchester, Caleb Thomas, 15, 166
Winterslow, 8, 19
wisdom, 2, 5, 53
wit, 54, 129–131
Wolff, Michael, 151, 179
women, 151
word order, 101, 109, 126, 133, 134
Wordsworth, William, 3, 94, 135, 149
written language, 135
Wu, Duncan, 20, 166, 167

York, 42, 156
Yorkshire, 119, 177

Zodiac, The, 117